Principles of Workers' Compensation Claims

Principles of Workers' Compensation Claims

Edited by

Donna J. Popow, JD, CPCU, AIC
Director of Curriculum
American Institute for CPCU/Insurance Institute of America

Third Edition · Fourth Printing

American Institute for Chartered Property Casualty Underwriters/
Insurance Institute of America
720 Providence Road, Malvern, Pennsylvania 19355

Third Edition • Fourth Printing • February 2007

Library of Congress Control Number: 2004-108337
ISBN 978-0-89463-175-7

Foreword

The American Institute for Chartered Property Casualty Underwriters and the Insurance Institute of America (the Institutes) are independent, not-for-profit organizations committed to expanding the knowledge of professionals in risk management, insurance, financial services, and related fields through education and research.

In accordance with our belief that professionalism is grounded in education, experience, and ethical behavior, the Institutes provide a wide range of educational programs designed to meet the needs of individuals working in property-casualty insurance and risk management. The American Institute offers the Chartered Property Casualty Underwriter (CPCU®) professional designation. You select a specialization in the CPCU program with either a commercial or a personal risk management and insurance focus, depending on your professional needs. In addition to this specialization, the CPCU program gives you a broad understanding of the property-casualty insurance industry.

The Insurance Institute of America (IIA) offers designations and certificate programs in a wide range of disciplines, including the following:

- Claims
- Commercial underwriting
- Fidelity and surety bonding
- General insurance
- Insurance accounting and finance
- Insurance information technology
- Insurance production and agency management
- Insurance regulation and compliance
- Management
- Marine insurance
- Personal insurance
- Premium auditing
- Quality insurance services
- Reinsurance
- Risk management
- Surplus lines

No matter which Institute program you choose, you will gain practical knowledge and skills that will help you to grow personally and professionally.

The American Institute for CPCU was founded in 1942 through a collaborative effort between industry professionals and academics, led by the faculty members at The Wharton School of the University of Pennsylvania. In 1953, the American Institute for CPCU merged with the IIA, which was founded in 1909 and which remains the oldest continuously functioning national organization offering educational programs for the property-casualty insurance business. The Institutes continuously strive to maximize the value of your education and qualifications in the expanding insurance market. In 2005, the Institutes extended their global reach by forming the CPCU Institute of Greater China (CPCUIGC). In addition, many CPCU and IIA courses now qualify for credits towards certain associate's, bachelor's, and master's degrees at several prestigious colleges and universities, and all CPCU and IIA courses carry college credit recommendations from the American Council on Education (ACE).

The Insurance Research Council (IRC), founded in 1977, helps the Institutes fulfill the research aspect of their mission. The IRC is a division of the Institutes and is supported by industry members. The IRC is a not-for-profit research organization that examines public policy issues of interest to property-casualty insurers, insurance customers, and the general public. IRC research reports are distributed widely to insurance-related organizations, public policy authorities, and the media.

Our textbooks are an essential component of the education we provide. Each book is specifically designed both to provide you with the practical knowledge and skills you need to enhance your job performance and career and also to deliver that knowledge in a clear manner. The content is developed by the Institutes in collaboration with insurance and risk management professionals and members of the academic community. We welcome comments from our students and course leaders because your feedback helps us to continuously improve the quality of our study materials. Through our combined efforts, we will truly be *succeeding together*.

Peter L. Miller, CPCU
President and CEO
American Institute for CPCU
Insurance Institute of America

Preface

Workers compensation laws are a crucial social welfare system for compensation of work-related injuries. Injuries, an inevitable part of industrial production, can be tragic for the worker, the worker's family, and the employer. An injury can ruin a worker's physical and financial health. The worker's family can be destroyed by the stresses of an injury. The employer has an enormous humanitarian and financial stake in the well-being of its employees.

If the payment of claims is an important purpose of most types of insurance, it is essential for workers' compensation. Workers' compensation is designed to be a no-fault system that ensures speedy compensation for work-related injuries.

Claim adjusters play an essential role in this important system. Insurers, insureds, self-insureds, and injured employees in particular depend on the diligence, efficiency, and expertise of claim adjusters. Traditionally, workers' compensation claim adjusters have learned on the job, but that approach has drawbacks. The quality of on-the-job training can vary by employer or even by supervisor. In general, the focus of on-the-job training may tend to be too narrow to be truly beneficial. For instance, workers' compensation training often has been regarded as a state-specific matter because of the differences in state laws.

This textbook reflects the belief that the similarities among state workers' compensation laws and procedures are more significant than the differences. Indeed, the study of common features helps students understand the unique aspects of any given state's laws and procedures. This textbook is designed for use in the American Institute for CPCU/Insurance Institute of America's AIC 34 course, which addresses workers' compensation and medical aspects of claims.

This text describes the evolution of employers liability and workers' compensation laws, the nature of the existing workers' compensation system, the standard insurance policy coverage, and the importance of safety and loss control. It explores compensability, the injuries and parties workers' compensation insurance covers, the calculation of benefits, and the administration of workers' compensation claims. The text concludes with a discussion of workers' compensation subrogation.

The Institutes appreciate the work of the following individuals who reviewed manuscripts for this text and made valuable suggestions for improvement:

Dennis D. Alves
Gordon Berger
Thomas E. Certain
Christopher Colavita, CPCU
Stephen Dansevich
Richard E. Ehret, CPCU
Elise M. Farnham, CPCU, ARM, AIM
Larry D. Gaunt, PhD, CPCU
William R. Gawne, MBA, CPCU
Eric H. Geisy, CPCU
Robert J. Gibbons, PhD, CPCU, CLU
Jonathan H. Gice, CPCU
Don Gordon
Alice Guttler
Mark J. Hartzer, Esq.
Christian Lachance, CPCU, AIC
Joe Long, CSSC
Samuel M. Meeks, CPCU, AIC
Lewis P. Palca, CPCU
E. Timothy Poindexter, Esq.
William E. Rogers, CPCU, ARM, CSP
Glenn Salka, AIC, ARM, SCLA
George W. Scherbak, CPCU
William C. Stewart, Jr., CPCU
David H. Stonehill, Esq.
John H. Sullivan, CPCU
Sandra Thomas CPCU, AIC, ARM
Jerome Trupin, CPCU, CLU, ChFC
Tony Vogel
David Weaver, CPCU, ARM
Ronald R. Wirsing

For more information about the Institutes' programs, please call our Customer Service Department at (800) 644-2101 or visit our Web site at www.aicpcu.org.

Donna J. Popow

Contributing Authors

The American Institute for CPCU and the Insurance Institute of America acknowledge with sincere gratitude the work of the following contributing authors:

David Appel, PhD

Kristin M. Bonner, CPCU

Michael Camilleri, Esq.

P.E. Nony Capellan, CPCU

Robert B. Dorsey

Marletta England, CPCU

Kimberly Campbell Hamilton, CPCU, ARM

Doris L. Hoopes, CPCU, AIC, AIM

James R. Jones, CPCU, AIC, ARM

James J. Markham, JD, CPCU, AIC

Brian Marx, CPCU, MA

Marjorie L. Mowrey, CPCU, AIC

Kevin M. Quinley, CPCU, AIC, ARM

Contents

Chapter 1

Direct Your Learning

The Workers' Compensation System

After learning the content of this chapter, you should be able to:

- Describe the common-law employer liability loss exposure.

- Explain how workplace injuries were handled before workers' compensation laws were enacted.

- Describe the goals of workers' compensation laws.

- Describe the common features of workers' compensation laws.

- Describe the various federal statutes dealing with compensation for workplace injuries, the workers subject to the statutes, and the remedies provided by the statutes.

- Given a case, identify any applicable federal statute and the remedy that would apply.

- Describe the various exceptions and challenges to the exclusive remedy concept.

Develop Your Perspective

What are the main topics covered in the chapter?

Workers' compensation is a topic that is important to workers' compensation adjusters, employers, and workers. This chapter discusses the common-law duties of employers to their workers and the defenses available to employers. It then outlines the common features of workers' compensation laws and discusses various federal workers' compensation statutes.

Identify the common-law duties your employer owes you.

- Have the workers' compensation laws changed those obligations?
- What common-law defenses are available to your employer?

Why is it important to learn about these topics?

To adjust a workers' compensation claim, an adjuster must be aware of the various state and federal statutes that create the need for workers' compensation insurance. An adjuster should understand how and why the exclusive remedy of workers' compensation can be challenged.

Research the workers' compensation laws specific to your state.

- What persons and employments are covered?
- What benefits are workers entitled to that differ from the federal statutory benefits?
- What challenges to workers' compensation as an exclusive remedy are allowed?

How can you use what you will learn?

Analyze the types of workers' compensation claims that might occur where you work.

- Depending on the type of employment, which workers' compensation statute would apply?
- To recover for their injuries under the common law, what do injured workers have to prove?
- Can a successful challenge to the exclusive remedy of workers' compensation be made?

Chapter 1

The Workers' Compensation System

Workers' compensation is a system that pays the lost wages and the medical and vocational rehabilitation expenses to injured workers for employment-related injuries and diseases and that pays death benefits to workers' dependents for employment-related fatalities. This system is based on workers' compensation laws that benefit the worker *and* the employer. These laws create a no-fault system whereby workers exchange the right to sue for certain damages in return for the employers' strict liability (meaning regardless of fault) for work-related injuries and diseases. These laws make workers' compensation the injured worker's exclusive remedy for injury or disease, except in limited circumstances.

This chapter discusses the liability that existed for employers before workers' compensation laws were enacted in the early twentieth century. It then describes modern workers' compensation laws, including federal compensation legislation. Workers' compensation is based primarily on state statutes, which have been enacted in all fifty states and U.S. territories and possessions. Despite some differences in state laws, they are generally similar.

The chapter also reviews the major features of the workers' compensation system and the challenges and exceptions to the exclusive remedy concept of workers' compensation.

Workers' compensation
A system that pays lost wages, medical and rehabilitation expenses, and death benefits to injured workers or their dependents for employment-related injuries and diseases.

EMPLOYERS LIABILITY LOSS EXPOSURES— AN OVERVIEW

The advent of workers' compensation changed many of the liability loss exposures faced by employers. These loss exposures include injuries and diseases that arise from employment and those that result from the employer's negligence. However, some of these loss exposures still fall outside the scope of the workers' compensation system. In some situations, workers must still prove that their employers were negligent in order to receive compensation for their work-related injuries or diseases. Many of the common-law duties that employers historically owed to workers still apply, and many of the traditional common-law defenses are still used by employers to refute liability. Common-law duties and defenses arose from case law, custom, and practice. Adjusters who understand how employers liability was historically determined should find it easier to understand the purpose and advantages of the current workers' compensation system.

History of Employers Liability

Understanding the history of employers liability helps to clarify the present role of the workers' compensation system and some of the issues associated with workers' compensation insurance. Workers' compensation laws departed significantly from the common law under which responsibility for an injury was based on fault. This departure stemmed from the historical inadequacies of the common law that prevented it from effectively providing workers with the legal remedies necessary to compensate them for work-related injuries.

Before the industrial revolution, the trades, the sea, and agriculture were the principal sources of employment. Tradesmen usually cared for their injured apprentices and journeymen to protect their investment in those workers, and shipowners and captains cared for their crew. Agricultural labor was so plentiful that farmowners did not feel obligated to care for injured workers.

With the industrial revolution, working conditions changed dramatically. New industries and manufacturing techniques arose, bringing together great numbers of workers, skilled and unskilled. These workers were exposed to new hazards caused by poor working conditions and the use of machinery for mass production. Workers who were injured or who became ill and the families of those who died had little recourse or protection. Over time, a body of common law developed defining the duties employers owed to their workers relating to safety in the workplace. In turn, courts defined employers' common-law defenses. These duties and defenses are discussed in the following sections.

Negligence and the Common Law of Employers Liability

To recover under common law for work-related injuries, a worker must prove that the employer was negligent, that is, that the employer's failure to use due care caused or contributed to the injury or illness. The following are the four essential elements that the injured worker must prove in a case based on negligence:

1. A legal duty owed
2. Failure to comply with the standard of care required by the duty
3. Proximate cause
4. Damages

To collect compensation, the worker must prove all of these elements. If any one element is missing, no recovery is allowed. The following section discusses common-law duties of employers, the first element of negligence.

Common-Law Duties of Employers

The common law requires that the employer exercise reasonable care for the safety of its workers. The following five specific duties have also been derived from this general duty of care:

1. Provide a safe place to work
2. Provide an adequate number of competent fellow workers
3. Provide safe tools and equipment
4. Warn the worker of inherent dangers
5. Make and enforce rules for the safety of all workers

The first specific common-law duty of employers, to provide a safe place to work, requires the employer to provide a physically safe building or work area, to maintain the work premises in reasonably safe condition, to provide proper housekeeping, and to inspect the work premises at reasonable intervals. The length of a reasonable interval depends on the nature of the work and the frequency with which unsafe conditions occur. Courts use the reasonably prudent person standard—what a reasonably prudent person would do under similar circumstances—to determine whether the employer has met this duty. For instance, a reasonably prudent person would not only make inspections to determine the presence of unsafe conditions but would also take immediate steps to remedy such conditions. In addition, a reasonably prudent person would comply with all state, county, and city safety requirements, as well as any federal safety standards.

The employer's duty to provide a safe place to work is not limited to the physical condition of the premises. It also extends to other circumstances that might be unsafe for workers. For example, an employer would fail in its duty of care if, after learning that a worker suffers from a respiratory condition that would be worsened by continued exposure to the work area, the employer allowed the worker to be further exposed to harm.

The second specific common-law duty of employers is to provide an adequate number of competent fellow workers. To accomplish this duty, the employer must exercise care in selecting and training all workers and must provide enough people for the required work. The extent of pre-employment screening and on-the-job training varies according to the required work.

The third specific common-law duty of employers is to provide safe tools and equipment. The machinery should be adequately guarded, properly maintained, and equipped with all standard safety features. The employer, however, is not bound to provide the newest and safest machinery possible. It is sufficient if the machinery provided can be used safely by a competent worker. Necessary safety equipment must also be provided, such as goggles for workers engaged in grinding, respirators for those exposed to noxious fumes or dusts, and hard hats for construction workers.

The fourth specific common-law duty of employers is to warn the worker of inherent dangers, that is work-related dangers of which the worker is unaware or that the worker would not discover by exercising reasonable care. Such dangers might include the presence of any toxic chemicals, radioactive materials, or hazards created by the use of certain dyes and chemicals.

Employers have no duty to warn workers of readily apparent dangers, because the employer has a right to assume that the workers, experienced or not, are aware of such dangers and are able to protect themselves against them. Accordingly, the employer is under no common-law duty to warn a worker of the dangers of fire from a gas stove, a caged lion in a zoo, or projectiles from a grinding wheel.

The fifth specific common-law duty of employers is to make and enforce rules for the safety of all workers. These rules must be adequate considering the dangers to which the workers are exposed. The greater the danger, the more rigid the rules must be. The employer must enforce the rules and must not tolerate repeated violations. Enforcement might require discharging workers who repeatedly violate the rules. The employer is not obligated to make and enforce rules for simple operations when the dangers, if any, are apparent to all. Workers are expected to protect themselves against such dangers without rules requiring them to do so.

Common-Law Defenses

If the employer fails to meet one or more of its duties and causes injury to a worker, then the worker has the right to seek recovery for damages against the employer. Three common-law defenses are available to the employer: assumption of risk, contributory negligence, and the negligence of a fellow worker.

Assumption of risk, one common-law defense, can be applied if two conditions apply to the facts of the case at the time of the injury:

1. The worker was aware of the existence of the risk and understood the extent of the danger.
2. The worker voluntarily exposed himself or herself to the danger.

The worker is expected to be aware of any danger that is apparent. If the worker has accepted employment where apparent dangers exist, the worker is deemed to have voluntarily exposed himself or herself to the danger and is therefore barred from recovering for any resulting injury. The same is true when an employer fails to meet a duty and a worker who is aware of this failure continues to work. The worker will be held to have assumed the risk of injury.

However, a worker cannot be held to have assumed a risk of which he or she is unaware. For example, if a worker is unaware that radioactive materials are used in another section of a plant and if the worker suffers an injury from exposure to radiation, it cannot be said that the worker assumed this risk.

The same is true when a worker's duties involve contact with chemicals that are unfamiliar to the average worker in the plant.

Contributory negligence is another common-law defense available to employers. The common-law rule is that if the worker's contributory negligence to exercise care for his or her own safety is responsible *to any degree* for causing the accident, the worker is barred from recovery for resulting injury even though the employer's negligence also contributed to the injury. Therefore, at common law, a workers' momentary lapse in behavior could eliminate recovery even though the employer's negligence largely contributed to the accident or to the extent of the injury.

Contributory negligence
A common-law principle that prevents an injured person from recovering damages if that person contributed in any way to his or her own injury.

A variation of the contributory negligence defense, known as comparative negligence, has largely replaced the contributory negligence defense. **Comparative negligence** is based on the principle that the worker's contributory negligence is not a complete defense and does not completely bar recovery. Rather, the injured worker can recover damages, but the amount of recovery is reduced by the amount of the injured worker's own negligence. Comparative negligence laws enable workers to recover a portion of their damages even when they are partially at fault.

Comparative negligence
A principle that allows an injured party, if he or she contributed to the loss, to recover damages that are reduced in proportion to the injured party's negligence.

The two forms of comparative negligence statutes are *modified* and *pure*. Both require a jury to reach a verdict about the percentages of negligence, if any, applied to the plaintiff and the defendant. Under modified comparative negligence, plaintiffs' recoveries are reduced by the percentage of their fault, but they recover nothing when their fault exceeds the defendant's fault. Under the pure form, plaintiffs can always recover damages as long as they are not 100 percent at fault. For example, an injured plaintiff can be 90 percent at fault and still recover 10 percent of damages under a pure comparative negligence law. Under pure comparative negligence, a plaintiff is barred from recovery only when the defendant is totally blameless.

Some states define contributory negligence to include assumption of risk. In such cases, the defendant is barred from using assumption of risk as a defense separate from a negligence defense.

Negligence of a fellow worker is a third possible common-law defense available to employers. Under this defense, the employer is not liable for an injury caused solely by a fellow worker's negligence. This defense is an exception to the general rule of *respondeat superior*, under which the negligence of a worker acting within the course and scope of employment is imputed to the employer. This rule has been criticized, but courts still apply it in the absence of legislation relevant to the issue.

Respondeat superior
A legal doctrine making an employer liable for the torts of a worker that are committed within the scope of the worker's employment.

A **fellow worker** is defined as a worker of the same rank as the injured worker. An injured worker's supervisor is not ordinarily held to be a fellow worker because the supervisor is an agent of management whose negligence is, therefore, imputed to the employer. Some courts have gone further, refusing to apply the fellow worker defense to any member of management who would

Fellow worker
A worker of the same rank as the injured worker.

be deemed responsible for carrying out the employer's duties to provide a safe workplace, to select competent fellow workers, and to warn workers of the inherent dangers of the work. Some courts have also held that a worker of another department is not a fellow worker. Generally, however, the courts have been reluctant to apply the fellow worker defense except in very clear-cut situations.

After having proven that the employer owed a duty of care and that this duty was breached, the injured worker would also have to show that he or she was injured and that the employer's negligence caused the injury.

WORKERS' COMPENSATION LAWS

The current workers' compensation system arose out of the inadequate common-law remedies for injured workers. Workers' compensation provides for the prompt payment of defined benefits for work-related injuries, irrespective of a determination of fault.

Under this new legal concept, the cost of occupational injury and disease was to be assessed against the employer even when the employer was neither negligent nor otherwise responsible under the common law or statute. The workers' compensation laws balanced the interests of both employer and worker. Workers relinquished their existing legal remedy, the right of a tort action for negligence against the employer and, with it, their right to recover damages for pain and suffering or inconvenience. The employer relinquished various defenses and became obligated to respond to the worker's injury according to the terms of the workers' compensation act. The law provided relative certainty about the amount to be paid for work-related injuries.

Original compensation laws were meant to address the specific social problem of inadequate remedies for injured workers and were therefore directed only at industries whose operations were considered hazardous. State laws defined what was hazardous, and little uniformity existed among those laws. Over time, state laws evolved to cover more types of employers without regard to hazardousness.

Goals of Workers' Compensation Laws in the United States

Today, all fifty states, the District of Columbia, and U.S. territories and possessions have workers' compensation laws. However, common-law principles still apply to those employments not covered under workers' compensation laws.

The general goal of workers' compensation laws is to alleviate the plight of the injured worker. The following box describes these laws' specific goals.

Goals of Workers' Compensation Laws

1. Pay adequate benefits promptly to injured workers or their dependents, according to a fixed and predetermined schedule

2. Eliminate the delays and costs of litigation to the worker and to society

3. Establish a guaranteed benefit payment to be secured by a form of insurance

4. Promote industrial safety by demonstrating to employers the relationship between accident prevention and the reduced cost of workers' compensation benefits

5. Pay for medical services

Workers' compensation laws provide specific and immediate benefits to injured workers. Injury schedules attempt to make payments largely automatic, minimizing the frequency of adversarial proceedings between workers and employers. Compensation hearing officers and judges often cite the public policy benefits—immediately covering injured workers and discouraging litigation—as justification for extending coverage in close or doubtful cases. Adjusters should understand this judicial inclination when evaluating workers' compensation claims.

Common Features of Workers' Compensation Laws

The workers' compensation laws of the fifty states, the District of Columbia, and U.S. territories and possessions have the following common features:

- Choice of law provision
- Persons and employments covered
- Injuries and diseases covered
- Benefits provided
- Methods of financing benefits
- Procedure for obtaining benefits
- Administration of benefits

Choice of Law Provision

A significant feature of workers' compensation laws is the choice of law provision. In any given case of an employment-related injury, the laws of numerous states might apply if the circumstances of employment (the place of injury, hire, or employment; the location of the employer; or the residence of the worker) occur in different states or when a contract specifies which state workers' compensation law will apply. Generally, the laws of the states in which the injury occurred, in which the employment usually occurs, and in which the worker was hired all apply to a loss. The worker cannot receive duplicate benefits but can select the state with the most generous benefits.

Because the facts of cases involving multiple states can be complex, the adjuster faced with such a case should obtain a legal opinion about which states' laws apply.

Persons and Employments Covered

Another feature of workers' compensation laws is the description of the persons and employments covered. Generally, an employer's legal obligations for occupational injury or disease extend to employees only, not to independent contractors. This distinction between an employee and an independent contractor is crucial. Some people who are called independent contractors are considered employees by the courts. The essential distinction between employees and independent contractors is that the employer has the right to control and direct the activities of an employee, both in the work to be accomplished and in the methods and means by which the result is obtained.

While the original workers' compensation laws were aimed at specific industries, today, workers' compensation statutes cover most public and private employments whether or not they are hazardous in the traditional sense of the term. Most state workers' compensation laws exclude domestic and farm workers, who therefore retain their common-law rights to sue employers for damages from work-related injuries.

Injuries and Diseases Covered

A third feature of workers' compensation laws is the description of injuries and diseases covered. The purpose of workers' compensation laws has always been to provide benefits only for **occupational injuries**; that is, injuries that arise from the worker's employment. It would be difficult to rationalize coverage for non-occupational injuries and diseases under a program financed exclusively by the employer.

Occupational injury
An injury that arises from a worker's employment.

State laws define occupational injury to include all of the elements listed in the following box.

Elements of a Compensable Injury
- The worker suffered an injury caused by an accident.
- The accident arose out of employment.
- The accident occurred in the course of employment.

Although the specific exclusions vary by state, many state compensation statutes exclude coverage for the following:

- Injuries that are intentional or self-inflicted
- Injuries caused by the worker's intoxication
- Injuries caused by the worker's willful violation of safety regulations

Some occupational diseases are also covered by workers' compensation as specified in a state's workers' compensation statutes. The details about compensability for occupational injuries and diseases are discussed in a subsequent chapter.

Benefits Provided

A fourth feature of workers' compensation laws is the description of the benefits provided. Four types of workers' compensation benefits are payable to the injured worker or the worker's dependents. See the following box.

Types of Workers' Compensation Benefits

1. Payments for lost wages

2. Payments for medical services

3. Rehabilitation services

4. Death benefits

Disability or indemnity payments are designed to compensate for lost wages. Injured workers typically receive two-thirds of their pre-injury weekly wage subject to a maximum set by the state. The maximum weekly benefits paid to injured workers have increased over time. The maximum benefit typically equals 66.66 percent of the state's average wages.

Most states require a waiting period, ranging from three to seven days, before loss benefits become payable to an injured worker. This period is designed to reduce compensation costs by eliminating compensation for job-related disabilities of short duration and to discourage malingering. If a worker's disability extends beyond a specified number of weeks (usually two or three), called the retroactive or retro period, wage loss benefits are paid back to the date of the injury, eliminating the effects of the waiting period.

There are two ways of classifying disability extending beyond the waiting period: (1) as either temporary or permanent and (2) as either partial or total. Temporary total disability payments are made to a worker who cannot work at any occupation during the period of recovery but who is expected to return to work. Temporary partial disability payments are made to a worker who is able to work on a limited basis but who is expected to return to regular job duties. Permanent disabilities can also be partial or total. Permanent partial disability involves injuries that prohibit a return to work in the same job function. Permanent total disability involves an injury that prevents the injured worker from ever working again.

A second type of workers' compensation benefit is payment for medical services. Almost all states cover 100 percent of necessary medical expenses without limits, deductibles, or co-payments. Medical benefits account for more than 53 percent of the total payments under workers' compensation.[1] See Exhibit 1-1.

EXHIBIT 1-1

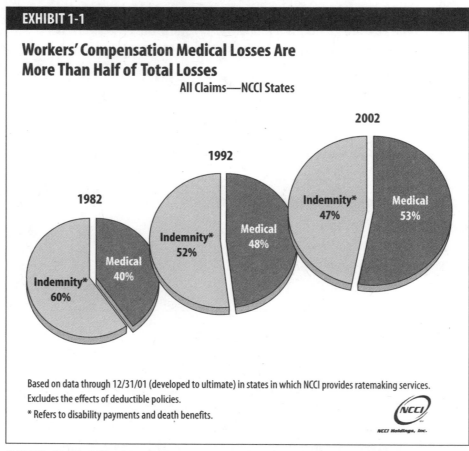

Workers' Compensation Medical Losses Are More Than Half of Total Losses
All Claims—NCCI States

1982
Indemnity* 60%
Medical 40%

1992
Indemnity* 52%
Medical 48%

2002
Indemnity* 47%
Medical 53%

Based on data through 12/31/01 (developed to ultimate) in states in which NCCI provides ratemaking services.
Excludes the effects of deductible policies.
* Refers to disability payments and death benefits.

NCCI
NCCI Holdings, Inc.

Rehabilitation services are the third type of workers' compensation benefit. Early workers' compensation laws covered medical care to injured workers but no further services, regardless of the extent of recovery from disability. When treatment ran out or no further benefit from it was apparent, permanent total disability was often inevitable. With advances in physical and rehabilitative medicine, paramedical services, and vocational training facilities, permanent total disability is no longer accepted as the final result in every case of serious injury. Injured workers are now entitled to the appropriate level of rehabilitation services as part of their compensation.

Rehabilitation programs are a means to reduce the long-term effect and, therefore, the cost of disabling injuries by providing vocational training or physical therapy to the injured worker so that the person can return to gainful employment. Rehabilitation also includes such services as-training to drive a specially equipped car.

Although not all states include specific rehabilitation provisions in their workers' compensation laws, rehabilitation is available in all states. Many insurers have been leaders in conducting rehabilitation programs for disabled workers, often providing rehabilitation benefits well beyond those legally required. Such services can reduce the ultimate loss costs by returning workers to full employment who might otherwise continue to receive benefits indefinitely. Equally important is the social benefit of helping disabled workers feel that they are contributing to society.

A fourth type of workers' compensation benefit is the death benefit. Like disability payments, death benefit payments vary by state. In more than half the states, the duration of these payments is limited; for example, payment ends when a widow remarries or when minor children reach a specified age. About one-fourth of the states adjust the benefits annually to correspond with increases in prices or wages. In addition to income replacement benefits, all states pay a burial allowance.

Methods of Financing Benefits

Another feature of workers' compensation laws concerns the methods of financing the benefits available under the laws. Most workers' compensation laws require employers to demonstrate financial ability to pay any claims that may arise. Possible methods of meeting this financial obligation are shown in the following box. Not all of these methods are legal in all states. Adjusters should be aware of the methods allowed in the states in which they handle claims.

Methods of Financing Workers' Compensation Benefits

1. Voluntary private insurance

2. Insurance through assigned risk plans

3. Insurance through state funds

4. Qualified self-insurance plans

5. Excess insurance

One method an employer can use to meet its workers' compensation obligation is to purchase insurance from a private insurer licensed to write workers' compensation coverage in the state. In return for the premium, the insurer promises to pay the benefits and assume most administrative duties required by law for work-related injuries.

Assigned risk plans are a second method of financing workers' compensation benefits. An assigned risk plan is a state-organized pool of workers' compensation insurers who are required to accept businesses that are unable to find insurance in the voluntary market; for example, some businesses cannot obtain private insurance because they do not meet insurer underwriting criteria. Because of the compulsory nature of workers' compensation, a firm without insurance could be forced out of business by the penalties imposed. An employer rejected by private insurers can apply to the assigned risk plan in the appropriate state to obtain coverage.

State funds are a third method of financing workers' compensation benefits. Twenty-five states offer and fund workers' compensation insurance. Territorial funds are in effect in Puerto Rico and the U.S. Virgin Islands. These funds provide the benefits required by workers' compensation laws. Although controlled by the state government, these state and territorial funds operate essentially the same way that private insurers do. The most significant differences are that state funds, unlike private insurers, accept any good-faith applicant for insurance in the state and that no assigned risk plan is necessary.

State funds can be competitive or monopolistic. Twenty states' funds sell workers' compensation insurance in competition with private insurers and are therefore called **competitive state funds**. An employer in these states can purchase insurance from either a private insurer or the state fund. See Exhibit 1-2 for a list of the states with competitive state funds.

Competitive state funds
State funds that sell workers' compensation insurance in competition with private insurers.

EXHIBIT 1-2			
States With Competitive State Funds			
Arizona	Kentucky	Missouri	Oregon
California	Louisiana	Montana	Pennsylvania
Colorado	Maine	New Mexico	Rhode Island
Hawaii	Maryland	New York	Texas
Idaho	Minnesota	Oklahoma	Utah

© 2001 International Risk Management Institute, Inc. Reproduced with permission of the publisher, International Risk Management Institute, Inc., from *IRMI Workers Comp*. Further reproduction prohibited.

Five states (North Dakota, Ohio, Washington, West Virginia, and Wyoming) plus Puerto Rico and the U.S. Virgin Islands require all workers' compensation insurance to be placed with the state or territorial fund. The states and territories license no private insurer to write workers' compensation coverage, and their funds have no competition. Their funds, called **monopolistic or exclusive state funds** provide workers' compensation coverage, but not employers liability coverage.

Monopolistic or **exclusive state funds**
State funds that are the only licensed source of workers' compensation coverage.

A fourth workers' compensation financing method is through qualified self-insurance. Almost all states allow employers to retain (self-insure) the risk of workers' compensation losses if they demonstrate the financial capacity to do so. To qualify as a self-insurer, an employer must post a surety bond or other collateral with the workers' compensation state administrative agency to guarantee the security of benefit payments. In addition, most states require evidence of an ability to administer the benefit payments and services mandated by the law. Self-insurance is usually practical only for large employers. Most states also allow self-insured groups, usually a group of employers that are in the same or a similar business, to qualify for self-insurance. The requirements for self-insured groups are similar to those for individual self-insurers.

Excess insurance is a fifth workers' compensation financing method. Excess insurance, in this case, is insurance purchased over and above the amount of the employer's self-insurance. An employer that qualifies for self-insurance might also decide to purchase excess insurance to cover catastrophic losses. Some states also require excess insurance above a permitted self-insured retention level.

Procedure for Obtaining Benefits

Workers' compensation laws require the worker to notify the employer of the injury or accident within a specific period (usually thirty days) in order to obtain benefits. Notice is usually given to a supervisor, manager, or human resources personnel. The worker's failure to give timely notice of the injury is not necessarily fatal to the claim; the timely notice requirement is often ignored if the employer witnessed or had reason to know about the injury. The notice requirement is also set aside if the late notice does not prejudice the employer's right to investigate the accident. Additionally, workers' compensation laws contain a statute of limitations provision, usually one year. Failure to file a claim within the statute of limitations time period renders the claim unenforceable.

Administration of Benefits

Broadly speaking, the traditional objective of workers' compensation claim administration has been to ensure that injured workers know their rights and promptly receive the benefits to which they are entitled. The principal administrative feature of workers' compensation laws is to provide a simple, convenient, and inexpensive method of settling the claims of injured workers and their dependents. Full and prompt payment when due is a key characteristic of the workers' compensation system. If payments are not made, the system must provide a speedy and effective method for settling controversies.

Generally, two bodies administer benefits in the United States—the state courts and special commissions or boards. State workers' compensation commissions and boards were created to settle disputes in a quasi-judicial manner that operates like an informal court. In all states, appeals of board rulings are heard by state courts. However, in a few states, the courts conduct the initial administration of workers' compensation claims, hearing and determining claims and issuing judgments in the same way that they would in any other type of case. The administration of workers' compensation by a commission or compensation board is far from perfect but is usually better than court administration because it is faster than the civil trial process.

One of the important advantages of the workers' compensation system is that claim handling is usually done by a third party, such as an insurer. The employer bears the legal obligations toward its workers established by the compensation law but rarely handles the workers' claims. This separation of duties protects the employer-employee relationship, particularly when claims are questioned or defenses are raised. In recent years, increasingly more employers have chosen to self-insure their workers' compensation loss exposures through retention plans. Consequently, the services of third-party claim administrators have become more important.

Federal Compensation Statutes

All fifty states, the District of Columbia, and U.S. territories and possessions have workers' compensation laws that cover a large percentage of the work force. Nevertheless, state workers' compensation laws do not apply to everyone. Persons employed by federal institutions or those who work on navigable waterways, on federal lands, or on federal projects abroad or within the District of Columbia are covered by the federal laws discussed next and summarized in Exhibit 1-3.

EXHIBIT 1-3

Remedies for Occupational Injuries Other Than State Workers' Compensation Laws

Employees Subject to Remedy	Source of Remedy	Nature of Remedy
Maritime workers, with some exceptions (such as the master or crew of a vessel)	Longshore and Harbor Workers Compensation Act (LHWCA)	No-fault benefits as defined by the statute
(1) Civilian employees at U.S. military bases acquired from foreign governments (2) Civilian employees working overseas under contracts with agencies of the U.S. government	Defense Base Act	Same as LHWCA
Workers on fixed offshore drilling and production platforms on the Outer Continental Shelf of the U.S.	Outer Continental Shelf Lands Act	Same as LHWCA
Civilian employees of "nonappropriated fund instrumentalities" on U.S. military bases, such as stores and theaters	Nonappropriated Fund Instrumentalities Act	Same as LHWCA
Members of a vessel's crew	Jones Act	Negligence suit against employer
	Death on the High Seas Act	Survivors may sue employer for death occurring beyond a marine league from the shore of any state.
	Maintenance and cure	Vessel owner must pay food, lodging, and medical care, irrespective of fault, until maximum medical cure achieved.
	Vessel owner's breach of warranty of vessel's seaworthiness	Negligence suit against vessel owner
	Moragne remedy	Wrongful death action against vessel owner
Employees of interstate railroads	Federal Employers' Liability Act (FELA)	Negligence suit against employer
Migrant and seasonal farm workers	Migrant and Seasonal Agricultural Worker Protection Act	Suit against employer if employee is not covered by workers' compensation insurance
Nonmilitary employees of the U.S. government	Federal Employees' Compensation Act	No-fault benefits as defined by the statute

Longshore and Harbor Workers Compensation Act

Congress enacted the **Longshore and Harbor Workers Compensation Act (LHWCA)** in 1927 in response to a Supreme Court ruling that federal admiralty jurisdiction was supreme and state compensation laws could not extend to accidents on the navigable waters of the United States. The immediate effect of this ruling was to leave longshore workers without compensation for work-related injuries. (A longshore worker is a land-based person employed to load and unload vessels. The term stevedore is also used to describe such a worker.)

To address the problem, Congress enacted the LHWCA, modeling it after state workers' compensation statutes. Workers subject to the LHWCA lost the right to sue in return for gaining the right to collect medical, disability, and death benefits as defined in the statute. In 1972 the LHWCA was expanded to cover any person engaged in longshore operations and any harbor worker, including ship repairers. The LHWCA was again revised in 1984 to liberalize the rules regarding occupational disease, add several coverage exclusions, and restrict death benefits.

The LHWCA provides for the payment of workers' compensation benefits for employment-related accidental injury, occupational disease, or death of a covered worker of a maritime employer. Although its provisions are similar to state workers' compensation laws, benefits under LHWCA are generally more liberal then those allowed by state laws. The Supreme Court has decided that coverage under the LHWCA is meant to supplement, rather than supplant, coverage for injuries that previously would have been covered under state workers' compensation law. A worker can seek coverage under both state law and the LHWCA, although no double recovery is generally allowed. However, because of concurrent jurisdiction and other gray areas between state laws and the LHWCA, many employers need to obtain insurance for both loss exposures. To be covered under the LHWCA, an injured worker must satisfy both a situs test and a status test.

The **situs test** requires that the location of the injured worker at the moment of injury be on navigable waters or certain adjoining areas, which include piers, wharves, dry docks, terminals, building ways, marine railways, or other areas used in loading, unloading, repairing, dismantling or building a vessel.

The term "navigable waters" is not defined but generally means any waters that are in fact navigable and that, by themselves or by uniting with other waters, form a continuous highway over which commerce may be conducted with other states or foreign countries. A strict reading of the LHWCA also appears to limit situs to injuries occurring within U.S. territorial waters, leaving those injured on the high seas, even when traveling between U.S. ports, uncovered. However, the courts have held that the purpose of the LHWCA favors a liberal interpretation that extends coverage under the LHWCA to the high seas, so long as the injury does not occur in foreign territorial waters.

Longshore and Harbor Workers Compensation Act (LHWCA)
A federal law providing workers' compensation benefits to longshore workers, stevedores, and harbor workers, including ship repairers.

Situs test
A test that a claimant must satisfy to be covered under the LHWCA; it requires that, at the time of injury, the claimant must have been on navigable waters or on adjoining areas such as piers, wharves, dry docks, terminals, building ways, marine railways, or other areas customarily used in loading, unloading, repairing, dismantling, or building vessels.

Status test
A test that a claimant must satisfy to be covered under the LHWCA; it requires that, at the time of injury, the claimant must have been "engaged in maritime employment."

The 1972 amendments to the LHWCA also introduced a **status test** that focuses on the worker's overall occupation. The status test requires that the worker be "engaged in maritime employment," which includes any longshore worker or any other person engaged in longshoring operations and any harbor-worker, including a ship repairman, ship builder, and ship-breaker (one who dismantles ships for scrap). As the shipping industry has changed to container-ization (shipping multiple goods in large containers), the term "maritime employment" has been liberally interpreted. It includes activities that form an integral part of the loading and unloading operations that longshoremen perform, such as cargo checking and warehousing, as long as some portion of the worker's job duties involve the loading or unloading operation. Therefore, any worker whose employment involves any part of the process of the five types of maritime activity specifically mentioned in the LHWCA—loading, unloading, repairing, building, or dismantling ships—satisfies the status test. However, the injury must occur at a covered situs. A traditional maritime worker who is injured on a non-maritime situs is excluded from coverage.

The LHWCA completely excludes several other types of workers, including the following:

- Masters or members of a crew of any vessel. (These workers may claim benefits as "seamen" under the Jones Act and general maritime law discussed later in this section. The LHWCA and Jones Act are mutually exclusive remedies.)
- Persons engaged by a master of a vessel to load or unload or repair any small vessel less than eighteen tons net.
- Officers or employees of the United States, of any U.S. government agency, of any state or foreign government, or of any of their subdivisions.

In addition, the following persons are excluded from receiving LHWCA benefits if they are covered *under a state workers' compensation law:*

- Individuals employed exclusively to perform office, clerical, secretarial, security, or data processing work.
- Individuals employed by a club, camp, recreational operation, restaurant, museum, or retail outlet.
- Individuals employed by a marina who are not engaged in construction, replacement, or expansion of the marina other than routine maintenance.
- Individuals who meet all of the following requirements: (1) employed by suppliers, transporters, or vendors; (2) temporarily doing business on the premises of a maritime employer; and (3) not engaged in work normally performed by employees of that maritime employer. To be excluded under this category, a worker must meet all three criteria. An example might be a truck driver who has made a delivery to an ocean cargo terminal or a shipyard.
- Aquaculture workers.
- Individuals employed to build, repair, or dismantle any recreational vessel under sixty-five feet in length.

These classes of workers, however, will qualify for LHWCA coverage if they are not covered under a state workers' compensation law. Therefore, organizations whose workers could be eligible for LHWCA benefits should have both LHWCA and state workers' compensation coverages in place. LHWCA coverage can be added by endorsement to the standard Workers Compensation and Employers Liability Insurance Policy.

The LHWCA also has a small vessel exemption designed to reduce the liability of small boatyards. This exemption is available upon certification by the U.S. Secretary of Labor. However, the small vessel exemption applies only to workers not working over navigable waters or on an adjoining pier; wharf; dock; facility over land for launching vessels; or facility over land for hauling, lifting, or dry-docking vessels. Similarly, if the boatyard happens to engage in building, dismantling, or repairing a large vessel, its workers would be entitled to LHWCA coverage in any period during which work was done on a non-qualifying vessel.

Some federal statutes extend LHWCA benefits to additional classes of workers. Four such statutes are described in the next section:

1. Outer Continental Shelf Lands Act
2. Nonappropriated Funds Instrumentalities Act
3. Defense Base Act
4. War Hazards Compensation Act

Two federal statutes, the Jones Act and the Death on the High Seas Act, provide legal remedies to a vessel's crew members or their survivors.

Recent world events have raised concern and uncertainty about workers' compensation loss exposures to workers assigned to work in politically unstable parts of the world. Two federal statutes discussed in the next section—the Defense Base Act and the War Hazards Compensation Act—may help address some of those concerns.

Outer Continental Shelf Lands Act

The **Outer Continental Shelf Lands Act (OCSLA)** is the first of four federal statutes that extend the benefits of the LHWCA to additional categories of workers: those engaged in exploring and developing natural resources on the outer continental shelf. For purposes of this extension to the LHWCA, the term "employee" does not include masters or members of the crew of any vessel or officers or employees of the United States, any state or foreign government, or any agency or subdivision. Typically, employees subject to OCSLA are workers situated on offshore artificial islands or drilling and production platforms. OCSLA defines the outer continental shelf as the submerged lands of the United States adjacent to the coast but outside the area of a particular state's territorial boundaries. The territorial boundaries of Florida and Texas extend to ten nautical miles from their coastlines, and those of all other coastal states extend to three nautical miles from their coastlines. No concurrent state workers' compensation remedy exists for these workers. Therefore, coverage under this LHWCA extension is exclusive.

Outer Continental Shelf Lands Act (OCSLA)
A federal statute that extends the benefits of the LHWCA to workers engaged in exploring and developing natural resources on the outer continental shelf.

Nonappropriated Fund Instrumentalities Act

Nonappropriated Fund Instrumentalities Act (NFIA)
Federal statute that extends the benefits of LHWCA to civilian employees of the United States whose salary and other benefits are paid with funds generated from government operations rather than funds appropriated by the Armed Services.

The second federal statute that extends LHWCA coverage, the **Nonappropriated Fund Instrumentalities Act (NFIA)**, extends benefits to U.S. civilian employees whose salary and other benefits are paid with funds generated from government operations rather than funds appropriated to the Armed Services by Congress, therefore making these employees ineligible for coverage under the Federal Employees Compensation Act. These employees work primarily at sales facilities on domestic military bases, such as post exchanges, stores, restaurants, daycare centers, movie theaters, and other government-operated revenue-generating facilities. U.S. citizens and permanent residents of the United States or its territories or possessions are covered for such employment outside the United States.

Defense Base Act

Defense Base Act (DBA)
Federal statute that applies the benefits of LHWCA to employees of federal contractors outside the continental United States, Alaska, and Hawaii.

The **Defense Base Act (DBA)** applies the benefits of the LHWCA to workers of federal contractors outside the continental United States, Alaska, and Hawaii. It provides workers' compensation benefits to civilian workers of private federal contractors doing work overseas in furtherance of U.S. foreign policy. Those covered under the DBA include civilians working on overseas military bases, working on overseas construction projects for the U.S. government or its allies, or fulfilling service contracts tied to such construction projects or national defense activity. Some differences exist between the LHWCA and the DBA. For example, the LHWCA minimum compensation benefits provision does not apply to DBA claims. This distinction recognizes the fact that many domestic and foreign overseas workers are paid wages much lower than their U.S. counterparts. Unlike the LHWCA, the DBA supersedes application of state workers' compensation law and is an exclusive remedy. However, like the LHWCA, the DBA specifically excludes masters or members of the crew of any vessel.

War Hazards Compensation Act

War Hazards Compensation Act (WHCA)
Federal statute enacted to supplement the Defense Base Act and shift the costs of workers' compensation from those engaged in such work and injured by a war risk hazard to the U.S. government.

The **War Hazards Compensation Act (WHCA)** was enacted to supplement the DBA and shift the costs of workers' compensation to the U.S. government for those engaged in work outside the continental United States, Alaska, and Hawaii and injured by a war-risk hazard. A war-risk hazard means any hazard arising during a war, during an armed conflict in which the United States is engaged, or from any missile or weapon fired by a hostile force or person. The act provides workers' compensation for several categories of persons employed outside the continental United States for injuries resulting from a war-risk hazard, whether or not the injured party was in the course of employment at the time of the injury. Essentially, the WHCA provides protection equal to the DBA: twenty-four hours a day, seven days a week for any hazard arising during a war or an armed conflict between military forces in which the United States is engaged.

Other Federal Statutes

The **Federal Employers' Liability Act (FELA)**, which applies to employees of interstate railroads, was enacted when many states were first contemplating workers' compensation statutes. FELA allows workers (or the survivors of deceased workers) to sue their employers for occupational injuries resulting from the employer's negligence. FELA uses a comparative negligence standard; contributory negligence reduces but does not bar recovery. It also eliminates assumption of risk as a defense in suits subject to FELA, making the employer liable for the negligence of all its officers, agents, and workers. That provision eliminates the fellow-worker defense as well. In short, FELA permits injured workers to sue their employers without being subject to the traditional employer defenses. Intrastate railroads that connect to interstate railroads by way of sidings or interchanges are considered instruments of interstate commerce and are thus also subject to FELA.

The **Migrant and Seasonal Agricultural Worker Protection Act** provides various protections to migrant and seasonal agricultural workers, including the right to sue their employers for occupational injury or illness if they are not covered by workers' compensation insurance. The **Federal Employees' Compensation Act** provides workers' compensation benefits for nonmilitary workers of the federal government. The federal government self-insures this loss exposure.

The Jones Act and the Death on the High Seas Act permit crew members or their survivors to sue a negligent vessel owner/employer for damages, thereby providing a remedy that is fundamentally different from the no-fault approach of state workers' compensation statutes and the federal compensation statutes previously discussed. Additional remedies for crew members and their survivors are provided by general maritime law, which has been created by legal traditions and court decisions rather than by federal statutes. The liability under each act and additional legal remedies are discussed next.

Section 33 of the Merchant Marine Act of 1920, commonly called the **Jones Act**, grants crew members a cause of action against their employers for negligence that results in injury or death. The Jones Act allows the personal representative of a deceased crew member to claim damages on behalf of the crew member's survivors.

Jones Act recoveries are subject to the rule of pure comparative fault. That is, recovery is reduced in proportion to the crew member's share of negligence. If, for example, the vessel owner was 40 percent at fault and the crew member was 60 percent at fault, the crew member's recovery will be reduced by 60 percent. Only if the crew member is 100 percent negligent is recovery barred. However, if the vessel owner has violated a statute enacted for the crew's safety, a finding of comparative fault under the Jones Act is prohibited. The statute of limitations period for a Jones Act claim is three years, and it begins when the crew member discovers the critical facts of his or her injury and its cause.

Federal Employers' Liability Act (FELA)
Federal statute that allows employees of interstate railroads or their survivors to sue their employers for occupational injuries or death that result from the employer's negligence.

Migrant and Seasonal Agricultural Workers Protection Act
Federal statute that allows migrant and seasonal workers to sue their employers for occupational injury or illness if the workers are not covered by workers' compensation insurance.

Federal Employees' Compensation Act
Federal statute that provides workers' compensation benefits for nonmilitary employees of the federal government.

Jones Act
Federal statute that grants vessels' crew members or their survivors a cause of action against their employers for negligence that results in injury or death.

Maintenance
As defined in the Jones Act, food and lodging.

Cure
As defined in the Jones Act, medical treatment.

Death on the High Seas Act (DOHSA)
Federal statute that provides legal remedies to survivors of a vessel's crew for death that occurs beyond a marine league from the shore of any state.

Generally, damages in Jones Act cases fall under the same rules that apply in other maritime personal injury actions and in nonmaritime actions as well. The Jones Act award to an injured crew member might include all damages attributable to the physical injury, including medical expenses, if not paid as **maintenance** (food and lodging) and **cure** (medical treatment), past and future pain and suffering, past and future mental anguish, impaired enjoyment of life, lost earnings, impaired earning capacity, and past and future economic loss, if any, other than lost earnings.

Damages that may be recoverable in wrongful death actions under the Jones Act include funeral expenses, loss of financial support, loss of services, loss of wages to the date of the decedent's death, and the decedent's medical expenses and pain and suffering before death. Damages for loss of consortium (the right of a spouse to the company, help, and affection of, and sexual relations with his or her mate) are not recoverable under the Jones Act for either injury or death.

The **Death on the High Seas Act (DOHSA)** provides an additional remedy for survivors of deceased crew members. (The remedy is also available to survivors of any persons, whether crew members or not.) DOHSA allows recovery for death caused by wrongful act, neglect, or default occurring on the high seas, defined as beyond a marine league from the shore of any state. DOHSA also provides a remedy if a vessel's unseaworthiness caused the death of a crew member. The damages recoverable under DOHSA are essentially the same as those recoverable under the Jones Act and, as with the Jones Act, damages for loss of consortium are not recoverable under DOHSA.

Three additional remedies are available for injured crew members, based on general maritime law rather than statutes:

- Maintenance and cure
- Suit for breach of the vessel owner's warranty of seaworthiness
- The Moragne remedy

Under the first general maritime law remedy, the employer, typically a vessel owner, is legally obligated to pay the costs of providing maintenance and cure for any person who is injured or who becomes ill while serving as a member of the vessel's crew, regardless of fault. The employer must pay maintenance and cure until "maximum medical cure" is achieved. The employer's obligation ceases when future treatment will not improve the crew member's medical condition. The only defenses that a vessel owner can assert are (1) that the crew member intentionally concealed an illness or injury at the inception of employment; (2) that the injury was a result of the crew member's own willful misbehavior, deliberate act, or indiscretion; or (3) that the crew member inexcusably delayed reporting the injury or illness, impairing the vessel owner's ability to assert a defense.

A second maritime law remedy available to injured crew members is a suit alleging breach of the vessel owner's warranty of seaworthiness. Both the vessel owner and the vessel operator are liable for damages resulting from injuries sustained by crew members because of the unseaworthiness of the vessel or because of a failure to supply and keep the vessel's appurtenances, gear, and equipment in proper order.

A third maritime law remedy, the Moragne remedy, stems from the case of *Moragne v. States Marine Lines, Inc.*[2] In this case, the U.S. Supreme Court created a remedy for wrongful death on navigable waters. This remedy covers deaths within territorial waters as well as deaths on the high seas. It also provides for recovery for deaths caused by either negligence or the vessel's unseaworthiness. Noncrew members can also qualify for the Moragne remedy; however, they are not entitled to the warranty of seaworthiness.

EXCEPTIONS AND CHALLENGES TO WORKERS' COMPENSATION AS EXCLUSIVE REMEDY

As previously discussed, workers' compensation is intended to be the exclusive remedy for injured workers by providing a quick, dependable source of compensation to workers for work-related injuries. The worker loses the right to sue the employer, and the employer loses certain common-law defenses. However, some statutes allow exceptions to workers' compensation's exclusive remedy. The exceptions are as follows:

- Employer's intentional acts
- Loss of consortium
- Dual capacity claims
- Subsidiary worker status

- Third-party-over actions
- Failure to provide benefits
- Title VII or ADA discrimination claims
- Fellow worker doctrine

Employer's Intentional Acts

Bodily injury intentionally caused or aggravated by the employer is not covered by workers' compensation insurance. The rationales for this exception to the exclusive remedy are that an intentional tort is not an accident and that the injury does not arise out of the course of employment.

Bad-faith claim handling might be considered an intentional act and thus an exception to the exclusive remedy. Insurers and employers that self-insure their workers' compensation loss exposure might be liable to injured workers for improperly handling claims as specified in unfair claim settlement practices acts. Bad-faith claims are less likely to be allowed if state workers' compensation statutes include penalties for improper claim handling. Adjusters should carefully evaluate each state's statutes when assessing an insurer's loss exposure to bad-faith actions.

> ### Intentional Act Claim
>
> Bercaw was robbed and killed while delivering pizzas for Domino's Pizza. Bercaw's relatives sued Domino's for wrongful death because of intentional endangerment. They claimed that Domino's should have known delivery drivers were exposed to attacks and should have taken precautions to prevent such attacks. The court dismissed the lawsuit because workers' compensation was the exclusive remedy, and the decision was affirmed on appeal. For an injury to be considered intentional, the employer must have specifically intended its actions to injure the worker. Bercaw's relatives did not prove that Domino's intended for robbers to attack Bercaw.[3]

Wrongful discharge and sexual harassment might also be considered intentional acts and outside the exclusive remedy protection. Employment practices liability policies should cover these loss exposures. Finally, deliberate and serious safety regulations violations can expose employers to liability excluded by workers' compensation insurance. Those violations might be considered intentional acts that subject the employer to liability in tort.

Loss of Consortium

Loss of consortium

The loss of benefits that one spouse is entitled to receive from the other, including affection, assistance, and conjugal fellowship; it includes loss or impairment of sexual relations.

Loss of consortium is the loss of benefits that one spouse is entitled to receive from the other, including, affection, assistance and conjugal fellowship, and includes loss or impairment of sexual relations.[4] An injured worker's spouse might claim damages from the employer for loss of consortium because of the worker's injuries. Generally, either statutes or court decisions reject loss of consortium claims.

> ### Loss of Consortium Claim
>
> Raney, a hospital custodian, contracted hepatitis B from needle pricks while emptying trash cans. Her husband sued for loss of companionship. Her husband and children sued the hospital for having to undergo tests and vaccinations and for their fear of contracting hepatitis B.
>
> The court dismissed the loss of companionship claim because workers' compensation is the exclusive remedy for claims based on injuries to a worker. However, the court awarded damages for the claim for tests, vaccinations, and fear of contracting hepatitis B because those claims did not result from Raney's actual work injury or her inability to do anything she did before contracting hepatitis B.[5]

Dual Capacity Claims

A **dual capacity claim** occurs when a worker contends that the employer acts in a capacity other than that of employer and therefore the worker is entitled to pursue a claim in tort separate from a workers' compensation claim. For example, if a worker uses and is injured by defective equipment that the employer has manufactured, the worker might sue the employer under products liability. Very few courts have allowed dual capacity claims.

Dual capacity claim
Claim in which an employee contends that the employer was acting in a capacity other than that of employer and that, therefore, the employee is entitled to pursue a claim in tort separate from a workers' compensation claim.

Dual Capacity Claim

Bitar worked for Beirut Bakery, Inc. Wakim, the sole owner of the bakery, also owned the building and the parking lot on which the bakery was located. Bitar slipped on the ice while throwing trash into a bin in the parking lot and received workers' compensation benefits from Beirut Bakery, Inc.

Bitar sued Wakim as the landlord for failing to maintain a safe parking lot. Wakim contended that workers' compensation was the exclusive remedy. Although Bitar worked for Beirut Bakery, Inc., Wakim owned the corporation, and Wakim's capacity as owner was not distinct from his capacity as landlord.

The court agreed with Wakim, and the decision was affirmed on appeal, that Wakim and Beirut Bakery, Inc., were so closely related that they should be treated as the same entity. Workers' compensation was the exclusive remedy for Bitar's injuries.[6]

Subsidiary Worker Status

Some states permit an injured worker of a subsidiary corporation to sue the parent corporation in tort. Such a suit might be successful, depending on the legal structure of the subsidiary and of the parent and on the basis of the parent's alleged negligence. The suit would also depend on how the parent corporation was negligent. For example, if the parent corporation manufactured a product that injured the worker, the worker might successfully sue the parent corporation if the subsidiary corporation was not involved in manufacturing the product.

Third-Party-Over Actions

A **third-party-over action** can arise when an injured worker sues and recovers from a negligent third party. The third party, in turn, sues the employer for at least partial recovery based on joint negligence of the employer. The construction industry with its reliance on independent contractors and commercial landlords is often the target of third-party-over actions.

Third-party-over action
Action that arises when an injured employee sues and recovers from a negligent third party and the third party, in turn, sues the employer for at least a partial recovery based on the employer's joint negligence.

For example, assume that a worker was injured by a production machine that the employer, with knowledge of a safety defect, allowed the worker to operate. The injured worker sued the machine manufacturer, seeking a larger judgment than the benefits that would be permitted under the workers' compensation law. The manufacturer then sued the employer, asserting that the employer was also negligent in permitting the machine to be operated under unsafe conditions.

The employer's Commercial General Liability (CGL) policy might apply if the contract between the manufacturer and the employer places liability on the employer. The CGL employers liability exclusion does not apply to liability assumed by the insured under an insured contract. To illustrate the effect of this exception, assume that the employer had agreed in the sales contract to indemnify the machine's manufacturer for damages the manufacturer would be required to pay for injuries caused by the machine and involving the employer's negligence. Assuming that the sales contract was an insured contract as defined in the policy, the employer's CGL policy would protect the employer against the manufacturer's action for indemnity, even though the claim involved injury to the insured's own worker. However, if the indemnification language does not appear in the sales contract, the CGL would exclude the third-party-over action. Employers can protect themselves from this loss exposure by purchasing employers liability insurance, which is part of the workers' compensation policy.

Failure to Provide Benefits

If an employer does not provide workers' compensation benefits, an injured worker can sue the employer in tort. If the employer violates workers' compensation laws, the employer cannot expect to take advantage of exclusive remedy protection.

Title VII or ADA Discrimination Claims

The Americans with Disabilities Act (ADA) of 1992 created a separate cause of action (right to seek recovery) for discrimination against disabled persons, including workers who are disabled by work-related injuries. Such discrimination is also a violation of civil rights laws, such as Title VII of the Civil Rights Act of 1964 as expanded under the Civil Rights Act of 1991, and is outside the scope of workers' compensation insurance. Workers' compensation insurance does not cover those discrimination actions. Workers can bring separate suits for violations of their civil rights, for wrongful discharge, for sexual harassment, or for employment discrimination. Some of these suits include claims of bodily injury and sometimes seek workers' compensation payments, creating a conflict of law between the federal Title VII laws related to discrimination and the state workers' compensation laws.

ADA law and workers' compensation law cross paths when disabled workers can return to their jobs only after their employer has modified their work requirement. To reduce the number of lost work days, employers are eager to return workers to work after an injury, even when doing so requires the employer to find light duty work or to modify the tasks required of the worker.

The employer's expectation is that the worker will eventually return to the same level of activity as before the injury. If the worker is unable to do so, however, the employer might consider the worker permanently and totally disabled for that job and might prefer to find a replacement. At this point, the worker might make a claim under the ADA demanding that the employer make a "reasonable accommodation" and allow the worker to continue to perform the modified version of the job. The employer might have difficulty arguing that the job modification is unreasonable if the worker has continued under the modified version of the job for an extended period and if the employer has not been harmed. The resolution of this situation can be complicated by conflicts of the federal ADA law and the state workers' compensation laws. These complicated legal issues require adjusters to seek the advice of legal counsel.

Fellow Worker Doctrine

In most states, the exclusive remedy doctrine protects employers when a worker's injury is caused by the negligence of a fellow worker. However, several states have specified exceptions to the exclusive remedy. One such exception is when the fellow worker who caused the injury is the injured worker's supervisor. If the supervisor is found negligent, the employer might be deemed responsible for the injury.

SUMMARY

Before the development of a workers' compensation system, the common law defined the duties employers owed to their workers. If an employer did not meet these duties and, as a result, a worker was injured, the worker had the right to sue the employer for damages.

Workers' compensation evolved as a result of the inadequacies of the common law in addressing worker injuries. The goals of the workers' compensation system are as follows:

1. To pay adequate benefits promptly to injured workers or their dependents
2. To eliminate delays and litigation costs
3. To establish a guaranteed benefit
4. To promote industrial safety
5. To pay medical services

These goals are accomplished by making the system "no fault," limiting the defenses that employers can raise, and limiting the circumstances in which workers can sue their employers. Workers' compensation laws vary by state. However, they all have the following common features:

1. Choice of law provision
2. Persons and employments covered

3.   Injuries and diseases covered

4.   Benefits provided

5.   Methods of financing benefits

6.   Procedures for obtaining benefits

7.   Administration of benefits

Federal statutes govern some compensation issues. Persons who are employed by federal institutions or who work upon navigable waterways or federal lands, including federal projects abroad or within the District of Columbia, are covered by the federal laws. Federal laws differ significantly from state workers' compensation laws in terms of compensability and benefits. Some federal compensation laws still require workers (such as railroad workers covered under FELA and seamen covered under the Jones Act) to prove employer negligence.

Several exceptions and challenges can be made to workers' compensation as the exclusive remedy of the injured worker, including intentional acts, loss of consortium, dual capacity claims, subsidiary worker status, third-party-over actions, the employer's failure to provide benefits, discrimination claims under the Americans with Disabilities Act and the Civil Rights Act, and the fellow worker doctrine.

The next several chapters will provide a more in-depth description of the provisions of workers' compensation laws. Knowing these provisions is important to adjusters because they will be called upon to decide if a claimant is a worker within the meaning of the workers' compensation law and if the injury or disease is covered. They will also be asked to calculate the amount and duration of benefits to be paid.

CHAPTER NOTES

1.   2003 National Council on Compensation Insurance, Inc.

2.   *Moragne v. States Marine Lines, Inc.*, 398 U.S. 375, 1970 AMC 967 (1970).

3.   *Bercaw v. Domino's Pizza, Inc.*, 630 N.E.2d 166 (Ill. App. 2 Dist. 1994).

4.   *Black's Law Dictionary*, 7th ed. (St. Paul, Minn.: West Publishing Co., 1999).

5.   *Raney v. Walter O. Moss Regional Hospital*, 629 So.2d 485 (La. App. 3 Cir. 1993).

6.   *Bitar v. Wakim*, 536 N.W.2d 583 (Mich. 1995).

Chapter 2

Direct Your Learning

Compensability: Covered Employments and Injuries

After learning the content of this chapter, you should be able to:

■ Given a case, determine the employment status of a given worker.

- Describe the elements of an employment relationship.

- Describe the following special employment relationships:

  - Statutory employees

  - Lent employees

  - Joint and dual employments

- Identify situations or employments that are typically excluded from workers' compensation insurance.

- Describe the noninsurance ways in which employers can transfer the workers' compensation loss exposure.

■ Given a case, determine if the injury is covered by workers' compensation insurance.

- Describe the compensability requirements of "accidental" or "by accident" for a claim for workers' compensation benefits.

- Describe the workers' compensation coverage for injuries that are not accidental.

- Identify the injuries typically covered and not covered by workers' compensation statutes.

■ Given a case, determine whether the employment and injury are covered by workers' compensation statutes.

Develop Your Perspective

What are the main topics covered in the chapter?

This chapter focuses on two elements of compensability: covered employments and covered injuries. To determine compensability, the adjuster must determine if the injured worker is an employee under the statute and if the injury sustained is a covered injury under the statute. The adjuster will also have to determine if the accident or injury or disease is included in the workers' compensation statute.

Review the workers' compensation statute in your state.

- What is the definition of an employee?

- What is the definition of an independent contractor?

Why is it important to learn about these topics?

Adjusters must understand the definitions of covered employments and covered injuries when handling workers' compensation claims. Failure to distinguish between what is covered by the workers' compensation statute and what is not can lead to mishandled claims.

Review the workers' compensation statute in your state.

- What injuries and diseases are covered?

- Why are certain injuries excluded?

How can you use what you will learn?

Analyze a workers' compensation claim in your state and determine if the first two elements of compensability are met.

- Is the injured worker a covered employee?

- Is the injury covered? Why or why not?

Chapter 2

Compensability: Covered Employments and Injuries

Workers' compensation statutes require employers to provide a certain amount of economic security to injured workers. In return, workers relinquish the right to sue their employers. Both state and federal statutes protect specific classes of workers but do not cover some employments and injuries; therefore, for some injured workers, suing their employers continues to be their only remedy.

To fully understand workers' compensation, an adjuster must understand which employers and workers fall within the scope of the workers' compensation law. Not everyone who performs work is an employee. Employers can choose to use "other than employees," such as independent contractors, for their businesses. This chapter describes the distinction between employees and independent contractors. Some employments are exempted from the scope of various workers' compensation statutes even though such workers are clearly employees.

Workers' compensation covers most, but not all, work related injuries. Generally, workers' compensation statutes require injuries to be "accidental" to be compensable. This chapter explains how the meaning of this requirement evolved. Workers' compensation statutes give special consideration to some types of injuries for which the accidental nature can be difficult to prove or disprove. These injuries, discussed at the end of this chapter, include occupational disease, cumulative trauma, hernias, hearing loss, and psychological injuries.

THE EMPLOYMENT RELATIONSHIP

Workers' compensation statutes are designed to protect all employees except those specifically excluded by the statutes. Not all workers are employees. A worker's status as an employee depends on the existence of an employer-employee relationship. The employer might be an individual, a partnership, a corporation, or any other entity. The employee is the individual who has consented to perform personal services for the employer in exchange for consideration. This consent implies that the employee has agreed to be under the employer's direction and control.

Elements of the Employer-Employee Relationship

Workers' compensation obligations are determined not by who is at fault but by whether the worker is an employee subject to the workers' compensation statute and whether the injury or disease is connected to the employment. Numerous factors determine whether someone is an employee. These factors relate to one of three essential elements of an employer-employee relationship: control, consent, and consideration.

Control is the first element in distinguishing employer-employee relationships from "other than employee" relationships. Control includes the employer's right to do the following:

Control
For workers' compensation purposes, the employer's right to give work assignments, direct how the work is to be done, and hire and discharge workers.

1.   Give work assignments
2.   Direct how the work is to be done
3.   Hire and discharge the worker

Consent
For workers' compensation purposes, a worker's voluntary acceptance of the terms of employment and the worker's competency to enter into such an agreement.

Consent, the second element, means that the worker voluntarily accepts the terms of the employment and is competent to enter into such an agreement as long as the agreement has a lawful purpose. Some workers' compensation statutes expressly exclude a spouse working for a spouse, children working for their parents, prison inmates working to serve their sentences, and workers employed in illegal trades because these workers might not be able to consent to the working relationship.

Consideration
For workers' compensation purposes, something of value an employer gives to a worker in exchange for work.

Consideration, the third element, means that services are not gratuitously given. The employer gives the worker something of value in exchange for the work. Consideration need not be monetary or tangible. Typical employment involves an employee's providing personal services in exchange for wages. However, meals or room and board can also be consideration sufficient to establish a valid employment relationship. Other types of exchanges can be consideration, such as working in exchange for using the facilities at a health club or golf club. Volunteers working for nonprofit organizations often do not receive money, yet many state workers' compensation statutes include volunteers in their definition of employee. Because of the many variables associated with control, consent, and consideration, each state has developed an extensive body of case law to interpret the meaning and applicability of statutory definitions.

Motivations for Employers to Consider "Other Than Employee" Workers

Issues that arise in considering the elements required in an employment relationship include what distinguishes an employee from an "other than employee" worker and why an employer might prefer to have "other than employee" workers. Employers increasingly use temporary contract workers and independent contractors as they look for ways to reduce expenses.

Employers often prefer to consider workers "other than employee" workers for several reasons, including the following:

- *Reduced workers' compensation premiums.* Because premiums are based on an employer's payroll, employers can reduce their employee payroll by treating workers as "other than employees." Adjusters might discover this practice while conducting their investigations and must determine whether an injured worker is an employee entitled to workers' compensation benefits even though the worker might not be classified as such.

- *Reduced employee benefits.* "Other than employee" workers are usually not entitled to any employee benefits. Therefore, companies save on the costs of providing and administering those benefits.

- *Reduced taxes and tax withholding.* The employer is not responsible for Social Security and unemployment taxes on "other than employee" workers, as they are for employees. Employers must also withhold their employees' taxes and pay them to the IRS.

- *Reduced administration costs.* Putting short-term employees on payroll can be cumbersome. To avoid the paperwork, some companies will consider short-term workers to be "other than employee" workers.

- *Reduced loss exposures for employment practices liability.* Some companies try to avoid liability for discrimination in hiring and wrongful discharge by engaging workers as "other than employee" workers.

Even though companies might find it beneficial to consider workers to be "other than employees," the employer's classification alone does not determine the issue. If the facts show that the elements of an employer-employee relationship exist, then absent a specific statutory exclusion, courts will find coverage.

Distinctions Between Employees and Independent Contractors

One of the most common "other than employee" workers is the **independent contractor**. An independent contractor is someone who contracts with another to perform some task. Independent contractors select their own methods to accomplish tasks. When examining the relationship between an employer and a worker, courts tend to presume that the relationship is that of employer-employee under workers' compensation statutes unless the facts establish that the worker is an independent contractor. This presumption is consistent with the remedial purposes of compensation legislation—to indemnify injured workers regardless of fault and without excessive legal action. The courts consider the totality of the circumstances, including the factors shown in the following box and discussed in more detail next, to determine if someone is an employee. The IRS uses similar criteria to make its determination. The descriptive names used by the IRS for these factors are in parentheses.

Independent contractor
A person who contracts with a principal to perform some task, according to his or her own methods, and who is not under the principal's control regarding the physical details of the work.

Factors to Consider to Determine a Worker's Status
- Control over the details of work (Instructions)
- Special skills
- Tools, materials, and equipment (Significant investment)
- Place of work (Work done on employer's premises)
- Method of compensation (Payments)
- Integration of services into business operation
- Training requirements
- Duration of relationship (Continuing relationship)
- Time constraints (Full-time requirements—Set hours of work)
- Availability of services to the public (Working for more than one firm)
- Right to discharge
- Right to quit
- Right to hire subordinates (Hiring assistants)
- Personal service requirement (Services rendered personally)
- Reporting requirements
- Order of sequence set
- Expenses
- Realization of a profit or loss
- State-specific distinctions

Control Over Details of Work (Instructions). The right to control is regarded as the most crucial distinction between employees and independent contractors. An employer has the right to control not only the result of an employee's work but also how that result is accomplished. An independent contractor is simply given specifications for the final product or result. The means of accomplishing the result or the pattern and sequence of completing the final product are left to the independent contractor's judgment. The right to control is the decisive test of the employment relationship; the actual exercise of such a right is not as important. An employer might not exercise the right to control because a worker is experienced and competent, but that does not change the employer-employee relationship.

Special Skills. Employers often hire independent contractors when they need a specialized skill or service that their employees cannot provide. Employees might not have the skill or training for the job, or it might not be economically feasible for the employer to invest in developing the necessary expertise. Specialized skills, taken with other factors, might suggest that a worker is an independent contractor.

For skilled professionals, such as doctors, nurses, lawyers, and architects, the test of whether they are employees or independent contractors is not the extent of the employer's control over a worker's process or professional discretion. The test is, instead, how much control the employer can exercise over the time the professional works for the employer's benefit versus the time the professional works for his or her own benefit. For example, a doctor who works full-time for and is paid a salary by a hospital is an employee even though the hospital's administrators cannot tell the doctor how to perform surgery. A professional worker who performs duties that are more administrative than professional, such as a doctor employed as a hospital administrator, is also more likely to be an employee than an independent contractor.[1]

Tools, Materials, and Equipment (Significant Investment). Investment in tools, materials, and equipment also helps to distinguish between an employee and an independent contractor. Employees are usually hired only to perform work; the employer furnishes tools, materials, and equipment needed to complete the work. Many independent contractors invest in their own tools and equipment and furnish the materials needed for their work. This investment, particularly if substantial, can suggest independent contractor status. However, furnishing tools, materials, and equipment alone is not enough to make a worker an independent contractor. For example, carpenters, hairdressers, and chefs often bring their own hand tools to work, but other factors, such as employer control over work processes and details, might still indicate that these workers are employees.

Place of Work (Work Done on Employer's Premises). Workers who are required to work on the employer's premises are likely to be deemed employees. Workers who can choose where they work are more likely to be deemed independent contractors, other factors aside. With more employees working from home and telecommuting, this factor is less likely to determine the issue, particularly because many independent contractors work at the employer's premises.

Method of Compensation (Payments). Workers paid by the hour, week, or month are likely to be considered employees. However, some independent contractors receive payment at regular intervals as part of a lump sum payment for completion of the job. The rationale for this test is that compensation based on a unit of time spent on the job indicates employer control of the worker's use of time spent at work.[2] Determining a worker's status is more difficult when payment is by commission or on a piecework basis. Both employees and independent contractors can receive compensation in these forms.

Integration of Services Into the Business Operation. If the service performed is an integral part of the employer's business, the worker is likely to be an employee. This factor, known as the "relative nature of the work test," simplifies the analysis of the employment relationship. Rather than focusing on the mechanics of the work to determine the extent of control or the right to control, this factor focuses on whether the services provided are an integral part of the employer's business. For example, a piece worker who assembles clothes for a clothing manufacturer would probably be regarded as an employee even if she performs her work at home, sets her own hours, and is paid by the piece. Assembling clothing is the essential activity of a clothing manufacturer, and the workers who perform such work are considered employees. In contrast, a landscaper who tends the grounds of the clothing manufacturer is likely to be regarded as an independent contractor even if a substantial portion of the worker's time is devoted to that employer. The case in the box provides an example of an "independent contractor" that is in reality an employee.

Independent Contractor Versus Employee

A dairy hired a cheese maker. Because cheese making is a specialized skill, a contract was written designating the cheese maker an independent contractor, to be paid piecemeal and to work without supervision or set hours. The contract also stated that the dairy was interested only in the final product. Nevertheless, the relationship was determined to be that of employer-employee, not employer-independent contractor, because the cheese maker's job was considered an integral part of the dairy business.[3]

Training Requirements. If a worker is required to attend meetings or to receive training in how to perform a given task, the employer is probably interested in both the final result and the means by which the result is accomplished. Workers subject to such training are likely to be employees.

Duration of the Relationship (Continuing Relationship). If the worker's services are recurrent, even if performed at irregular intervals, the relationship is more characteristic of employer-employee than independent contractor. However, a worker who is otherwise a bona fide independent contractor does not lose that status by providing regular and continual services.

Time Constraints (Full-Time Requirements—Set Hours of Work). An independent contractor might be given a schedule to complete the job. In contrast, imposing specific time constraints, such as set hours of work and full-time devotion to the job, creates the appearance of an employer-employee relationship.

Availability of Services to the Public (Working for More Than One Firm). A worker who advertises his or her services, offers them to anyone needing such specialized skills, and regularly provides them to more than one employer at a time is likely to be an independent contractor. Conversely, a person working solely or substantially for one employer is likely to be an employee.

Some independent contractors must meet licensing requirements to perform work for the general public. If a worker is hired because a special license is required for the job, and if the worker offers the licensed services to others, then the worker is likely to be an independent contractor. However, many kinds of employees, such as adjusters, lawyers, and insurance producers, also have licenses. Additionally, a worker performing a service that is integral to the employer's business might be regarded as an employee even if the worker also works for others.

Right to Discharge. If an employer can dismiss a worker, the worker is an employee, not an independent contractor. This test can be decisive because the right to discharge indicates the right to control. However, this test is neither absolute nor always conclusive because not all independent contractors have written contracts that contain cancellation provisions. For example, a housekeeper might be engaged on a verbal contract and with the understanding that cancellation can occur at any time. Although the right to discharge is a key test, courts are reluctant to rule out exceptions.

Right to Quit. If the worker can terminate the employment at will without incurring any legal liability for a contract breach, the relationship is likely that of employer-employee.

Right to Hire Subordinates (Hiring Assistants). If a worker can hire, supervise, and pay assistants to complete a job, then control rests with the worker, who would likely be considered an independent contractor.

Personal Service Requirement (Services Rendered Personally). If the employer specifically designates the worker who must perform the services, then the employer is probably interested not only in the result but also in the methods used to accomplish the desired result, and the worker is likely an employee. Hiring an independent contractor does not normally allow the employer to dictate who will do the job, although such a right might exist in some cases.

Reporting Requirements. If the worker is required to submit oral or written reports at regular intervals while performing the job, the employer likely has a degree of control over the worker. Consequently, the worker is likely to be an employee.

Order or Sequence Set. If a worker must perform services in the order or sequences set by the employer, the relationship is most likely an employer-employee relationship.

Expenses. If the employer pays the worker's business and/or travel expenses, the worker is usually an employee. The employer, to be able to control expenses, retains the right to regulate and direct a worker's business activities. Conversely, a worker who is paid on a project basis and who includes incidental expenses in the "bid amount" for the project is generally an independent contractor.

Realization of Profit or Loss. A worker who can realize a profit or suffer a loss as a result of providing services to a company is generally an independent contractor, although this factor is not by itself decisive.

State-Specific Distinctions. Thirteen states define independent contractors in their workers' compensation statutes. Exhibit 2-1 provides an example of one state's definition.

EXHIBIT 2-1

Sample Independent Contractor Provision

Wisconsin Workers Compensation Act (102.07(8b)):

An independent contractor is not considered an employee of an employer for whom the independent contractor provides services if all of the following criteria are met:

- The independent contractor maintains a separate business with his or her own office equipment, material, and other equipment.

- The independent contractor holds or has applied for a federal employer identification number with the federal Internal Revenue Service (IRS) or had filed business or self-employment tax returns with the IRS based on that work or service in the previous year.

- The independent contractor operates under contracts to perform specific services for specific amounts of money and under which the independent contractor controls the means of performing the work.

- The independent contractor incurs the main expenses related to the service performed under contract.

- The independent contractor is responsible for satisfactory completion of the work under contract and is liable for failure to complete the work.

- The independent contractor receives compensation for the work under contract on a commission, per job, or competitive bid basis, and not on any other basis.

- The independent contractor may realize a profit or suffer a loss under contracts to perform work.

- The independent contractor has continuing or recurring business liabilities or obligations.

- The success or failure of the independent contractor's business depends on the relationship of business receipts to expenditures.

International Risk Management Institute, Inc. (IRMI), *IRMI's Workers Compensation State Laws,* 2001, p. VIII. E Wisconsin - 2. Reproduced with permission of the publisher, International Risk Management Institute, Inc., from *IRMI Workers Comp.* Further reproduction prohibited.

Wisconsin requires an independent contractor to meet *all* of the listed criteria. Other states do not have such strict requirements, and most states do not define independent contractor. They rely instead on common-law criteria, such as the factors previously described, to make the distinction. Case 2-2, found later in the chapter in the section "Lent Employees," illustrates how a court in a state that does not define independent contractor examines an employment relationship to determine whether a worker is an employee.

Special Employment Relationships

Certain types of employees and relationships raise important questions about the nature or existence of an employment relationship and of coverage under workers' compensation statutes. Those employers and relationships include statutory employees, lent employees, and joint and dual employments.

Statutory Employees

The preceding discussion focused on the tests to determine whether a worker is an employee or an independent contractor. Workers' compensation statutes do cover some independent contractors, called *statutory employees.*

A statutory employee situation arises when a general contractor hires a subcontractor (an independent contractor) who is uninsured for workers' compensation, and one of the subcontractor's employees is injured. Because the purpose of the workers' compensation system is to provide a remedy to all employees exposed to employment hazards, most state statutes impose workers' compensation obligations on general contractors. The injured worker in these situations is considered a statutory employee, and the general contractor is the statutory employer. Although it might appear that the general contractor is unjustly burdened, this result must be understood in the context of the primary purpose of the workers' compensation system—to compensate employees and their dependents regardless of fault. Furthermore, imposing vicarious liability (liability of an employer for acts of an employee) on the general contractor is justified because the general contractor presumably has control over which subcontractor to hire and has the responsibility to insist that the subcontractor be insured.

When a case involves a hierarchy of contractors and some at various levels are uninsured, the workers' compensation statute generally moves up the hierarchy until it finds the first insured contractor. Workers' compensation obligations are imposed solely on that contractor. The assumption is that control flows downward, so liability flows upward.

A risk management technique for general contractors under these circumstances is to require proof of workers' compensation insurance from a subcontractor before the subcontractor can bid on a job. Additionally, the workers' compensation statute does not absolve the irresponsible subcontractor. Most states allow the insured contractor legal remedies against the uninsured subcontractor to recoup losses paid for the subcontractor's injured employee.

Lent Employees

Lent employees also raise special workers' compensation questions about which employer is responsible when one employer assigns one of its regular employees (called the lent employee) to work temporarily for another employer (called the special employer). The lending employer is called the general employer. The typical employment situation arises when a temporary employment agency contracts one of its workers out to another employer.

When a general employer lends an employee to a special employer, the special employer becomes liable for workers' compensation only if all of the following three conditions are met:

1. The employee has made a contract of hire, expressed or implied, with the special employer.
2. The work performed is essentially the special employer's work.
3. The special employer has the right to control the details of the work.

Also, when all three of these conditions are met, *both* the general and special employers are liable under workers' compensation.[4] The crucial element is control. The special employer becomes liable only if an actual transfer of control occurs; otherwise, the worker is considered an independent contractor, but still an employee of the general employer.

Another issue related to lent employees is which employer, if not both, is immune from common-law suits by virtue of the workers' compensation exclusive remedy doctrine. States have differed on the issue of immunity. Some states make workers' compensation the exclusive remedy against both the general and the special employers, but other states allow common-law suits against either the general or the special employer who did not provide the statutory workers' compensation benefits. The case in the box examines a special employment relationship.

Temporary Workers—Independent Contractor or Special Employee?

Ms. Shoemaker worked for a temporary employment agency, which paid Shoemaker and confirmed her assignments. The agency sent Shoemaker to work for Westwood Pharmaceuticals as an assembly-line packing worker.

As a temporary worker, Shoemaker had to wear a visitor's pass and enter the plant through a separate door from the permanent workers. Westwood did not have the right to fire temporary workers, but it could bar them from the plant at any time. Shoemaker did the same work as the permanent workers and was supervised by Westwood's staff.

While working on the assembly line, Shoemaker was injured. She sued Westwood for negligence. Westwood claimed that it was Shoemaker's special employer and that Shoemaker should be entitled only to workers' compensation benefits (not general damages). Both Westwood and the employment agency agreed that the employment agency was the general employer.

Initially, the Workers' Compensation Board had determined that Westwood was not a special employer. The court overturned this decision, ruling that Westwood was a special employer because of the following:

- Westwood controlled Shoemaker's activities on its premises.
- Westwood's staff told Shoemaker what to do and how to do it.
- Westwood furnished Shoemaker with her equipment.
- Shoemaker performed the same duties as permanent workers.
- Westwood could bar her from the plant at any time.

Note: In this case, the worker did not want to be considered an employee of Westwood because her potential damages would be greater in a tort claim than under the workers' compensation statutes. Westwood sought immunity from the common-law suit by seeking status as a special employer.[5]

Joint and Dual Employments

Workers might have more than one employer. Employers might share workers through joint employment or dual employment.

The key element of a joint employment is that a worker performs the same personal services for two or more employers at the same time. If the worker has an employer-employee relationship with all employers, the employers are jointly and severally liable for workers' compensation benefits. If any of the key criteria of an employer-employee relationship are missing for a particular employer, that employer is not included among those jointly liable. That employer is excused from paying workers' compensation benefits but also loses immunity from common-law suits. Some states impose joint and several liability on joint employments, and other states apportion liability among employers.

The following hypothetical case is an example of a liability question arising from a joint employment. A film company rented an airplane and a pilot from an airline corporation. During filming, the airplane crashed. Both the film company and the airline corporation directed the pilot's activities during the filming, and therefore both employers could be held liable for workers' compensation benefits. Because no state allows double recovery to the worker, the adjuster should consult with legal counsel to determine which employer would be liable in this case.

Dual employments are different from joint employments. In dual employments, a worker performs separate and distinct services for two employers at different times. The only employer responsible for workers' compensation benefits and immune from common-law suits is the employer whose interests were being advanced at the time of the worker's injury. An example of dual employment would be a security guard who works for two separate employers, a bank and a hotel. If the guard is hurt in a robbery attempt at the bank, the hotel is not liable for workers' compensation benefits because the worker's activities at the time of the injury were related solely to the employment with the bank. The case in the box deals with a dual employment claim.

Concurrent Employers—Who Pays?

Febe started work with Riverboat Casino on October 11, 1992, dealing "double-deck black jack." On April 20, 1993, she took a second job dealing "single-deck black jack" at Harold's Club. She worked forty hours a week at Riverboat and twenty to twenty-five hours at Harold's. In July of 1993, it was determined that Febe was suffering from tendonitis caused by the repetitive motion of shuffling cards. Febe filed a claim with both employers. Each employer blamed the other for Febe's condition. Although there is a difference between the motions of dealing single decks versus dealing double decks, medical experts were unable to determine which employment caused her injury. The court decided to apportion financial responsibility between Riverboat and Harold's based on the wages Febe earned from each.[6]

Note: The employers also unsuccessfully argued that the "last injurious exposure rule" applied to this claim. The court stated that this rule applied only to successive employers, not to concurrent employers. The "last injurious exposure rule" is discussed later in this chapter.

Exempted and Limited Employments

Not all workers are employees, and not all employees are subject to the workers' compensation statutes. Certain employees are legislatively exempted; others are judicially excluded because they fail to meet one or more of the criteria of an employer-employee relationship. Employment relationships that are exempt from state workers' compensation statutes vary greatly by state. Various exemptions have evolved as a result of judicial interpretations. A chart of the state-by-state list of employments that are exempt from the state's workers' compensation statutes can be found in the U.S. Chamber of Commerce Analysis of Workers Compensation Laws. Adjusters should know the exemptions of the states in which they adjust claims. Some typical exempted employments are listed in the following box.

Typical Exempted Employments

Domestic workers	Real estate salespersons
Farm workers	Casual workers

In addition to those exempted employments listed, some states exempt employments for the following:

- Religious and charitable organizations
- Sole proprietors, partners, and corporate officers
- Intrafamily employments
- Employers having fewer than a minimum number of employees
- Public and federal employments

Other miscellaneous exclusions found in some states are described later in this chapter.

Domestic Workers

Domestic workers, such as servants, maids, and gardeners, are hired to work in a home or to maintain a household. These workers typically meet the criteria for being employees; that is, the elements of control, consent, and consideration and the other employment criteria likely exist in their relationship with their employer. However, their employment usually has no business purpose. Some state workers' compensation statutes use the terms "trade" or "industry" to mean a business purpose. Courts have concluded that the workers' compensation system does not apply to every odd job performed for a homeowner.

The U.S. Chamber of Commerce Analysis of Workers' Compensation Laws shows the states that have statutory exclusions in one form or another for domestic employees. Some states exclude them only under certain conditions or only in conjunction with other factors. For example, states that generally cover domestic employees might still exclude them if the employment is part-time or if the employment fails to meet the required minimum number of employees.

Agricultural Employment

Agricultural employments do not always have the elements of an employer-employee relationship. Many labor exchanges and gratuitous services are performed for farmers by family members and friends. Consequently, agricultural employments are generally excluded from workers' compensation statutes. Another reason for the agricultural exclusion is the difficulty of complying with administrative requirements. Small farms have little or no payroll recordkeeping and may employ only a small number of seasonal workers.

Some states are eliminating the agricultural employment exemption because the distinction between agricultural employments and nonagricultural employments has become blurred. This uncertainty can arise when the agricultural operation is an integral first stage in the industrial production of consumer goods, such as for a vineyard that grows the grapes, then processes them into wine and bottles the wine. If an agricultural process is a stage in a manufacturing process, the employment might lose its agricultural standing and its statutory exclusion.[7]

Instead of analyzing the nature of the employer's operation as farm or nonfarm, the courts interpret agricultural exclusion statutes according to the character of the employee's work and if and at what stage it is part of an industrial process. The test applied is whether the work involves handling an agricultural raw material or a finished agricultural product. The latter would give the work a commercial character that eliminates the agricultural exclusion. Because of the changing character of agriculture, states that still have statutory farm exclusions generally allow farmers to elect to have their employees covered under workers' compensation statutes.

Real Estate Salespeople and Brokers

Real estate salespeople and brokers often simultaneously represent more than one firm and do not follow a pattern of work or work hours established by their employer. They are compensated substantially from commissions and many operate under a contract specifying that they are independent contractors. Although courts do not generally honor such independent contractor designations in what is an otherwise employer-employee relationship, many states have recognized the special relationship between realty companies and their sales force and have expressly excluded real estate sales occupations. Therefore, real estate sales personnel are excluded even if the circumstances of their employment indicate that they are employees.

Casual Employments

When the relationship between the worker and the employer is not continuous or recurrent, the worker might not be considered an employee for compensation purposes. Some states have set temporal or monetary thresholds to define "casual" employments. For example, a state may exclude a handyman who has worked fewer than fifty-two hours during the preceding ninety days or who has earned less than $100 during the same period.

Some states have abandoned the casual employment exclusion altogether. Most apply the casual employment exclusion only if the employment is also outside the employer's usual business. Typical statutory language defining the casual employment exclusion reads "casual and not in the employer's trade or business."

States that exclude casual employment only when the work is also outside the employer's usual business apply the casual employment test to the nature of the work, not to the worker-employer relationship. For example, if a building owner hires a worker for one job, such as painting a building, the employment might not be continuous or recurrent. However, if maintaining the building is shown to be an integral part of the employer's business, the employment does not meet the definition of "casual" employment, and the worker is a covered employee.

The primary reason for excluding casual employments is administrative. Workers' compensation benefits are calculated based on past earnings and are provided on the assumption that such earnings are regular and continuous.

Determining the benefit rates for employments with irregular and nonrecurring earnings would be difficult and impractical.

Also, compensating workers more than what they would normally earn from irregular, unpredictable employments might create moral and morale hazards. **Moral hazard** is a condition that increases the likelihood that a person will intentionally cause or exaggerate a loss. **Morale hazard** is a condition of carelessness or indifference that increases the frequency or severity of loss. If a transient worker who takes only odd jobs is injured and paid regular weekly benefits, the payments could significantly exceed the worker's usual income and eliminate the incentive to get off disability, thereby creating a morale hazard. This incentive might also increase the temptation to file fraudulent claims, increasing the moral hazard.

Moral hazard
A condition that increases the likelihood that a person will intentionally cause or exaggerate a loss.

Morale hazard
A condition of carelessness or indifference that increases the frequency or severity of loss.

Religious, Charitable, and Nonprofit Employments

Only a few states exempt religious, charitable, and nonprofit employers from workers' compensation obligations because of the nonbusiness character of the employment. Recognizing that such organizations employ paid, nonvolunteer workers, the majority of states do not exclude them. In the absence of an explicit statutory exclusion, courts find coverage for such workers because their work generally meets the criteria of an employment relationship.

Sole Proprietors, Partners, and Corporate Officers

A moral hazard exists when the employer is also the employee. Most states exclude sole proprietors, partners, and corporate officers from workers' compensation obligations. However, to recognize the fact that companies have working partners and officers, these states allow employers to elect inclusion, or to be automatically covered unless they opt not to be. Corporate officers in particular often receive the same coverage as any employee because many officers perform nonexecutive, supervisory, and even manual work. Unless a corporate officer is also the business's owner, the officer is an employee subject to the control of the corporation and its stockholders. Generally, corporate officers are covered unless they elect not to be. About half the states offer this option.

Excluding sole proprietors and partners is common because the employer-employee distinction is difficult to establish in this situation. A few states permit them to elect coverage. In other states, the owners' proprietary interests in the business and their separate legal standing as business entities prevent them from losing their status as employers and becoming employees. However, the exclusion becomes problematic when it involves working partners, such as a partnership of lawyers, or joint venturers (a group of people jointly involved in a commercial enterprise). Excluding working partners is especially problematic when they are placed on the payroll, the basis from which compensation premium rates are determined.

Intrafamily Employments

Only a few states still exclude family members working for a family business. The exclusion is based on the assumption that such arrangements might not involve consideration or consent. Usually the exclusion specifies the circumstances that must exist for the exclusion to apply.

Minimum Number of Employees

Some states set a minimum number of employees before workers' compensation applies to an employment. States recognize that many informal and casual employment relationships exist, particularly in agricultural and domestic settings, for which the general tests of employment cannot be conclusively applied. Statutes vary, but many use three to five employees as the threshold for exemption. Just as for casual employments, the primary reason for this statutory exclusion is administrative. Requiring small businesses to keep and maintain the records necessary to administer and comply with workers' compensation requirements becomes impractical.

This minimum number criterion is arbitrary. Employers might move in and out of the statute's technical scope as the number of their workers fluctuates. To overcome this problem, statutes usually include the term "regularly employed," requiring employers who regularly maintain a certain number of employees above the minimum number to provide workers' compensation benefits even when the number of employees drops below the minimum.[8]

Public and Federal Employments

To recognize the distinction between private and public employment, particularly regarding public officials who have some sovereign power, state workers' compensation statutes do not always make workers' compensation benefits compulsory for public employees. States differ substantially in this area. Some states include all public employees. Some exclude certain public employees and include others. Some exclude only elected officials. In addition to the rationale that public employees exercise sovereign power, other reasons to exclude public officials are that they act independently of any master (employer) and that they are answerable only to the laws they are sworn to serve and uphold.

Miscellaneous Exclusions

Most states exclude workers in illegal employments by statute or as a matter of public policy even absent a statutory exclusion. However, the distinction must be made between a worker employed in an illegal trade and a worker employed illegally. If the trade is illegal, such as operating an illicit drug lab, it is not a covered employment. If the illegality is a function of the employment relationship, such as a minor employed in an otherwise lawful enterprise, a valid employment relationship for the purposes of workers' compensation statutes exists. Remember that the purpose of the statutes is to compensate injured workers.

Another exclusion some states recognize concerns members of the clergy. To avoid confusion and unnecessary litigation, many states have made specific statutory exclusions for this profession, whether they are paid or not.

Other employments frequently excluded from workers' compensation are professional and amateur athletes and officials, jockeys, and taxicab drivers. Using the usual tests of coverage, college athletes can argue that they are employees. They are under the school's control, they generate revenue from their work, and they are given consideration in the form of scholarships and the like. However, because the states did not intend to expand workers' compensation to amateur athletes, they are excluded by statute. Jockeys are in the same category, although they could arguably also be properly classified as independent contractors. The employment status of taxicab drivers can be ambiguous. Because the facts usually suggest that taxicab drivers are independent contractors, some state legislatures have removed the uncertainty by a statutory exclusion.

Noninsurance Transfer of the Workers' Compensation Loss Exposure

The cost of workers' compensation insurance is a significant item in any organization's budget. Consequently, risk managers and other corporate officers continually explore alternative risk management techniques to transfer the financial effect of this loss exposure.

Independent Contractor Agreements

One risk management technique for dealing with workers' compensation loss exposure is to hire independent contractors instead of employees, thereby transferring the workers' compensation statutory obligations to the independent contractor. However, courts frown on attempts to circumvent workers' compensation obligations through contracts if the workers are in fact employees. Courts will not enforce a written contract under such circumstances, particularly if the independent contractor does not have workers' compensation insurance coverage. Additionally, as previously discussed, contractors might become liable under certain conditions for the workers' compensation obligations of uninsured subcontractors.

Independent contractor agreements can be created, but to be enforceable, they must meet the following two criteria:

1. An employer-independent contractor relationship must exist in fact, not simply in name and form.
2. The work subject to the agreement must not be of the type normally performed by an employee.

Arrangements to Hire the Equipment and the Owner-Operator

Another noninsurance transfer technique has been used in the trucking industry. Many shipping companies own the trailers and hire as independent contractors owner-operators who own tractors. A shipping company typically has a significant investment in the trailers and might insist on certain rights of control, such as giving instructions and requiring the trailers to display the shipping company's name. Under such circumstances, if the tractor owner is injured and has no insurance, the shipping company will likely be responsible. Some states, however, consider truck owners-operators to be independent contractors, irrespective of the criteria defining their employment relationship.

Worker-Lessor Arrangements

Another approach employers might use to transfer the workers' compensation loss exposure is to try to establish that the worker is in a distinct business or occupation. In arrangements of this kind, a company owns equipment and leases it to a worker at an agreed price. The worker is not paid with wages but earns profits based on the income generated from the equipment's use minus the costs of leasing the equipment. An example of this arrangement would be a carpet cleaning company that rents steam cleaning equipment to persons who use this equipment in the carpet cleaning business. A close examination of this arrangement might reveal evidence of control, including the employer's signs on the equipment and detailed instructions about where, when, and how the worker must perform the services. Such factors might lead to the conclusion that the workers are employees.

Employer-Landlord Arrangements

Some companies try to circumvent workers' compensation obligations by configuring landlord and tenant-like relationships. For example, oil companies charge gas station operators rent and make the operators responsible for all operating expenses. This technique has been somewhat successful, but it has generally failed when the arrangement has allowed the oil company to terminate the relationship at will. Courts generally equate the right to discharge with the right to control.

Judicial Response to Noninsurance Transfers

A common thread runs through the courts' analysis of the preceding noninsurance transfer techniques. Whenever the worker is not able to bear the costs of the workers' compensation premium, the courts will go out of their way to find coverage. The test used by the courts appears to be the answer to the question: Is the worker able to independently bear the risk of an industrial injury? If the answer is negative, the courts are likely to reject employers' attempts to transfer workers' compensation loss exposures by hiring "independent contractors."

Having established which employments are usually covered by workers' compensation statutes and which are excluded, this chapter continues with a description of the next requirement for coverage: a covered injury.

COVERED INJURIES

Workers' compensation statutes do not list every type of on-the-job injury. They usually describe broad categories of injuries. Rather than list all of the conceivable covered injuries, the following section describes injuries in the following six categories:

1. Accidental injuries
2. Occupational diseases
3. Cumulative trauma
4. Hernias
5. Mental injuries
6. Excluded injuries

Accidental Injuries

In some states, an injury must be accidental to be compensable under workers' compensation. The wording "accidental" or "by accident" appears in most states' workers' compensation statutes. Adjusters must understand how each state defines and interprets the term "accidental injury" and whether the term "by accident" is included in the statutory definition of compensable injury. The "by accident" requirement is a remnant of employers' liability law, which required the event or occurrence causing injuries to be fortuitous and traumatic. The injury could be neither expected nor intended by the injured worker. The statute's definition of compensable injury is significant because it indicates two essential conditions of an accident that must exist before injuries are covered: (1) unexpectedness and (2) a definite time, place, and cause.

Unexpectedness Requirement

The unexpectedness requirement raises the question of whether an injury must be unexpected regarding both cause and result or whether an unexpected result alone, from the injured worker's standpoint, is enough to meet the requirement for coverage. Does the unexpectedness requirement permit compensation for an injury caused by normal and usual strains on the job under a strict and narrow statutory definition of "injury by accident"?

In the past, some courts interpreted the statutory definition of "injury by accident" literally and stringently. Injuries involving usual, normal, and routine work strain were not covered because they failed to meet the narrow statutory definition. A back injury caused by repetitive lifting of heavy boxes, for example, was not deemed to have been caused "by accident." Over time, however, the courts have made gradual concessions. Most states began to award coverage for injuries caused by normal strain at work, moving away from the strict interpretation of the "by accident" language. Recognizing the no-fault, strict liability concept built into the workers' compensation system, the majority of states now require the injury or disease to be unexpected only from the worker's standpoint. The injury or disease must also arise out of and in the course of employment.

The "accidental" or "by accident" requirement is therefore satisfied merely by an unexpected result. Most states now agree that any injury that the worker does not intend is accidental, even if the cause is not unexpected, unusual, or abnormal.

Definite Time, Place, or Cause

Some states have interpreted their workers' compensation statutes to require that causes of injuries and injuries themselves must be traceable to a definite time, place, and event. States that strictly construed the terms "injury" and "accident" as used in their workers' compensation statutes had difficulty awarding compensation for injuries resulting from nonspecific events or for work-related injuries that occur over an extended period. States with more liberal definitions permit coverage of these types of injuries.

Occupational Disease

Occupational disease
Disease that is caused by and is peculiar to an industrial setting.

Another category of injury, **occupational disease**, raises specific issues. An injury that is unexpected and definite in time, place, and cause is clearly compensable (provided, of course, that it also arises out of and in the course of employment). Traumatic injuries such as cuts and broken bones are obviously compensable because they meet all the criteria. However, assessing the compensability of nontraumatic occupational diseases can be problematic because these injuries may not be traceable to a definite time, place, or event.

Coverage for Occupational Diseases

Unlike traumatic injuries, the causes of diseases are not always clear. Determining that a disease is work-related can be difficult. Proof of a condition is not proof of causation. Although courts have largely abandoned the distinction between an industrial injury and an occupational or work-related disease, many states still have separate occupational disease laws that enumerate covered occupational diseases or define a covered occupational disease. Occupational disease statutes serve mainly to distinguish between diseases that are caused by and are peculiar to the industrial setting and the ordinary diseases of life. Occupational diseases are covered; ordinary diseases are not unless a direct causal connection to the workplace and the activities of the worker can be established. Although all occupational diseases are covered, the following box lists three that are commonly mentioned in workers' compensation statutes.

Common Occupational Diseases

1. *Pneumoconiosis.* A lung disease characterized by a fibrous inflammation of the lungs or chronic hardening of lung tissue resulting from dust inhalation.

2. *Asbestosis.* A form of pneumoconiosis resulting from protracted inhalation of asbestos particles. Exposure to asbestos particles has been associated with the later development of lung cancer. The latency period can be twenty years or more.

3. *Silicosi* by small, separate nodules forming in the lungs. In advanced cases, emphysema with respiratory impairment can develop.[9]

Coverage Triggers for Occupational Diseases

Occupational disease statutes and court rulings have provided guidelines to determine when an injury is presumed to have occurred so that a loss date can be assigned for purposes of insurance coverage. The loss date triggers the applicable insurance policy. Depending on the state, the loss date can be one of the following:

- The date of last injurious exposure to the harmful stimuli on the job. This is often the last day of employment.

- The date the disease or generalized condition becomes disabling.

- The date the disease first manifests itself.

- The date the injured worker is notified by a doctor that he or she is suffering from a work-related disease.

In specific cases, the applicable state ruling must be determined. To illustrate, the trigger for the onset of an occupational disease in Georgia is "Within 1 year of the date when the employee knew or should have known of the existence of an occupational disease, but in no event more than 7 years after the last injurious exposure."[10] The last injurious exposure rule holds that an employee exposed to harmful stimuli must seek workers' compensation from the last employer that exposed the employee to the harmful stimuli. (See box for example.)

Loss Date Trigger—Last Injurious Exposure Rule

The injured worker worked for one employer for more than five years as an electrician. He experienced problems with his right hand, but he did not consult a physician or file a workers' compensation claim. The injured worker left this employer to start his own business doing the same work as an electrical contractor. Six weeks after leaving, his hand worsened, and he sought medical treatment. It was determined that he had nerve entrapment syndrome as a result of cumulative trauma. The court applied the last injurious exposure rule and held that his current employer (his own company) was responsible for his workers' compensation benefits.[11]

Accidental Infectious Disease as an Occupational Disease

Infectious diseases are common to the general population and are not easily traceable to employment hazards. However, if the cause of an infectious disease is traceable to a specific incident(s) at or related to work, then contracting the disease meets the definition of an accident and qualifies as a covered injury. For example, if contracting typhoid fever could be traced to polluted water in a factory, then the illness is a covered injury. However, state courts would deny coverage if the state occupational disease statute limits coverage for occupational injuries to those specifically named and the disease suffered is not listed.

Allergy as an Occupational Disease

Allergic reaction to hazards in employment presents a special problem because of the personal nature of allergies. Not all workers react the same way, if at all, to stimuli in the employment environment. Consequently, some state courts have denied allergic conditions as a covered injury or disease. However, most states now recognize allergies as a covered occupational disease if (1) the employment caused the allergic reaction, (2) the hazard causing the allergic reaction is peculiar to an employment, and (3) the employment exposes the worker to the hazard to a greater degree than other employments in general.

As an example, an allergy problem known as latex sensitivity has become common among healthcare workers. OSHA standards requiring healthcare workers to wear surgical gloves more frequently and for longer periods of time to help prevent the spread of infection contributed to the rise in this allergic reaction. Approximately 2 percent of the general population is sensitive to latex.[12] Although the normal latex allergy reaction is itching, swelling, skin redness, and sometimes asthma, some experts claim that latex allergies can be lethal.[13] The Centers for Disease Control estimates that anywhere from 4.5 percent to 21 percent of healthcare workers are affected by adverse reactions to latex.[14] The latex allergy meets the three criteria listed in the previous paragraph and would be compensable in most states.

Cumulative Trauma Injuries

Cumulative trauma, repetitive-motion injury, or repetitive-stress injury
A condition that occurs as a result of repetitive motion, stress, or trauma.

Sometimes a condition is traceable to a certain time period and to separate incidents, but not to identifiable points in time and place. Many such conditions, known as **cumulative traumas**, **repetitive-motion injuries**, or **repetitive-stress injuries**, occur because of repeated stress or trauma to the same body part. For example, a worker suffering from a repetitive-motion injury might identify the origin of the condition as a special project at work for which specific tasks were performed. The project might have lasted for a defined period, but the worker cannot pinpoint the exact task or the specific exposure that caused the condition because of the ongoing nature of the injury. Billions of dollars are spent each year on workers' compensation benefits for repetitive-motion injuries.

An estimated 45 percent of workers' compensation claims are related to repetitive-motion injuries. Carpal tunnel syndrome is the most noted type of repetitive-motion injury. This condition is characterized by a soreness, tenderness, and weakness of the muscles of the thumb caused by pressure on the medial nerve at the point at which it goes through the carpal tunnel of the wrist. Cumulative trauma is one suspected cause of this condition.

However, only a small percentage of all repetitive-motion injuries are full-blown carpal tunnel syndrome. Carpal tunnel syndrome attracts the most attention because of the high cost to treat it. Payments for carpal tunnel claims range from $29,000 to $75,000 on the East and West Coasts and $12,000 to $20,000 in the Midwest.[15]

Injuries involving cumulative trauma can include back injuries, heart and vascular conditions, loss of hearing, and disabilities to extremities. Older workers who suffer from the normal degenerative process of aging make many of these claims. Consequently, several states do not permit damages for cumulative trauma claims. Other states provide coverage but exclude injuries resulting from general conditions that have no traceable cause. Adjusters must be familiar with their state-specific laws on cumulative trauma to make correct claims decisions.

Hearing Loss

Loss of hearing as a result of explosion or a traumatic head injury clearly meets all of the requirements of a covered injury. States gradually began recognizing hearing loss caused by protracted exposure to industrial noise as a covered injury or disease. States handled the problem of pre-existing, nonoccupational causes by apportioning benefits by cause and by establishing funds to give employers relief if they were found liable. Nonetheless, adjusters must investigate hearing losses in those states that accept hearing loss workers' compensation claims. An example of a hearing loss claim is in the following box.

Hearing Loss—Causal Connection to Workplace?

A man who worked for Oscar Mayer Food Corporation for twenty-three years on the meat processing floors made a workers' compensation claim because of a gradual loss of hearing. He claimed that the areas he worked in were very noisy and that for the last three years he had worn protective earmuffs. The man's doctor supported his claim, but the doctor's credibility was called into question because she had made an error in reading the hearing test results when determining her diagnosis. Another doctor could not determine the cause of the man's hearing loss and noted that

---

Continued on next page.

factors outside of work could have contributed to the condition. The man's claim was denied, and a court affirmed the denial for the following reasons:

1. The level of noise at the factory had not been measured and proven to be a risk to workers.

2. The doctor had made errors in her diagnosis.

3. Outside factors could have caused or contributed to the hearing loss.[16]

Hernias

Another type of injury that presents special coverage problems because of how they develop are hernias. A hernia is a rupture in connective tissue or a wall cavity that allows an organ to protrude. Hernias are caused by a weakness in the muscle tissue and a strain. The weakness can be congenital or can develop suddenly from trauma or strenuous effort. Consequently, a significant number of states have specific statutory provisions that govern workers' compensation coverage for hernias. States differ in their specific requirements for compensability, but they generally agree on the following:

1. The hernia must result from a sudden effort, severe strain, or trauma.
2. The hernia must appear suddenly, and the employer must be notified promptly.
3. The hernia's onset must be accompanied by severe pain.
4. A pre-existing rupture or protrusion must not be evident.
5. The injured worker must promptly seek medical care.

Hernias are one injury to which most states still apply the requirements of unexpectedness and capability of being traced in time and place to both the cause and result of the injury. A special provision generally found in workers' compensation statutes limits the length of time benefits are payable for a hernia. Twenty-six weeks is a common limitation.

Mental Injuries

Mental injuries are another type of injury that presents difficulties for the adjuster who is trying to determine compensability. Workers' compensation statutes were drafted to cover only injuries and diseases. Many states initially covered only injuries involving damage or harm to the body. Liberal interpretations of the workers' compensation statutes, along with advances in medical science relating to causes of mental illness, have allowed the courts to expand coverage to emotional conditions not accompanied by bodily injury or disease. A common example is coverage for an emotional breakdown because of an unusual emotional trauma at work.

Little or no dispute about coverage arises when the nonphysical injury is caused by physical violence. Some dispute arises when an emotional trauma causes a physical injury. Most controversial are nonphysical injuries that result from nonphysical causes. A convenient conceptual framework to determine coverage divides such cases into the following three categories:

1. Physical-mental
2. Mental-physical
3. Mental-mental

The physical-mental category includes mental suffering or mental consequences caused by physical injuries. These mental injuries are usually covered. A typical example is a worker who develops traumatic neurosis after a physical injury. The unexpectedness of the injury and the injury's time, place, and cause are clearly established.

The mental-physical category includes physical symptoms caused by a mental stimulus. As long as the mental stimulus can definitely be attributed to work, these injuries are covered. An example would be unusual job-related tension that leads to a heart attack. The character of the mental stimulus and the suddenness and definiteness of the physical injury are relevant factors in determining coverage. Questions can arise about whether the injury was accidental within the statute's definition of an injury. Factors considered in answering that question include whether the mental stimulus was unusual, traumatic, gradual, or sustained and whether the physical injury was immediate or protracted.

The mental-mental category includes mental injuries caused solely by a mental stimulus, such as stress. States are sharply divided about how to treat this category, and the issue has prompted much litigation. Because of the liberal interpretation of the workers' compensation statutes, state courts are moving toward finding coverage for injuries in the mental-mental category. Many states have already recognized that mental injuries meet the definition of "bodily injury."

State statutory definitions of an "injury" might include the term "bodily" and might include the term "personal" when describing covered injuries. The criteria required to prove a mental injury are contingent on the specific wording of state workers' compensation statutes and court interpretation of that wording. States fall roughly into four categories regarding compensability of mental injuries:

1. States that cover mental injuries only when they result from a compensable physical injury (physical-mental injury category)
2. States that require an unusual, work-related cause for the mental injury
3. States that require the cause to be predominantly work-related
4. States that do not specifically address mental injury in their statutes and that rely on case-by-case court decisions

Adjusters must recognize the rapid changes occurring in mental injury legislation and in court interpretations of that legislation. Adjusters should ascertain the current status of mental injury statutes and case law in the states in which they adjust claims and should review the statutory language or consult with legal counsel to understand the nuances.

Many states define "injury" with wording that excludes all mental injuries except those accompanied by or resulting from physical trauma (physical-mental). The exact wording varies by state but can be similar to that found in the Oklahoma law, which reads, "Mental injuries are not covered under the Act unless they are caused by a compensable physical injury except in the case of rape that arises out of and in the course of employment. (85-312.(c)).[17] See the following box for a mental injury claim made in Oklahoma.

Mental Injury Claim Alleging a Physical Injury

During an undercover investigation, a police officer suddenly felt weak, dizzy, and nauseated. He perspired profusely and experienced strong chest pains. He was taken to a hospital, where the doctors determined that he was suffering from a panic attack. A psychologist diagnosed his condition as severe panic disorder. He was treated for two and one-half months. He continued to take medication for the disorder and continued to perform his normal duties as an Oklahoma City police officer, but he occasionally had minor panic attacks. Four years later, his condition worsened. He had trouble controlling his aggressive impulses and could not continue working as a police officer. He applied for workers' compensation benefits because his psychologist stated that his panic disorder was the result of job-related stress. The case eventually went to the Oklahoma Supreme Court, which denied workers' compensation benefits because his condition was a mental injury that did not result from a physical injury as required in the state law.[18]

Other states in the physical-mental category have no statutory language referring specifically to mental injuries, but court decisions have reached the same result.

More states are expanding coverage to include mental injuries with no physical injury whatsoever. This expansion of coverage is one of the important issues facing workers' compensation insurers today. Mental injuries in those states are compensable if they have been caused by unusual stress. Injuries caused by unusual stress are covered; those caused by usual stress are not. Although the wording varies by state, many states in this group have wording similar to that in the Missouri statute: "Stress-related mental injuries are not considered to have arisen in the course and scope of employment unless the stress is work-related, unusual, and measured by objective standards and actual events (287.102.8)."[19] Some states add an additional criterion: the unusual event must be sudden rather than occurring over a period of time. Many of the states in this category do not cover mental injuries resulting from personnel-related actions in hiring, promoting, or discharging employees. The following box illustrates such a claim.

Mental Injury for Unusual Stress

A sales manager for Hershey Chocolate Corporation doubled her workload when she was told to handle a poorly performing district in addition to her own district. The assignment required her to hire and train new salespeople. She increased her workweek from fifty-five to seventy hours and continued to feel overwhelmed.

She began to suffer insomnia and anxiety and developed stomach pains. Her doctor diagnosed her as having major depression, and she was eventually given electric shock therapy because she did not respond to medication.

She applied for workers' compensation benefits. The workers' compensation board granted her benefits, stating that the doubling of her workload amounted to abnormal work conditions. Hershey appealed the decision and it was affirmed. Hershey then appealed to the Supreme Court of Pennsylvania which reversed the decision, finding that an increased workload after promotion did not constitute abnormal working conditions.[20]

The most liberal state statutes permit workers' compensation benefits for mental injuries as long as they can be proven to be job-related. For example, Michigan law reads, "Injuries of this nature are compensable only when arising out of actual, not perceived, events of employment and if significantly aggravated or accelerated by the employment (418.301 (2))."[21]

Some states, such as Iowa, whose statutes do not address mental injuries, have adopted the standard outlined in the previous paragraph through court decisions. The case in the following box is an example.

Pure Mental-Mental Injury Claim

The injured worker had been employed as an insurance adjuster for more than thirty years when his employer merged with another insurer. The worker retained his job and continued as an adjuster, but the merger caused changes in claim-adjusting procedures, and the adjuster's workload increased. He suffered depression and was hospitalized and treated extensively. He sought workers' compensation benefits, claiming that he had been the victim of intimidation because the company was attempting to force him to quit before retirement. His claim was denied, and, on appeal, expert testimony was presented to indicate that his condition was work related. The court agreed and granted recovery of benefits. The court also concluded that the worker had experienced more stress than had his co-workers in similar positions.[22]

This case illustrates the potential for workers' compensation claims in states that have the most liberal standard. It also provides a reminder for adjusters to be familiar with the laws and most recent court decisions in states that do not have a uniform standard and that decide claims on a case-by-case basis.

EXCLUDED INJURIES

The term "injuries not covered" is somewhat misleading because it is not the injury itself that is excluded, but the cause of the injury. Because the purpose of the "no fault" workers' compensation system is to compensate injured workers regardless of the worker's own negligence, few circumstances exclude coverage. However, some circumstances are so egregious that states do not permit the injured workers to be compensated. Nearly all states designate some injuries as not covered, but the causes of such injuries and the details related to them vary. Injuries that are not covered fall into the following five broad categories of causes, which vary by state. See the following box.

Categories of Injuries Not Covered

- Injuries intentionally self-inflicted

- Injuries sustained while attempting to injure another person

- Injuries caused by the worker's intoxication

- Injuries caused by the worker's willful misconduct

- Injuries caused by the worker's willful failure to use a safety device

---

The details about these categories of injuries are discussed in a later chapter. Almost all states exclude self-inflicted, intentional injuries. Likewise, almost all states exclude or limit some injuries caused by the worker's intoxication. Some states allow a claim to be reduced by a specified amount when the worker's intoxication caused the accident. More states exclude injuries caused by the use of narcotics. Although several states have wording that excludes coverage for willful misconduct, they do not define the term. Some states exclude coverage for injuries suffered as a result of the worker's willful failure to use a safety device. That exclusion is sometimes held to be inapplicable if the employer had failed to consistently enforce the device's use.

SUMMARY

Claim adjusters must understand what employees and what injuries are covered by the workers' compensation system. They must also recognize the nature of the employment relationship. The existence of an employment relationship depends on three factors: control, consent, and consideration. Workers not in an employment relationship, such as independent contractors, are excluded from employee status and, therefore, from workers' compensation coverage. Determining whether a worker is an independent contractor or an employee is important, but often difficult, and is based on many factors. The common law regards the extent of control an employer has over a worker as the most significant factor. However, many scholars of workers' compensation law use the nature-of-the-work test, which treats workers as employees if their work is integral to the employer's business. That test generally results in broader coverage.

To transfer the financial burden of workers' compensation loss exposure, employers consider several risk management techniques, including independent contractor agreements, arrangements to hire equipment with owner/operators, worker-lessor arrangements, and employer-landlord arrangements. Courts, however, tend to extend coverage under such circumstances if the worker cannot independently bear the cost of industrial injury.

States may also exclude other types of employees from workers' compensation coverage, including statutory employees, lent employees, and joint and dual employments. Various types of employments are excluded from some compensation laws, including domestic workers; farm workers; real estate salespeople; casual workers; employees of religious, charitable, or other nonprofit entities; proprietors of businesses; family members; employers having fewer than a statutory minimum number of workers; and public employees.

Following some evolution in case law, the workers' compensation coverage requirement that injuries be accidental has come to mean that the result of the injury must be unexpected or unintended from the employee's point of view. Striking a co-worker with one's fist is not accidental from the aggressor's point of view, but it is from the victim's.

Occupational diseases and cumulative traumas are treated specially under occupational disease statutes, which distinguish occupational diseases from ordinary diseases of life. Likewise, special statutes might address injuries such as hernias that can also occur outside employment.

Many courts have created special standards of compensability for mental injuries. Other courts apply to mental injuries the same standards of compensability as those that apply to physical injuries even though mental injuries might present difficult issues of causation. Despite the intent of the workers' compensation system, some injuries are excluded when the cause of the injury is the injured person's or the employer's specifically defined misconduct. Self-inflicted injuries are considered nonaccidental in nature and are therefore excluded from coverage.

The next chapter continues to build on the elements needed to determine compensability by discussing the meaning of "arising out of and in the course of employment."

CHAPTER NOTES

1. Arthur Larson, *Larson's Workers' Compensation, Desk Edition* (Newark, N.J.: Lexis Nexis, 2003), § 62.06 (2) [a].
2. Larson, § 61.06.
3. *Green Valley Cooperative Dairy v. Industrial Com.*, 27 N.W.2d 454 (Wis. 1947).
4. Larson, § 67.01.

5. *Shoemaker v. Manpower Inc.*, 635 N.Y.S.2d 816 (N.Y. 1996).

6. *Riverboat Hotel Casino v. Harold's Club*, 113 Nev. 1025, 944 P.2d 819 (Nev. 1997).

7. Larson, § 75.03[1].

8. Larson, § 74.02.

9. *Tabor's Cyclopedic Medical Dictionary*, 16th ed. (Philadelphia, Pa.: F.A. Davis Company, 1985).

10. U.S. Chamber of Commerce, 2002 Analysis of Workers' Compensation Laws, p. 31.

11. *Collett Electric v. Dubovic*, 911 P.2d 1192 (Nev. 1996).

12. Michael Tetto, "Latex Rubs People the Wrong Way," *Best's Review—Property/ Casualty*, January 1997, p. 96.

13. Mark Emmons, "Latex Can Be Lethal," *Chicago Tribune*, September 13, 1996, Dow Jones Interactive Publications Library, http://interactive.wsj.com, Publications Library (Subscriber Only).

14. Caryle Murphy, "Latex Allergy Can Be an Occupational Hazard," *The Washington Post*, July 16, 1996, Dow Jones Interactive Publications Library, http://interactive. wsj.com, Publications Library (Subscriber only).

15. Sara Marley, "Repetitive Motion Claims Increase," *Business Insurance*, February 14, 1994, p. 3.

16. *Scheurmann v. Oscar Mayer Foods Corp.*, 515 N.W.2d 546 (Iowa 1994).

17. International Risk Management Institute, Inc., *IRMI's Workers Compensation State Laws*, 2002, p. VIII.E Oklahoma - 4.

18. *Osborne v. City of Okla. City Police Dep't.*, 1994 OK 105, 882 P.2d 75 (1994).

19. International Risk Management Institute, Inc., *IRMI's Workers Compensation State Laws*, 2001, VIII.E Missouri - 3.

20. *Hershey Chocolate Co. v. W.C.A.B.*, 638 A2d 336 (1994).

21. International Risk Management Institute, Inc., *IRMI's Workers Compensation State Laws*, 2001, VIII.E Michigan - 4.

22. *Dunleavey v. Economy Fire & Casualty Co.*, 526 N.W.2d 845 (Iowa 1995).

Direct Your Learning

Compensability: Arising Out of and in the Course of Employment

After learning the content of this chapter, you should be able to:

■ Describe the "arising out of" requirement of the statutory standard for workers' compensation compensability, including:

- The "increased risk" principle

- The "but for" principle

■ Describe the "in the course of" requirement of the statutory standard for workers' compensation compensability, including:

- The elements of an injury's relationship to work

- The activities that are not work-related but that might give rise to compensable injury

■ Describe the statutory standard exceptions for workers' compensation compensability, including:

- Willful misconduct and safety rule violations

- Intoxication

- Self-inflicted injury

■ Given a case, determine if an injury arises out of and in the course of employment.

Develop Your Perspective

What are the main topics covered in the chapter?

This chapter discusses two additional requirements for determining compensability under a workers' compensation statute: this injury must (1) arise out of employment and occur (2) in the course of employment. Workers can be injured while at work, and the injury might be completely unrelated to work and therefore not compensable under workers' compensation.

Consider the language of the statute.

- What is the difference between "arising out of employment" and "in the course of employment"?
- What types of claims does this language attempt to exclude?

Why is it important to learn about these topics?

Adjusters must investigate claims to determine whether the injury or illness claimed arose out of and in the course of employment. Many situations are fact sensitive and depend on the case law of the applicable state.

Analyze the workers' compensation statute for the state in which you work.

- What is the standard for compensability?
- What types of situations that give rise to injury are excluded by statute?

How can you use what you will learn?

Imagine that a co-worker has suffered a heart attack while at the office.

- Is the injury compensable under the workers' compensation statute in your state?
- Is the co-worker's employment covered under the statute?

Chapter 3

Compensability: Arising Out of and in the Course of Employment

As previously discussed, not every accidental injury to an employed worker is covered by workers' compensation. The compensation system was created to make employers responsible for the cost of injuries related to employment. A previous chapter described the employments and injuries covered by workers' compensation statutes. This chapter discusses the relationship that must be found between the injury and the employment for workers' compensation to apply.

The requirement that limits workers' compensation to work-related injuries is easy to apply in most cases. However, courts continue to refine the distinction between work-related and nonwork-related injuries. Litigation occurs frequently because the applicable legal rules are general, and specific facts usually determine a case's resolution.

Most states require that, to be compensable, an injury must "arise out of and in the course of employment." Courts have provided many interpretations of this requirement, not all of them consistent. Nevertheless, because courts in the various states have been interpreting the same phrase, a working consensus about its meaning and application has evolved.

This chapter explains how courts have interpreted the phrase "arising out of and in the course of employment" and have applied each element of it. Much of the apparent inconsistency among courts is explained by the different facts of each case and by the differences in each court's standards for compensability. Most courts judge an injury's compensability by its degree of work-relatedness, and many depart from the official legal standard, "arising out of and in the course of employment," when an otherwise strong relationship exists between an injury and employment.

Because of the variability of the outcomes based on the facts of each compensation case, courts have developed general principles that apply to the compensability analysis. Nevertheless, some situations have defied the application of general principles. This chapter describes and illustrates the general principles and some exceptions to them.

STATUTORY STANDARD

The usual statutory standard for compensability has two requirements: the injury must be one (1) "arising out of" and (2) "in the course of" employment. They are separate requirements that must be separately satisfied. In most cases, both requirements are either satisfied or not satisfied. However, some cases meet either one or the other requirement; that is, an injury arises out of employment but does not occur in the course of employment, or, conversely, an injury occurs in the course of employment but does not arise out of the employment. While courts consistently hold that both requirements should be separately satisfied, courts in some cases overlook the failure of a case to meet one test when the other test is clearly satisfied.

The "arising out of and in the course of" standard is not universal. Some states require compensation for injuries that occur "in the course of and resulting from" employment, a standard that is essentially the same as the statutory standard. Other states require that injuries "result" from employment, a standard similar to the "arising out of" requirement alone. A few states require only that an injury occur "in the course of" employment. This standard of compensation is more liberal than the statutory standard because in these states it does not matter *how* the injury arises, as long as it occurs in the course of employment. Also, a state can apply an even more liberal standard, injuries "arising out of *or* in the course of employment" (emphasis added), allowing compensation in cases that meet either one of the two requirements.

"ARISING OUT OF" REQUIREMENT

The "arising out of" requirement concerns an injury's cause. An injury is considered to have arisen out of the employment if it was caused by some circumstance of the employment. Determining the exact meaning of this concept has been a difficult task for courts. In the compensation context, cause does not mean proximate cause, which is the tort standard for determining liability. Tort law is more concerned than compensation law with culpability. Consequently, determining compensability under workers' compensation depends not on the fact that the injury was foreseeable but instead on whether the injury arose out of the employment.

Increased Risk Principle

Most courts deem an injury to have arisen out of employment if the injury resulted from a risk to which the worker was more subject than the public is. For example, although the public is exposed to the danger of being struck by an automobile, a worker whose job requires being on the street more often than the public is in greater danger of being struck. Any injuries to this worker caused by an automobile accident would be deemed to have arisen out of the employment. Similarly, a laborer required to work outdoors might experience the same weather as everyone else but experiences it more frequently and for a longer duration. Any injuries caused by exposure to heat or cold would be considered to have arisen out of employment and would, therefore, be compensable.

Increased Risk Cases

A garbage truck driver was struck by an apple thrown from a passing school bus. The court ruled that the injured worker was at greater risk for this injury because of his employment, that, therefore, the injury arose out of the employment. Compensation was granted.[1]

A worker regularly made large deposits of money to the bank for her employer, a precious metals dealer. While making one such deposit, the worker was assaulted and robbed. The court ruled that the injury arose out of the employment because the employment exposed the worker to an increased risk of robbery.[2]

A cocktail waitress at a hotel in a high crime area of the city was sexually assaulted in a public restroom. The court ruled that the assault arose out of the employment because the employment exposed the injured worker to a higher risk of crime.[3]

A worker's job involved sales and collections. While waiting in his car outside a customer's office, the worker was shot by two assailants who admitted that they had seen him earlier with a large sum of money and that they had intended to rob him. The court held that collecting and holding large sums of money was a condition of the worker's employment and that, therefore, the assault arose out of the worker's employment. Compensation was awarded.[4]

An off-duty policeman, after identifying himself as a policeman, was shot by a gunman. The court ruled that when shot, the injured worker was acting as a policeman and was required by law to do so. Compensation was awarded.[5]

"But for" Principle

Certain states have further liberalized the interpretation of "arising out of," to allow compensation whenever an injury results from a risk related to employment. Regardless of whether the risk was the same in type and degree as that faced by the public, courts in these states ask whether the worker would have been exposed to the risk "but for" the employment. If not, the resulting injuries are compensable. Therefore, under the "but for" principle, when a worker is exposed to a risk because of the employment, any resulting injuries are compensable.

This interpretation is also called the **positional risk doctrine**.[6] According to the doctrine, whenever the employment places the worker in the time and place in which an injury occurs that would not have otherwise occurred, the injury is compensable. For example, a worker who is struck by a stray bullet while running an errand for his employer would be compensated. Although the stray bullet is unrelated to the employment, the employment has placed

Positional risk doctrine
Some state courts' interpretation of the "arising out of" clause that would require workers' compensation coverage when a worker's employment has placed the worker in the time and place in which an injury occurs and when the injury would not otherwise have occurred.

the worker in the position to be injured. The injury is therefore considered to have arisen out of the employment.

The "but for," or positional risk, principle allows compensation in all cases except when the injury is caused by factors that would have operated regardless of the employment. For example, death caused by a cerebral hemorrhage would not be compensated just because it happens at work. The location of the occurrence is not relevant. Likewise, when someone is assaulted at work by a personal enemy or by a jealous spouse, the connection with work is coincidental, and any resulting injuries are not compensable.

Cases on the "but for" Requirement

A road-grader operator's work required him to be outdoors in the cold. Because of his diabetic condition, the worker wore electric socks to keep his feet warm. The socks injured his feet. The court ruled that the worker would not have been injured but for his employment, which required him to be out in the cold.[7]

While entering his car after lunch, a salesman was shot and killed by a stranger who acted without provocation. The court awarded compensation because the salesman would not have been at the place of attack at that time but for his employment.[8]

A worker contracted tuberculosis from a co-worker. The two worked in extremely close proximity and, because of the noise in their workplace, had to have their faces within inches of each other and shout to be heard. Compensation was awarded because the worker would not have been exposed to tuberculosis but for the workplace conditions.[9]

Situations Having a Dubious Relationship to Employment

Cases in which the cause of injury is not related or has a dubious relationship to employment include claims based on street risk and positional risk, acts of God, exposure to the elements, health risks peculiar to the injured worker, heart attacks, mental injuries, and assaults. These cases are fact-sensitive. When encountering such cases, adjusters should consult counsel or review the applicable state's case law.

Street Risk

Street risk
Term used to describe all dangers characteristic of public streets, including traffic accidents; defective street and sidewalk surfaces; criminal assaults; and random encounters with people, animals, or objects that share the street.

Street risk includes all dangers characteristic of public streets, including traffic accidents; defective street and sidewalk surfaces; criminal assaults; and random encounters with people, animals, or objects that share the street. The difficulty of awarding compensation for injuries resulting from street risk is that everyone who uses the streets, employed or not, faces such risks. Nevertheless, courts award compensation for injuries caused by street risk to workers whose jobs require them to be on the street more often than the public. Such workers include traveling salespeople, police, delivery personnel, road repair crews, and trash collectors. Many courts award compensation to workers injured on the street in the course of employment (1) regardless of whether the worker must regularly travel the streets or (2) even if injury occurs during the only visit to the streets ever made by a worker. Courts apply the "but for" requirement of causation to street risk injuries. But for the employment, the worker would not have been on the street and would not have been injured. However, the worker must be in the course of employment when injured. A typical case arises when a worker runs an errand for the employer. For example, after leaving the workplace where she worked as a bookkeeper, a woman was attacked while depositing mail for her employer. The court applied the street risk doctrine and ruled that the worker's injuries would not have occurred but for the employment.[10] However, a worker on the street for personal reasons during the working day cannot expect compensation.

Positional Risk

The positional risk doctrine is a generalization of the "but for" principle to any cause of injury, not just street risk. Courts that apply this doctrine award compensation when an injury would not have occurred but for the employment (assuming the worker is in the course of employment). For example, a bee flies into an open window at a workplace and stings a worker, who suffers a severe allergic reaction. But for the employment, the worker would not have been in a position to be stung. Compensation is awarded even though the employment itself might not present an increased risk of bee stings and therefore did not directly cause the sting. A significant minority of states apparently apply the positional risk doctrine, though not always identifying it as such.

Positional Risk Injury

A miner who was required to return a lamp to his employer's office slipped on ice on the road. The court ruled that the employment required the worker to be on the road and that the injury would not have occurred but for employment and was, therefore, compensable.[11]

Acts of God

Acts of God include such natural phenomena as lightning, floods, hail, tornadoes, hurricanes, and earthquakes. The issue concerning compensation for injuries caused by these phenomena is similar to that associated with awarding compensation for injuries caused by street risk: the risk does not really arise out of the employment. Most acts of God affect entire communities. Even those having a more localized effect, such as lightning and hail, are not directly associated with employment.

Acts of God
Natural phenomena, such as lightning, floods, hail, tornadoes, hurricanes, and earthquakes.

Courts have resolved this issue in the same way they have resolved the street risk issue. All courts award compensation to someone whose job increases the exposure to acts of God,[12] such as agricultural workers, construction workers, and other outdoor workers. However, this approach does not apply to all acts of God. Hurricanes devastate entire communities regardless of place of employment. Earthquakes likewise affect entire communities and may pose a greater danger to indoor workers than to outdoor workers.

As with injuries related to street risk, a significant minority of courts award compensation whenever the employment causes the exposure to the act of God, regardless of whether the employment itself poses an increased risk. For example, if employment puts someone in the path of a tornado, that person should be compensated for resulting injuries whether or not the overall risk was greater than that of the public.

Acts of God Injury Cases

While in the course of employment, a person was struck by lightning in an open, level field. The court awarded compensation, ruling that the person's employment created a greater risk from acts of God than other employments do.[13]

A man was killed at his place of employment by a tornado that affected 60 percent of the community and caused casualties at the man's workplace at about the same rate as it did in the community. Compensation was denied.[14]

Exposure to the Elements

When temperatures are extreme, anyone exposed to the elements might suffer injuries such as frostbite or heatstroke. Workers such as sanitation workers and parking lot attendants are required to stay outdoors in extreme weather, to a greater extent than the public is. When such workers suffer injury as a result of the elements, courts deem the injury to have arisen out of the employment.

Idiopathic Conditions and Other Medical Conditions

Certain accidents and the resulting injuries are caused by medical conditions peculiar to the victim and unrelated to the employment. For example, a worker might lose balance and fall because of an inner ear problem. A medical condition arising from an obscure or unknown cause or a medical condition peculiar to the individual is called an **idiopathic condition**. In the workers' compensation context, an idiopathic injury is one that arises solely from within the worker and not from any circumstance of the employment.

Idiopathic condition
A medical condition arising from an obscure or unknown cause or a medical condition that is peculiar to an individual.

By definition, idiopathic injuries should not be compensable. Although all courts are prepared to accept this principle, adjusters often encounter two types of claims associated with idiopathic injuries.

- The first type of claim occurs when an injury appears to be idiopathic, but the worker claims that the employment caused the injury. This kind of claim often involves heart attacks and psychological injuries. Adjusters who encounter an injury that appears to be idiopathic but is alleged to be work-related should immediately obtain expert assistance. Such claims usually involve complex medical issues as well as serious and expensive injuries.

- The second type of claim is for resulting injury. The worker does not claim compensation for an epileptic seizure, stroke, or heart attack but for resulting injuries. For example, a worker might faint because of an idiopathic condition and strike her head on an object in the work environment. The worker might make a compensation claim for the head injury, not for the underlying cause of the fainting.

Courts allow compensation for resulting injuries whenever the work environment creates a special hazard for someone afflicted with the worker's particular condition. If a person who works at heights or around dangerous machinery faints because of an idiopathic condition, the worker would be compensated for resulting injury. If the same worker simply falls to the floor and is injured, the worker probably would not receive compensation.[15]

Not all medical conditions are idiopathic. An idiopathic condition affects the worker on its own. A medical condition that makes a worker more vulnerable must interact with a workplace hazard to cause injury. The classic example of vulnerability is a weak back. Many workers have backs that are weak or in bad condition, and they suffer injury when they exert their backs in work-related activity.

Idiopathic or Other Medical Conditions Cases

A worker died of a heart attack while driving in the course of his employment. The court denied compensation, finding no evidence of an exertion or any other basis on which to attribute the heart attack to the employment.[16]

A worker suffered a fall that might have been caused by an idiopathic condition. She fell from a wooden platform, across a metal table, and onto a concrete floor. The court awarded compensation because of the increased danger caused by the work environment.[17]

While a worker was outside getting fresh air, he suffered a heart attack, fell into a pool of water, and drowned. The court found that the worker was in the course of employment when the incident occurred and that the fall and death resulting from a heart attack, an idiopathic condition, were compensable.[18]

Compensability for claims involving strokes and heart attacks is often difficult to determine because of contributing nonwork-related risk factors, such as high blood pressure, diabetes, smoking, a family history of heart problems, and coronary artery blockages. Evidence of such factors must be weighed against the work circumstances to determine the cause. However, stress does cause heart problems, and abnormal job stress can lead to heart attacks and strokes. One study concluded that the risk of myocardial ischemia (a precursor to heart attacks) more than doubled following periods of emotional stress.[19] Workers who suffer heart attacks at work usually claim that the heart attack followed a period of physical or emotional stress. Courts award compensation if the stress that caused the heart attack is extraordinary and unusual and is predominantly work-related.

Heart Attack Cases

A sixty-one-year-old car salesman got into a heated argument with the dealership's service manager over how a customer had been treated. Following the argument, the salesman became unsteady on his feet and suffered blurred vision. The next day the salesman went to the hospital, where he was diagnosed with a stroke. The stroke permanently impaired his ability to walk and talk. The salesman was given permanent total disability benefits. Doctors testified that the salesman had no other significant risk factors that could have contributed to the stroke; therefore, the stroke had to be work-related.[20]

A sixty-five-year-old man suffered a heart attack at work after moving several heavy boxes. The man had a family history of heart disease, and a doctor determined that he had coronary artery disease that had developed over several years. Three doctors examined him and testified that the physical strain from lifting the boxes might have caused the heart attack. However, a fourth doctor testified that the man's medical history was sufficient reason for the heart attack and that the heart attack was not work-related. The workers' compensation commission denied benefits.[21]

In weighing whether a heart attack is compensable, courts rely heavily on medical testimony and the circumstances preceding the attack. Courts look to concrete medical testimony showing at least a "probability" that the heart attack was more likely than not related to the worker's job. Indecisive medical testimony such as "the heart attack might possibly have been work-related" or "the work was a precipitating factor in the heart attack" is not usually sufficient to prove causation.[22]

Mental Conditions

As a previous chapter discussed, the circumstances that trigger compensable mental injury claims vary by state and depend on state workers' compensation statutes and case law. Some states require an accompanying physical injury for the mental injury to be covered. A more common requirement is that the mental injury be "substantially caused by work-related factors" and "caused by greater than normal" job stress. When investigating claims for mental injuries, adjusters must do the following:

1. Determine what coverage the state law provides for mental injury claims

2. Determine whether the circumstances meet the coverage requirements

3. Determine whether the injury is work-related

Many of the compensability issues that complicate heart attack claims also arise in psychological stress claims. Many mental injury claims involve factors not related to work that contribute to the mental injury. Further complicating the determination of compensability are subjective elements inherent in mental injury claims.

Mental Condition Cases

A supervisor at a manufacturing company was responsible for ensuring that equipment assembly and shipping occurred on time. His employer implemented a program to ensure that shipping deadlines were met and began calling the supervisor repeatedly at home to check on job deadlines. The supervisor, who considered himself a perfectionist, accepted this situation. After the company reduced its workforce, the supervisor began to worry that he would lose his job. During a meeting called after his department was unprepared for a scheduled inspection, the supervisor learned that he would be discharged. The following morning, he left a suicide note on his desk, went outside, and shot himself in the head with an air-powered nail gun. He survived and filed a compensation claim that was denied because of the willful intent to kill himself. Psychologists testified that the supervisor had a preexisting compulsive personality that made him more susceptible to depression and that his job put him at greater risk than members of the public for developing suicidal tendencies. The state industrial commission awarded him benefits.[23]

A sixty-four-year-old insurance agent filed for benefits, claiming that he could no longer work because of depression and work-related anxiety brought on by supervisors continually pressuring him to be more productive. Psychologists determined that a non-work-related physical ailment, as well as normal job stress, contributed to the agent's psychological condition. Benefits were denied because the agent could not prove that his job stress was greater than that usually found in a business environment.[24]

Abnormal stress is a usual standard that courts and compensation commissions examine in determining compensability in stress claims. Normal job stress is encountered by the public at large and is therefore not sufficient to trigger compensation. The abnormal stress standard varies by state. However, one common definition of abnormal stress is a traumatic event that is generally outside a worker's usual experience and an event that would evoke significant symptoms of distress to other workers in similar circumstances.

Assaults

Injuries caused by assaults to workers might be compensable, depending on the nature of the assault. Engaging in a fight might be deemed to be abandonment of the employment because being assaulted and fighting back is not considered part of most jobs.

Although compensation might be in doubt, the fact that an injured worker was the aggressor in a fight is generally not relevant. The compensation system is not based on fault. A worker's role as aggressor is relevant only when it constitutes willful misconduct. As previously noted, misconduct is found to be willful in compensation claims only when it is intentional. Such willfulness in the case of an assault would constitute criminal behavior. The spontaneous or heat-of-the-moment fights that tend to erupt in the workplace would not be deemed willful misconduct. Therefore, aggressors can usually receive compensation if the injury meets other requirements for compensation.

Spontaneous Assault Cases

After having his work corrected by a foreman, a worker sprayed the foreman in the face with paint. The foreman struck and kicked the worker, causing injury. The court rejected the aggressor defense and the willful misconduct defense and awarded compensation.[25]

While unloading a truckload of insulation, a worker was injured in a fight he provoked with a co-worker. The court rejected the aggressor defense and awarded compensation, ruling that the dispute arose out of the employment.[26]

Because of the nature of their work, certain workers are more likely to be assaulted than the public is. Such workers include police, armored car personnel, couriers of valuables, bill collectors, and people whose work requires them to be in high-crime areas. Injuries resulting from assaults against such workers are generally deemed to arise out of the employment and are therefore compensable.[27]

Many assaults on workers are committed by co-workers. These assaults might arise out of work-related disputes, such as those between supervisor and subordinate or between co-workers. They might also result from personal animosity. Assaults arising from work-related disputes are generally compensable even though fighting is outside the course of the employment.

Co-worker Assault Cases

A dispute arose between two furniture salesmen about which one would wait on a customer. One of the salesmen assaulted the other, and the second salesman sued the first for assault and battery. The court held that the assault arose out of the employment and remanded the case to the Bureau of Workers' Compensation for a compensability ruling.[28]

A co-worker asked the cook at a restaurant for some shrimp to give to a relative. The cook refused because it was against company policy. A brief shoving match ensued, and other workers separated the two. The cook then went outside to cool down. Fifteen minutes later, the cook's co-worker came outside and poured three gallons of scalding water over the cook's head, permanently disfiguring him. The insurer argued that, the fifteen minutes that had elapsed between the shoving match and the assault indicated that the attack was motivated purely by a personal grudge. The court rejected this argument, concluding that preventing a co-worker from stealing the employer's property is work-related.[29]

Even a thin connection to the job is often sufficient to award compensation.

Co-Worker Assault Cases—Connection to Job

A woman was on break in her employer's lunchroom when a co-worker accused her of spreading rumors about another worker. An argument followed and quickly escalated into a fight, and the woman was injured. The court awarded benefits to the woman because the fight happened on the employer's premises and because the subject of the alleged rumor was another worker.[30]

A hotel security guard owed money to a co-worker. The co-worker's boyfriend came to the hotel to help her collect the debt. A fight ensued between the boyfriend and the guard, and the guard was injured. The court overruled the workers' compensation commission's earlier decision and awarded the guard benefits because the boyfriend was not supposed to be on the premises and because the hotel owner had previously instructed the guard to tell the boyfriend to leave if he entered the premises. The court concluded that the fight was related to work because it was the guard's job to keep trespassers off the premises.[31]

One exception to finding compensability arises when the injured worker deliberately disobeys company policy and, consequently, is injured in an assault.

Co-Worker Assault Case: Disobedience of Company Policy

A worker had ongoing complaints about people taking his parking space at work. The owner informed the man that he had no right over others to his favorite spot and advised him to avoid confrontations over parking. Despite the warning, the man continued to assert that the spot was his and got into a scuffle with another person. During the scuffle, the man stubbed his toe on the curb. He was denied benefits because his deliberate disobedience of the warning placed his injury outside the scope of his employment.[32]

Compensation is much more difficult to assess in cases of assaults related to personal animosity between parties whose only connection is the employment. But for the employment, such parties would not assault other parties. Nevertheless, the employment duties and circumstances play no role in causing the assault. Those states that follow the positional risk doctrine would likely award compensation in such cases.

A similar analytical problem arises in cases of mistaken or unexplained assaults or assaults committed by an insane person. Again, the employment duties and circumstances play no role in causing the assault. Only those states that follow the positional risk doctrine are likely to award compensation in those cases.

Unexplained Assault Cases

A woman was assaulted by an unknown person in the laundry room of her employer, a nursing home. The woman was engaged in work duties when attacked, was not robbed or sexually assaulted, and had no known enemies. Compensation was awarded.[33]

A man was shot by a paranoid schizophrenic co-worker who believed the man was a hit man out to get him. The two parties had no contact with each other except through work. The court ruled that the injury arose out of the employment and awarded compensation.[34]

Assaults at the workplace that arise from purely personal motives are not compensable. For example, if a person who is clearly engaged in the course of employment is attacked and injured by a jealous spouse, the resulting injuries are not compensable. The cause of the injuries arose from outside the employment, and the fact that injuries were sustained on the job is sheer coincidence.

Cases of Assault Arising From Personal Motives

A man was attacked at work by his ex-wife's husband, who worked at the same auto assembly plant. The court found the animosity between the parties to be purely personal and unrelated to the employment. Compensation was denied.[35]

During her lunch break, a woman cashed her paycheck at a bank and returned to her employer's parking lot, where she was assaulted and robbed. The court ruled that the robbery was strictly personal and did not arise out of the employment. Compensation was denied.[36]

"IN THE COURSE OF" REQUIREMENT

The "in the course of" employment requirement refers not necessarily to the cause of an injury but to the circumstances of its occurrence, including the time and place in which it occurs and the activities in which the worker is engaged when it occurs. The course of employment is essentially the same as the common law scope of employment. A worker is within the course of employment whenever engaged in work-related or incidental work activities at the time and place required by the employment.

Work-Related Activities

A worker is within the course of employment when performing work-related activities. These activities include the job functions and any incidental activities that someone in that position would be expected to perform, such as setting up work, cleaning up, moving from one workstation to another, and helping co-workers.

An injury suffered by a worker in the course of employment will not necessarily arise out of the employment. For example, the death of a worker from a cerebral hemorrhage at work may well be within the course of employment. Yet the *cause* of injury is not employment related, so it does not arise out of the employment. On the other hand, a strike-breaking worker who is assaulted and injured at home by strikers may have sustained injuries that arise out of the employment but not in the course of it.

In most cases, however, the activities in which the worker is engaged are also the cause of injuries. For example, a worker who is injured while lifting boxes at work is injured in the course of employment because moving boxes is a work-related task. The injury also arises out of the employment because the risks of lifting boxes are a part of that job.

"In the course of employment" also refers to the time and place of employment, which are fixed for most workers. In these cases, determining whether workers are within the course of employment by where and when they are injured is easy. Generally, injuries that occur at work during work hours to workers with a fixed schedule are compensable.

It can be more difficult to determine compensability for injuries to workers who travel to various locations and work irregular hours. Such workers are within the course of their employment whenever they are engaged in work duties at a place and time required by the employment. However, because the time and place of employment are not fixed, whether an injury has occurred in the course of employment is not always clear. For example, the issue might arise in the case of a traveling salesperson who is injured in a hotel at 9 PM after completing the day's business.

A worker who performs work at a certain time and place for personal convenience is not necessarily within the course of employment. For example, a worker who takes work home and is injured while working at home is generally not deemed to be within the course of employment. Usually, such cases also raise issues concerning whether the injury arises out of the employment.

Determining Compensability

Courts generally maintain that "arising out of" and "in the course of" requirements must be fulfilled separately. Yet the results of a number of difficult cases suggest that this rule is not strictly enforced. Compensation has been awarded when the circumstances of a worker's injury have fulfilled one of the requirements but the other only weakly, if at all. For example, cases have occurred in which the cause of injury is completely unknown, but compensation has been awarded if the worker was diligently engaged in the course of employment when injured. Likewise, courts have awarded compensation to workers clearly not engaged in work activities when injured. In these cases, courts apparently look for a sufficient connection between the injury and the employment regardless of whether the "arising out of" and "in the course of" tests are each separately fulfilled. Strong evidence of one requirement might make up for a deficiency in the other.[37] Accordingly, adjusters who analyze compensation claims must consider the overall relationship of the injury to the employment.

Unless the employer or its insurer can prove that an injury is not work-related, most industrial commissions award compensation. This presumption of compensability places the burden of proving that an injury is not compensable on the employer or its insurer. New York's law explicitly includes a presumption that injuries are work-related.[38] Adjusters should expect compensation to be awarded whenever some relationship between an injury and the employment can be shown.

When determining whether an injury is related to work, adjusters should ask questions about the following four elements of an injury's work relationship:

- *Cause of injury*. What caused the worker's injury? This element of the work relationship is the essence of the "arising out of" test. An injury is deemed to be work-related whenever it *is caused by* some employment hazard.

- *Worker's activities*. What was the worker doing when injured? An injury is deemed to be work-related whenever the worker is directly engaged in job duties or is performing any activity incidental to the job duties.

- *Place of injury*. Was the worker injured on the employer's premises or at some place he or she was required to be because of work? Most injuries that occur on the employer's premises are deemed to be work-related.

- *Time of injury*. Was the worker injured during regular work hours or at some other time when the worker's services were required? An injury that occurs before or after regular work hours will require careful investigation to determine work-relatedness.

The more of these elements that indicate an employment relationship, the greater the likelihood that compensation will be awarded. When all four elements indicate a work relationship, an injury is clearly compensable.

When three of the four elements indicate a work relationship, compensation is likely. The cases most likely to be denied compensation are those in which the injury's cause (the "arising out of" test) is obviously unrelated to the employment, such as the previous example of the person who died suddenly on the job of a cerebral hemorrhage.

Cases in which only two elements indicate a work relationship are the most difficult to decide. Compensation is often, but not always, awarded in cases of this type. Suppose, during a lunch break on the employer's premises, the worker chokes on a sandwich brought from home. At best, only the time and place of the accident have any relationship to the employment. Courts are split on how this case would be decided.

Compensation is doubtful when only one element indicates a work relationship. Suppose the worker left the employer's premises during a scheduled lunch break and was injured in a car accident. Because only one element (the time of accident) would indicate a work relationship, compensation would likely be denied. Nevertheless, adjusters should not deny compensation in cases in which one element indicates a work relationship without legal advice.

The case in the box analyzes a claim having elements for and against compensation.

Analyzing Work-Relatedness

A card dealer at a casino left his poker table to clock out for the day. On his way to the time clock, he fell in a hallway and injured his knees and back. Medical testimony indicated that the cause of his fall was weakness in his legs resulting from multiple sclerosis. Witnesses confirmed that there was no condition in the hallway that caused the fall.

Elements supporting denial of compensation:

1. The fall and subsequent injury were not caused by an employment hazard but instead by the worker's unrelated disease.

2. The worker had completed his job duties and regular job hours.

Elements supporting compensation:

1. The place of the injury was the employer's premises.

2. The injury occurred when the worker was still performing an employer service (clocking out).

Without information about the case law of the state in which the injury occurred, it is difficult to predict whether a court would deem this injury compensable. In situations such as this one, adjusters should consult with legal counsel before deciding on compensability.

Relationship of Workers' Activities to Employment

The fact that a worker is not performing work duties when injured, by itself, is not usually sufficient reason to deny compensation. However, if the injury's cause or the injury's time and place are also unrelated to the employment, compensation will likely be denied.

Some cases that can present complications are injuries to workers on lunch breaks and coffee breaks; while taking breaks to rest, smoke, chat, or use the lavatory; at social affairs and sports events; while engaged in unauthorized activities, pranks, or practical jokes; and while deviating from business travel for personal reasons. The following discussion addresses the relationship of these activities to employment as interpreted under workers' compensation statutes.

Personal Activities

Workers interrupt their work to do many things, for example, to rest, chat with co-workers, and attend to their personal appearance. Generally, these personal activities are considered incidental to the employment even though they are clearly not work duties and even if the break might be longer than a few minutes or is not compensated by the employer.

The legal standard for granting compensation for injuries sustained during such activities is that the activity must be reasonable; it does not have to be necessary. Even if an activity's extent and duration have become excessive, courts and commissions will not necessarily deny compensation if the employer has known about and acquiesced to the activities.

Compensation might be denied when the facts of the case include additional circumstances unrelated to the employment. As discussed, workers who leave their employers' premises and are injured during lunch breaks are unlikely to receive compensation because their injuries would involve both a cause and place of accident unrelated to the employment. Similarly, workers who use breaks to engage in horseplay or pranks (discussed later); who try out tools, machinery, or equipment they are not authorized to use; or who wander onto parts of their employers' premises they are not authorized to enter are likely to be denied compensation. Additionally, if the cause of injury is unrelated to the employment (for example, if a worker is stabbed in the eye by a hairbrush bristle while brushing his or her hair), the worker is likely to be denied compensation.

Workers injured while sleeping on the job might not receive compensation, depending on the circumstances. Sleeping on the job is considered a more substantial abandonment of work duties than other personal activities. Sleeping is unlikely to have a defined beginning and end like a lunch break, and employers are unlikely to know about it or allow it. On the other hand, if the worker was sleeping during an unavoidable lull in work, or if the worker's fatigue followed long hours of work, courts are likely to deem the sleep incidental to the employment and compensable.

The outcome of any case that turns on the issue of personal activities depends substantially on the facts. In almost all such cases, the worker is injured on the employer's premises while not performing work duties. Adjusters who investigate claims for such injuries consider such factors as how reasonable and customary the worker's activity was, whether the employer knew of or permitted the activity, and whether the worker limited the activity to a reasonable time or instead extended it into a deliberate departure from work.

Personal Activity Injury Cases

A worker was a member of a grounds maintenance crew that regularly took swimming breaks between jobs. On one such break, the worker dived into a river and broke his neck. The court ruled the swimming to be an insubstantial deviation that was made necessary by the work conditions and awarded compensation.[39]

While a department store salesperson was shopping on the store premises during her lunch break, she tripped on a hanger on the floor and was injured. She filed a liability claim, but the court ruled that the injury had occurred in the course of employment and that workers' compensation was the only remedy.[40]

Social and Recreational Activities

Injuries occurring during social events and recreational activities connected with employment raise issues of compensability. Whether such injuries are compensable depends on the nature and extent of the employer's involvement in the activity and the benefit of the activity to the employer. These injuries have become so common that numerous state legislatures have enacted specific statutes concerning their compensability.

Many courts require that a recreational activity's circumstances meet at least one of three requirements to be considered in the course of employment:

1. The recreational activity must occur on the work premises during a recreation period.
2. The company must require workers to participate in the recreational activity.
3. The company must receive substantial direct benefit from the activity beyond the value of improved worker health or morale.

Adjusters must know which of these requirements apply in the states in which they handle claims. The following case illustrates the importance of knowing a specific state statute and applying it to the claim.

Recreational Activity Case and State Law

A worker was injured at a company-sponsored holiday party in Illinois. The party was on the employer's premises, held during normal work hours, and paid for by the employer, and the worker was paid for the time spent at the party. However, the court denied benefits because attending the event was optional. Illinois law specifically states that injuries occurring at optional employer events are noncompensable.[41]

Compensation is likely for injuries sustained during recreational activities that occur regularly on the employer's premises and with the employer's knowledge. This result is true even if the employer has not explicitly sanctioned the activity. Courts often deem a regular activity, such as a touch football game during lunch break, incidental to the employment and compensable. Courts might deny compensation for an injury resulting from a one-time or first-time activity, especially if the employer's knowledge of the activity cannot be demonstrated.

Recreational Activity Injury Cases

A worker suffered a ruptured kidney playing touch football on company property during an afternoon break. The employer had known of and had acquiesced to the football games for more than three months. The court ruled that the games had become incidental to the employment and awarded compensation.[42]

Continued on next page.

A worker was hurt in a softball game that occurred off the employer's premises during nonworking hours. The employer had paid the team's league entry fee and provided supplies and uniforms bearing the company logo. The company had a wellness program and awarded credits to workers who played on the team. Benefits were denied because the circumstances did not meet any of the three requirements.[43]

Injuries related to recreational activities away from the employer's premises might be compensable if the employer requires or expects worker participation in, or derives benefit from, the activity.[44] Compensation is granted to injured workers who are explicitly required to participate because the social or recreational activity has become a job duty. The requirement to participate need not be explicit. Many sales personnel are implicitly expected to entertain customers. Other types of workers might participate in company-sponsored social events only because the alternative is to report to work.

Employers might derive benefit from social or recreational activities at which customers or suppliers are entertained or when the event is part of an advertising or marketing effort. Injuries to workers who participate in such events, even voluntarily, are compensable. However, when the employer does not derive any real benefit, other than improved worker morale, and does not even tacitly require participation, the fact that the employer has organized or financed the activity does not create a work relationship substantial enough to require compensating resulting injuries. Most courts deny compensation when the employer merely encourages the activity.

Off-Premises Injury Cases

The court awarded compensation to a worker for injury occurring during a company softball game because the employer had organized and maintained the league, pressured the worker to play, paid for the equipment, publicized and encouraged the games, and made company time available to create schedules and league bylaws.[45]

A worker broke his leg while playing softball for a team sponsored by his employer. The employer had paid for the equipment and jerseys, but games occurred off the employer's premises and were played mainly for workers' enjoyment. Compensation was denied.[46]

Acts Outside Regular Duties

As previously discussed, under certain circumstances, workers can be compensated for injuries occurring while they are not engaged in work duties. This principle is applied to several situations, usually with the rationale that the activity in question is incidental to the employment or that it benefits the employer.

A worker who abandons work duties to help a co-worker with other work duties, even if forbidden to do so, remains within the course of employment. A worker who does so is advancing the employer's interests even if the worker's only intent is to help the co-worker. In contrast, a worker who abandons work duties solely to satisfy curiosity is likely not to be compensated for resulting injuries. Many courts would rule that workers who both abandon their own work and involve themselves with machinery, tools, or places that do not relate to their own work should not be compensated for resulting injuries. However, when a worker's lapse is momentary and spontaneous, some courts might overlook curiosity and might grant compensation for resulting injuries.

A worker ordered to perform personal errands for a superior would likely be compensated for resulting injuries. A few courts might disagree on the grounds that the errand is neither work-related nor something a superior is allowed by the employer to order. However, most courts would allow compensation because denial places the financial burden of the injury on the worker, not the employer, or because workers should not be put in the position of having to decide which orders from their superiors are appropriate and which are not. Injuries a worker suffers while running a personal errand for a co-worker, not a supervisor, would not be compensable.

Injuries a worker sustains while acting in an emergency are compensable if the employer benefits from the worker's actions or if the circumstances of the employment caused the worker to become involved in the emergency.[47] A worker injured while rescuing a co-worker or saving the employer's property from danger would be compensated. Rescuing a stranger has a much weaker relationship to the employment, but some courts have granted compensation even in those situations. More difficult yet are cases in which no real emergency exists but only a need for help, such as the case of a stranger with a broken-down car. Courts would probably not grant compensation for injuries resulting from such a situation unless ordinary standards of human behavior required the worker to become involved, such as if the broken-down car were in a remote, uninhabited area.

Pranks, Horseplay, and Practical Jokes

Workers sometimes leave their work duties to engage in pranks, horseplay, or practical jokes. They play hide-and-go-seek; chase one another; engage in play fights with tools, supplies, or trash; perform athletic or acrobatic stunts; sabotage the work stations of others; or prey on workers around them.

Unwilling victims of such behavior can receive compensation for their injuries. However, adjusters investigating these cases should be aware that, after being injured, a willing participant might deny participating in the activity and might pose as an innocent victim.

Compensation for instigators and willing participants is much less likely. Courts are most likely to grant compensation when the behavior is momentary and spontaneous, is induced by boring lulls in work, or has become an established and tolerated part of the work environment. Nevertheless, courts readily deny compensation in the absence of evidence that the behavior is an expected or an established incident of the employment.

Horseplay Injury Cases

While closing a service station, a seventeen-year-old attendant and another co-worker engaged in a sponge fight. The attendant tripped and fell through a glass door. The court ruled that, because horseplay frequently occurred at this workplace, an accident was almost inevitable under the circumstances. Compensation was awarded.[48]

A man was injured when he struck his face on a hand truck after throwing a piece of rubber tubing at a co-worker. The court ruled that such horseplay was not compensable unless it was part of a series of similar incidents so known to the employer that they had become part of the employment.[49]

Relationship of Injury's Time and Place to Employment

The time and place of a worker's injury are important in determining whether the injury is work-related. Generally, injuries occurring at the workplace during work hours are compensable, and those occurring away from the workplace outside regular work hours are not. Some important exceptions are discussed later in this chapter. The time and place of the accident are especially important in cases involving workers commuting to and from work, traveling workers, workers injured before being hired and after leaving employment, and resident workers.

Commute to and From Work

One of the most often stated rules of compensation law is that workers are not compensated for injuries sustained while commuting to and from work even though the trip would not have been made except for the employment. Generally, this rule holds true no matter how close to the employer's premises the worker is when injured. Determining the boundaries of the employer's premises is the key issue in applying the commuting rule.

For the purpose of the commuting rule, the employer's premises include all areas owned, occupied, leased, or controlled by the employer. Therefore, an injury occurring in a private parking lot owned by the employer would likely be compensated, while one occurring in the public lot of an office complex or shopping center in which the employer is located probably would not be compensated. Some courts have granted compensation for injuries occurring in areas over which the employer has some nominal control, such as common areas in an office building or sidewalks in front of the employer's premises. Other courts apply the premises rule conservatively and do not award compensation for injuries occurring in such areas.

Travel from one part of an employer's premises to another is covered because it occurs completely within the premises. Workers need not be injured at their workstations to receive compensation. Coverage begins when workers set foot on any part of the premises. Workers who travel from one employer location to another are engaged in business travel and are not governed by the commuting rule. Injuries to such workers are compensable. Nor does the commuting rule apply to workers who are injured on the way home if they are required by the employer to work when they arrive at home. However, the act of taking work home for their own convenience does not transform the worker's commute home into a business trip.

Commuting Injury Cases

A worker slipped and fell on an icy public sidewalk while reaching for the door to his employer's office building. The court ruled that the worker could not be compensated for travel to and from the workplace and that the worker had not been injured by any hazard of the employment. Compensation was denied.[50]

While leaving work, a worker fell in the lobby of the building in which his employer was a tenant. Benefits were awarded even though the employer did not own, control, or maintain the lobby area. The court reasoned that the lobby is different from sidewalks and parking lots in that the lobby is part of the employer's premises.[51]

As a rule that is frequently the basis on which compensation is denied, the commuting to and from work rule is subject to several exceptions. Transportation provided by the employer is an obvious exception. When the employer provides the means for commuting, the risks associated with employment begin as soon as the worker enters the employer's vehicle.[52] However, injuries are noncompensable if the employer merely reimburses or subsidizes the cost of commuting or if workers arrange their own car pools, because controlling the means of transportation does not rest with the employer.

Travel through dangerous areas, such as railroad crossings, that cannot be avoided when entering and leaving the employer's premises is also considered an exception to the commuting rule. The dangers of such places are considered a hazard of the employment.

Special Errands

Another exception to the commuting rule is for travel that in itself is a major part of the worker's duties. This exception is known as the special errand rule. For example, a worker who must journey to the workplace just to open doors or lock up would likely receive compensation for injuries sustained during that time. In this case, the major part of the worker's effort is the trip back and forth at the required times, and that trip is considered a required, work-related activity. Likewise, workers temporarily assigned to a distant facility of the employer might be compensated for injuries occurring in transit. However, merely working overtime or different hours does not invoke the special errand rule.

Special Errand Injury Cases

A worker was temporarily assigned by her employer to a location thirty miles from her usual workplace. She suffered injuries in an accident on the way back to her regular job location from this distant location. The court ruled that the injured worker was on a special errand because the reassignment was temporary and unusual, because of the distance involved, and because the worker was required to carpool with a co-worker. Compensation was awarded.[53]

A worker was injured while traveling home to change into a suit before going to a trade show that his employer required him to attend. Because the worker normally wore work clothes at work and was required by his employer to change clothes and attend the show, the court ruled that the worker was on a special errand and was entitled to compensation.[54]

Travel as a Regular Duty

Certain workers are required by their jobs to travel. They include delivery personnel, solicitors, truck drivers, repairmen, construction personnel, and salespeople. While traveling from one place of business to another, these workers are covered by workers' compensation. When it is clear that they are engaged in work-related duties, the absence of a fixed workplace should not jeopardize their compensation. Workers whose jobs require them to travel are covered by workers' compensation as soon as they leave for their first destination. This "door-to-door" coverage contrasts with the usual commuting rule for workers who work at fixed places.

Some workers' jobs require overnight travel. Most states extend twenty-four-hour compensation protection to such workers. They are covered continuously for all expected activities, including eating at restaurants, sleeping in hotels, and engaging in reasonable relaxation, until they return home.

Traveling Injury Cases

A worker was killed in a fire in a hotel in which he was conducting meetings and conferences for his employer. Compensation was awarded.[55]

A bus driver on an overnight trip was accidentally shot at a bar to which he had gone for drinks. The court ruled that the visit to the bar was a reasonable recreational activity, incidental to the employment, and awarded compensation.[56]

Some courts have denied compensation to overnight traveling workers when the worker has deviated substantially from expected activities, for example, becoming intoxicated at a place far removed from the business destination. However, both workers who travel during the workday and those who travel overnight sometimes make personal trips that take them outside the scope of workers' compensation coverage. When an injury occurs during an identifiable personal deviation from a business trip, compensation might be denied.

Dual Purpose Trips

Workers are covered by workers' compensation during a business trip. Sometimes people travel for both business and personal reasons. These trips are known in workers' compensation law as **dual purpose trips**. For example, a worker going home for the day is asked by the employer to pick up or drop off something. Some courts have weighed the relative importance of the business purpose and the personal purpose for the travel, and have awarded compensation only when the business purpose is more substantial than the personal purpose. However, this decision is subjective. One court might decide that the business purpose of a given case is more significant, while another court might decide the opposite.

Dual purpose trip
An employee trip having both business and personal purposes.

A commonly used rule for deciding such cases is set out in *Marks' Dependents v. Gray*, 167 N.E. 181 (N.Y. 1929): If a business purpose makes a trip necessary, the entire trip is deemed a business trip, no matter how substantial the personal motive for the travel. Alternatively, if the business trip would have been postponed but for the personal purpose, the trip is deemed a personal trip. The issue is whether the worker would be required to go on the business trip, not whether the business purpose is more substantial.

Dual Purpose Trip Injury Cases

A woman's husband was the president of the company she worked for. She accompanied her husband on a business trip that included a vacation in Yellowstone and Grand Teton National Parks. She was killed en route from the parks to a business meeting. Before she had been hired to work at the company, the woman had accompanied her husband on six of eight previous similar trips. The court ruled the trip to be personal, stating that no evidence had been presented that the company had required anyone to accompany the husband for business purposes.[57]

A man was killed en route from a job site to his home in Phoenix, 300 miles away, where he planned to spend the weekend with family. While in Phoenix that Saturday, he was also expected to pick up some fuel pump parts for his job. Co-workers admitted that delivery of the fuel pump parts would have been arranged during the work week had it not been for the man's trip home. The court found the trip to be personal and denied compensation.[58]

Sometimes a worker departs from a business trip to take a personal trip that is identifiable by a distinct deviation from the normal business trip route. Courts generally deny compensation for injuries when the worker has distinctly deviated from the business route and is injured during the deviation. Other courts allow compensation if the deviation is not substantial or if the worker has completed personal matters and is returning to the business trip route.[59] Adjusters faced with such cases should carefully investigate business locations and personal destinations and all alternative routes for reaching them. Determining whether a particular deviation is substantial depends on the distance, duration, and alternatives.

A distinct business deviation from a personal trip is considered a business trip until the worker returns to the personal trip route. A worker is therefore covered by workers' compensation throughout the business deviation even if it is not substantial and even if the worker has completed the work-related business and is returning to the personal trip route.

Deviation From Dual Purpose Trip Cases

A truck driver was killed while driving off the usual route between Buffalo, New York, and Sioux City, Iowa. The court ruled that even if the driver had stopped for personal reasons, he was returning to his business destination and awarded compensation.[60]

A worker had to travel from Pittsburgh (in western Pennsylvania) to Bethlehem (in eastern Pennsylvania) on business. He left several days early and visited New York City on vacation. While traveling from New York to Bethlehem, he was killed in a car accident in New Jersey. The court ruled that the worker was outside the course of his employment and denied compensation.[61]

The preceding two cases illustrate the principle that compensability in these kinds of cases depends on whether the worker is on an identifiable deviation from the business trip route at the time of injury or whether the worker has returned to the business trip route.

Time of Employment

Workers' compensation does not apply before the employment relationship begins or after it ends. The employment relationship begins when the parties agree to the employment and the worker is present at a place and time required by the employment. The employment agreement can be completely informal. The completion of personnel paperwork is not essential to confirm the employment relationship. The worker need not have begun any actual work duties to be in the course of the employment and to have a compensable claim, as long as the worker is at a place required by the job during a time required. After termination of employment, a person is entitled to reasonable time to remove personal belongings from the workplace and to collect any pay that must be collected in person.

Injuries occurring during any of these activities are covered. However, the person is not covered during subsequent and unnecessary visits to the workplace.

Off-Hours

Certain workers, including those at hotels, camps, resorts, and construction sites, are required or allowed to live on the employer's premises. These workers have twenty-four-hour coverage if they are continuously on call. Injuries to resident workers during off-hours are not necessarily covered by workers' compensation, particularly if they are not caused by the employer or the employer's premises.

Off-Hour Injury Cases

A worker employed at a remote job site slept in his van each night. The worker died from inhalation of carbon monoxide released from a charcoal grill that he had placed in the van and lit for warmth. Because it was reasonably necessary for the worker to stay at the job site, the court awarded benefits.[62]

STATUTORY STANDARD EXCEPTIONS

One of the clearest rules in workers' compensation law is that the worker's fault in causing an injury is generally irrelevant in determining the injury's compensability. Injuries are compensable if they arise out of and in the course of employment regardless of the worker's fault. The worker might receive compensation despite negligence, gross negligence, or even certain intentional wrongdoing. The few exceptions to this rule are discussed in this section.

Willful Misconduct and Safety Rule Violation

Slightly fewer than half the states have a specific statutory exception to compensation in cases of willful misconduct or safety rule violation. The other states deny workers' compensation benefits on the premise that such behavior removes the worker from the course of employment.

Courts have construed exceptions to compensation very narrowly. Compensation is usually denied only in cases in which the worker deliberately and knowingly violates a safety rule.[63] The worker must both know of the rule and intend to violate it before compensation is denied. In some states, the willful misconduct must be the injury's sole cause before compensation can be denied. Certain courts have allowed compensation, despite rule violations, in cases in which the employer had been aware of repeated rule violations but had failed to enforce the safety rule.

Courts have also allowed compensation when a worker has been injured while attempting to perform job duties by prohibited means.[64] According to these courts, workers injured while attempting to perform job duties should be compensated no matter how reckless and prohibited the means by which they do so.

Intoxication

Some states have statutory exceptions to compensation for injuries to an intoxicated worker. The specific application of this exception varies widely. Some states deny compensation to an intoxicated worker even if the intoxication had nothing to do with the injury. Other states deny compensation only if intoxication is the sole cause of injury, a condition that rarely occurs. Most states that recognize this exception require that the injury be "due to" intoxication.[65] Adjusters who discover that a worker was intoxicated when injured should carefully investigate all other circumstances of the injury and should obtain the advice of counsel before denying compensation.

Self-Inflicted Injury

Some states have a statutory exception to compensation in cases of self-inflicted injury. In states without such a specific exception, self-inflicted injury is considered to be outside the course of employment.

Courts interpret this exception carefully and usually apply it only to intentional and deliberate behavior. No matter how grossly reckless a worker might be, the worker can recover for injuries that are not *intentionally* and *deliberately* self-inflicted.

Courts have also allowed recovery in suicide cases when a compensable injury contributed to the suicide. Identifying such circumstances is a complex medical and legal issue. Those circumstances are most likely to occur in cases in which the original injury caused such severe suffering that the victim commits suicide as an escape.[66]

SUMMARY

Most state workers' compensation laws allow compensation only for injuries arising out of and in the course of employment. Court interpretations of this requirement vary among states. "Arising out of" employment and "in the course of" employment are considered two separate elements that must be proven separately. When both elements exist in a case, compensation is granted. Some states grant compensation when only one element is clearly proven. Some states require only that injuries result from employment.

The "arising out of" element relates to an injury's cause. Some courts apply the increased risk principle, granting compensation if a worker's risk of the injury is greater than the public's risk. Some courts use the "but for" or positional risk principle, granting compensation for an injury that would not have occurred but for the worker's employment.

Injuries resulting from the following causes commonly raise compensability issues relating to whether they arose out of employment:

- Street risk (exposure to the dangers characteristic of the street)
- Positional risk
- Acts of God (natural phenomena)
- Exposure to the elements
- Idiopathic conditions (medical conditions peculiar to the injured worker) and medical conditions
- Mental conditions
- Assaults

The "in the course of" employment requirement for compensability refers to the circumstances of an injury's occurrence. To determine if an injury occurred in the course of employment, an adjuster must investigate the facts of the claim and look for indications of a relationship between the employment and the injury in terms of the following:

- Cause
- Activity of the worker when injured
- Place of injury
- Time of injury

The more of those factors that are related to employment, the greater the chance that the injury is compensable. Cases that include the following circumstances might raise questions about whether an injury occurred in the course of employment:

- Personal activities
- Social and recreational activities
- Acts outside regular duties
- Pranks, horseplay, and practical jokes
- Commutes to and from work
- Special errands
- Travel
- Time of employment
- Off-hours

Most states, either through law or court decisions, make exceptions to workers' compensation in cases that involve willful misconduct or safety rule violations. Some states make exceptions for injuries to an intoxicated worker and for self-inflicted injuries.

Having determined what cases might be compensable, an adjuster must determine what benefits are due under the statute. The next chapter discusses the various types of benefits under workers' compensation statutes.

CHAPTER NOTES

1. *Crites v. Baker*, 276 N.E.2d 582 (Ind. App. 1971).

2. *R&T Investments Ltd. v. Johns*, 321 S.E.2d 287 (Va. 1984).

3. *Orr v. Holiday Inns, Inc.*, 627 P.2d 1193 (Kan. App. 1981).

4. *Craig v. Electrolux Corp.*, 510 P.2d 138 (Kan. 1973).

5. *Jordan v. St. Louis County Police Department*, 699 S.W.2d 124 (Mo. App. 1985).

6. Arthur Larson and Lex K. Larson, *Larson's Workers' Compensation* (Desk Edition), § 3.05, Vol. 1, 2003, LexisNexis.

7. *Baker v. Orange County Board of County Commissioners*, 399 So.2d 400 (Fla. App. 1981).

8. *Corken v. Corken Steel Products, Inc.*, 385 S.W.2d 949 (Ky. App. 1965).

9. *Vanderbee v. Knape & Vogt Mfg. Co.*, 210 N.W.2d 801 (Mich. App. 1973).

10. *Wayne Adams Buick Inc. v. Ference*, 421 N.E.2d 733 (Ind. App. 1981).

11. *Harlan-Wallis Coal Corp. v. Foster*, 277 S.W.2d 14 (Ky. 1955).

12. Larson, § 5.0.

13. *Reich v. A. Reich and Sons Gardens, Inc.*, 485 S.W.2d 133 (Mo. App. 1972).

14. *Mobile & O.R.R. v. Industrial Commission of Ill.*, F.2d 228 (E.D. Ill. 1928).

15. Larson, § 9.01.

16. *Collins v. Liberty Mutual Insurance Co.*, 561 S.W.2d 456 (Tenn. 1978).

17. *Ware v. State Workers Compensation Commissioner*, 234 S.E.2d 779 (W.Va. 1977).

18. *Kennecott Corp. v. Industrial Commission*, 675 P.2d 1187 (Utah 1987).

19. Elizabeth C. D. Gullette; James A. Blumenthal, PhD; Michael Babyak, PhD; Wei Jiang, MD; Robert A. Waugh, MD; David J. Frid, MD; Christopher M. O'Connor, MD; James J. Morris, MD; David S. Krantz, PhD, "The Effects of Myocardial Ischemia During Daily Life," *The Journal of American Medicine*, May 21, 1997.

20. *Steve Foley Cadillac v. Industrial Commission*, 670 N.E.2d 885 (Ill. 1996).

21. *Beeson v. Landcoast*, 862 S.W.2d 846 (Arkansas 1995).

22. *United Exposition Service Co. v. State Industrial Insurance System and Robert Keating*, 851 P.2d 423 (Nevada 1993).

23. *Weaver v. Proctor & Schwartz*, Docket No. 253209 (North Carolina Industrial Commission 1996).

24. *Troy v. Prudential Insurance Co.*, 649 N.Y.S.2d 746 (New York 1996).

25. *Geeslin v. Workers Compensation Commissioner*, 294 S.E.2d 150 (W.Va. 1982).

26. *Colvert v. Industrial Commission*, 520 P.2d 322 (Ariz. App. 1974).

27. Larson, § 8.01 [1] [a].

28. *Schwartz v. Golden*, 338 N.W.2d 218 (Mich. App. 1983).

29. *Beverly v. Ruth's Chris Steak House*, 682 So.2d 1360 (Alabama 1996).

30. *Baker v. Hudson Valley Nursing Home*, 649 N.Y.S.2d 105 (N.Y. 1996).

31. *Bryan v. Best Western/Coachmans Inn*, 885 S.W.2d 28 (1994).

32. *Dependable Messenger v. Industrial Commission*, 858 P.2d 661 (AZ 1993).

33. *B&B Nursing Homes v. Blair*, 496 P.2d 795 (Okla. 1972).

34. *Cedar Rapids Community School v. Cady*, 278 N.W.2d 298 (Iowa 1979).

35. *Devault v. General Motors Corp.*, 386 N.W.2d 671 (Mich. App. 1986).

36. *Rogers v. Workers Compensation Appeals Board*, 218 Cal. Rptr. 662 (1985).

37. Larson, § 29.

38. New York State Consolidated Laws, Workers' Compensation, Chapter 67, Article 2, § 21.

39. *B&B Cash Grocery Stores v. Wortman*, 431 So.2d 171 (Fla. App. 1983).

40. *Chen v. Federated Department Stores*, 489 A.2d 719 (N.J. Super. 1985).

41. *Glassie v. Papergraphics*, 618 N.E.2d 885 (Ill. App. 1 Dist. 1993).

42. *Mack Trucks, Inc., v. Miller*, 326 A.2d 186 (Md. App. 1974).

43. *Tucker v. Acme Boot Co.*, 856 S.W.2d 703 (Tenn. 1993).

44. Larson, § 22.05.

45. *Illinois Bell Telephone Co. v. Industrial Commission*, 334 N.E.2d 136 (Ill. 1975).

46. *Chilcote v. Blass, Riddick, Chilcote & Continental Insurance Co.*, 620 S.W.2d 953 (Ark. 1981).

47. Larson, § 28.00.

48. *Peet v. Garner Oil Co.*, 492 S.W.2d 103 (Mo. App. 1973).

49. *Ognibene v. Rochester Mfg. Co.*, 80 N.E.2d 749 (N.Y. 1948).

50. *Simpson v. Cady & Lee*, 293 N.W. 718 (Mich. 1940).

51. *Evans v. Coats & Clark*, 492 S.E.2d 807 (S.C. 1997).

52. Larson, § 15.

53. *Winn-Dixie Stores v. Smallwood*, 516 So.2d 716 (Ala. App. 1987).

54. *Green v. Workers Compensation Appeal Board*, 232 Cal. Rptr. 465 (Cal. App. 1986).

55. *Burton v. Broadcast Music, Inc.*, 250 N.E.2d 243 (N.Y. 1968).

56. *Voight v. Rettinger Transportation, Inc.*, 306 N.W.2d 133 (Minn. 1981).

57. *Storm v. Karl-Mil, Inc.*, 460 A.2d 519 (Del. 1983).

58. *Kriese v. Industrial Commission*, 554 P.2d 914 (Ariz. Ct. App. 1976).

59. Larson, § 17.

60. *Hilliker v. North American Van Lines, Inc.*, 207 N.Y.S.2d 753 (1960).

61. *Hess v. Catholic Knights of St. George*, 27 A.2d 542 (Pa. Super. 1942).

62. *Lujan v. Payroll Express, Inc.*, 114 N.M. 62, 834 P.2d 939 (N.M. 1992).

63. Larson, § 34.

64. Larson, § 33.

65. Larson, § 36.

66. Larson, § 38.

Chapter 4

Direct Your Learning

Statutory Benefits

After learning the content of this chapter, you should be able to:

■ Given a case, determine the appropriate type and amount of workers' compensation benefits.

- Explain when the following lost wage benefits are awarded and how those benefits are calculated:

  - Temporary total disability
  - Temporary partial disability
  - Permanent total disability
  - Permanent partial disability

- Explain how each of the following factors affects the benefits payable under workers' compensation:

  - Maximum rates
  - Minimum rates
  - Waiting periods
  - Retroactive periods

- Explain how benefits are determined for scheduled injuries.

- Distinguish between the following methods of determining loss of earnings capacity in cases of nonscheduled permanent partial disability:

  - Actual economic loss
  - Medically determined impairment

- Describe the scope, limitations, and duration of medical benefits.

- Describe the rehabilitation services provided under workers' compensation statutes.

- Describe the death benefits payable under workers' compensation.

■ Describe the factors affecting workers' compensation costs.

Develop Your Perspective

What are the main topics covered in the chapter?

Workers' compensation provides various benefits to injured workers. These benefits include lost wages, medical expenses, rehabilitation expenses, and death benefits. This chapter describes the benefits and explains how to calculate them.

Consider the financial consequences if you were injured at work.

- Who will pay your medical expenses?
- How will you meet personal financial obligations while out of work?

Why is it important to learn about these topics?

Calculating the appropriate amount of benefit to be paid is the responsibility of the workers' compensation adjuster. Additionally, having an understanding of the factors that affect the costs of workers' compensation keeps the adjuster mindful of the opportunities for cost control.

Calculate your benefits if you sustain a compensable injury.

- What type of benefits should you receive?
- When would your benefits begin?
- How long would your benefits continue?

How can you use what you will learn?

Adjust a workers' compensation claim.

- Determine what type of benefit should be paid.
- Calculate the amount of benefits to be paid.

Chapter 4
Statutory Benefits

The accurate and prompt payment of benefits is vital in workers' compensation claims. Disabled workers depend on compensation benefits to replace income during periods of disability and might also depend on other compensation benefits due them, including medical and rehabilitation benefits. Therefore, the adjuster must know the benefits prescribed by the applicable statute, when the benefits are due, how long the benefits are payable, and how much to pay. The adjuster must also be able to explain the benefit computation to the injured worker.

Paying benefits promptly sets the stage for a harmonious relationship between the injured worker and the adjuster. Accurately computing benefits avoids underpayment or overpayment. Underpayment, late payment, or inaccurate payments can cause anxiety and anger for the injured worker and might cause legal problems for the insurer. State workers' compensation agencies can impose penalties on insurers for unjustifiable delays in paying benefits.

Workers' Compensation Benefits

1. Wage loss benefits
2. Medical benefits
3. Rehabilitation benefits
4. Death benefits

Workers' compensation statutes provide the following four categories of benefits:

1. Wage loss benefits—to cover lost wages during the period the worker is medically unable to work and to compensate for any permanent residual disability or loss of earning capacity. Wage loss benefits fall into four categories. The two primary categories are benefits for temporary disability and benefits for permanent disability. These categories both have two subcategories: partial disability and total disability. The next section discusses each category.

2. Medical benefits—payments for medical treatment of the disability during the period the injured worker is medically unable to work. Medical benefits are furnished, usually without limit, as long as the medical care is reasonably necessary and related to the injury.

3. Rehabilitation benefits—payment for services to assist injured workers in reentering the labor force by helping limit the effects of the disability.

4. Death benefits—payments to the survivors of a worker who dies from a compensable illness or accident.

The purpose of this chapter is to identify and describe workers' compensation benefits in general, to describe the benefit categories, and to demonstrate how benefits are computed. Because benefits vary by state, adjusters are advised to consult the applicable law for the precise provisions that apply to a given case.

BENEFIT FACTORS

Four factors are used in computing workers' compensation benefits. The four factors are:

1. Average weekly wage (AWW)
2. Maximums and minimums
3. Waiting periods and duration of benefits
4. Retroactive benefits

Adjusters must understand these four factors to calculate benefits specified in a statute.

Average Weekly Wage

The AWW is a significant figure because it is the basis for computing various benefit rates. The AWW is calculated by averaging the worker's actual wages, including overtime, for a prescribed number of pre-injury weeks. Statutes are not uniform in the number of weeks prescribed. In addition, because tips, overtime, meals, lodging, car or fuel allowance, and other benefits might need to be included in the wages, determining a proper AWW is sometimes difficult. Workers' compensation statutes contain provisions for an administrative agency to resolve disagreements over the AWW.

In some states, wages from more than one job might be stacked to determine the AWW. For example, if the injured worker is employed full time as an accountant and part time as a salesperson, wages from both jobs would be totaled to determine the AWW. Other states allow stacking of wages only from similar employment. A worker employed as a full-time police officer and as a security guard on weekends might include wages from both jobs for consideration of the AWW. Certain states consider wages solely from the job the worker was performing when injured. In some states, spendable earnings (gross wages net of taxes) are used as a basis for the AWW. Those states base the compensation rate on 80 percent of spendable earnings or 66⅔ percent of gross wages, whichever is less. The injured worker's employer typically provides the wage history on a published form that simplifies computation. (See Exhibit 4-1.)

The worker's wage history might not extend to the prescribed number of weeks. Statutes outline alternate methods for determining the average weekly wage in such cases. For example, wages of "similar workers" might be used by averaging wage history from three to five workers in the same employment capacity with the same hourly rate. Many states accept whatever wage history is available. The object is to determine a fair indication of the disabled worker's pre-injury wages.

EXHIBIT 4-1

Wage History

STATE OF

Employer:

Please complete the weekly earnings schedule below for the employee you are reporting injured. Provide the weekly earnings for each of the 13 weeks, or all if less than 13 weeks, immediately preceding the date of accident.

Injured employee name   Social Security number

_____   _____

Week No.	Week Ending Month Day Year	Days Worked	Gross Amount Paid Including All Overtime
1			
2			
3			
4			
5			
6			
7			
8			
9			
10			
11			
12			
13			

Was this employee given free rent, lodging, board, tips, or other allowances in addition to the above earnings? If yes, state weekly value thereof.

$ _____

Signed _____

Illustrations of Computations of Average Weekly Wage

Glenda, a file clerk, is paid $13,000 per year. Her AWW remains constant at $250 ($13,000 ÷ 52 weeks).

George earns $6.50 per hour. He does not always work a full week. George is employed in a state where the AWW is based on a 13-week pre-injury history. Over the past 13 weeks, George's total gross income was $2,782; his AWW is $214 ($2,782 ÷ 13 weeks).

Jane, a waitress, earns $5.00 per hour plus tips. Jane is employed in a state prescribing a 52-week history as the basis for the AWW. Her earnings for 52 weeks total $10,400; she can verify $8,500 in tips received in that period; and she receives a meal valued at $4.00 each workday, totaling $1,040 for that period. Jane's AWW is $383.46 ($10,400 wages + $8,500 tips + $1,040 meals) ÷ 52 ($19,940 ÷ 52 = $383.46).

Bill, a maintenance worker for an apartment management company, receives an apartment in addition to his weekly salary of $400. The apartment is valued at $300 per month, or $75 per week. While Bill is disabled, he must pay rent for his apartment. In this case, the value of the apartment is added to Bill's income to arrive at Bill's AWW: $400 + $75 = $475.

Earl, a construction superintendent with a weekly salary of $500, also receives a car allowance of $125 per week that is added to his salary to yield an AWW of $625.

Maximums and Minimums

Each state's workers' compensation statute will specify an amount of benefit to be paid. For example, a statute may say that benefits for temporary total disability will be two-thirds of a worker's wage, subject to a minimum dollar amount and subject to a maximum dollar amount. Often, the maximum is 100 percent of the state average weekly wage. The minimum may also be expressed as a percentage of the state average weekly wage.

Waiting Period and Duration of Benefits

Each workers' compensation statute specifies a waiting period before lost wages benefits can be collected. Under this requirement, the injured worker must wait a prescribed time, usually between three and seven days, after becoming disabled before disability benefits begin. If a worker returns to work before the end of the waiting period, then lost wages benefits are not payable. (The waiting period does not apply to payment of medical expenses.)

Wage loss benefits are calculated by calendar days rather than workdays, that is, on a seven-day week. Therefore, workers who are disabled on days they normally do not work receive benefits for those days, but their wage loss benefits for each day are one-seventh of their weekly benefits. The calendar-day method is used because it equitably accommodates various work schedules and days of disability.

Wage loss benefits continue until the worker is able to return to work or a permanent disability settlement is reached.

Illustrations of Waiting Periods

Joe is injured on June 2; he is able to return to work on June 10. Joe works in a state imposing a three-day waiting period. He was paid his normal wages for the day of injury, June 2. Joe's benefits will not begin until June 6, three days after the injury. He would receive benefits for June 6, 7, 8, and 9—four days, or $\frac{4}{7}$ of a week. However, suppose Joe did not return to work until June 29. The retroactive period in Joe's state is fourteen days. Joe is out of work for twenty-six days, June 3 through June 28. Because he is disabled more than fourteen days, the waiting period does not apply, and Joe receives wage loss benefits from his first day of disability.

Eleanor is employed in a state with a seven-day waiting period and a twenty-one-day retroactive period. Eleanor is injured on March 4. She returns to work on March 8. Eleanor receives no wage loss benefits because her disability did not extend beyond the waiting period.

Ann is employed in the same state as Eleanor. Ann is injured on March 4 and is paid her regular wages for that day. She is able to return to work on March 15. She is eligible for wage loss benefits from March 12 through March 14 (for three days) because she must wait seven days (March 5 through March 11) for benefits to begin. If Ann had not been able to return to work until March 30, her disability would have extended past the twenty-one-day retroactive period, and she would have received wage loss benefits from the first day of disability, March 5.

Tom is injured in a state with a three-day waiting period and a fourteen-day retroactive period. His accident occurred at 8:05 AM on April 1; he is not paid his regular wages for the day of the accident. Tom returns to work on April 9; his waiting period is April 1, 2, and 3. Tom receives wage loss benefits for April 4, 5, 6, 7, and 8—five days, or $\frac{5}{7}$ of a week. Had he not returned to work until April 17, the waiting period would not have applied, and he would have received benefits from April 1 through April 16, sixteen days, or $2\frac{2}{7}$ weeks.

Retroactive Benefits

If a worker's disability continues beyond the waiting period and then beyond another specified date, called a retroactive date, benefits are paid retroactively back to the date of disability. That is, once the disability runs past the retroactive date, benefits for the previously uncompensated waiting period become payable. The period between the end of the waiting period and the retroactive date is known as the **retroactive period**.

WAGE LOSS BENEFITS

The majority of cases involving any lost time from work are **temporary partial disability (TPD)** cases: The injured worker might be away for a limited time or might be able to continue to work on a limited basis but eventually returns to full duties and hours. An injured worker with a **temporary total disability (TTD)**, however, is unable to perform any job duties for a specific period but ultimately makes a full recovery and can resume all job duties. This section describes wage loss benefits for both kinds of temporary disability.

Retroactive period
A period set by statute after which, if a disability continues, workers' compensation benefits are payable retroactively for the designated waiting period after the disability's onset.

Temporary partial disability (TPD)
A disability caused by a work-related injury or disease that temporarily limits the extent to which a worker can perform job duties; the worker is eventually able to return to full duties and hours.

Temporary total disability (TTD)
A disability caused by a work-related injury or disease that renders an injured worker unable to perform any job duties for a period of time; the worker eventually makes a full recovery and can resume all job duties.

Temporary Total Disability (TTD) Benefits

Compensation for temporary total disability is an income replacement benefit payable to workers during the time they are temporarily totally disabled because of compensable injuries or illnesses. The compensation provides income to replace the disabled worker's regular wages. The TTD rate, commonly paid weekly, is based on a percentage of the worker's gross average weekly wage (AWW). The percentage is typically 66⅔ percent. Adjusters should refer to the applicable statute for the exact rate to use in a particular state. Certain states increase the TTD rate by an additional amount for dependents. For example, Massachusetts allows an additional weekly amount per dependent for workers whose compensation benefit is below a specified amount. The increased benefit cannot exceed the state maximum. The TTD wage loss benefits in all states are subject to both a maximum and a minimum.

TTD Maximums and Minimums

The maximum TTD wage loss benefit is normally computed as a percentage of the state average weekly wage (SAWW). The SAWW is specified in the workers' compensation statute and is usually determined by dividing total wages reported by employers by the average number of workers annually reported, and dividing that figure by fifty-two. The maximums increase annually as the SAWW increases.

Minimum TTD wage loss benefits vary widely. In some states, if the worker's AWW is below the minimum, the base for the TTD benefit changes from the SAWW to 100 percent of actual wages. In other states, 80 or 90 percent of actual wages is used as the base, and in others, after-tax wages are used. Because of these variations, adjusters should consult the applicable state statute.

TTD Benefit Waiting Period and Duration

A worker is not eligible for TTD until after a statutory waiting period. Temporary total wage loss benefits continue until the worker is able to return to work. A few states impose a time or dollar limit on temporary total disability wage loss benefits.

TTD Benefit Calculations—Cases

To compute the TTD benefit, an adjuster must have the following information:

1. Date of injury—obtained from the employer
2. AWW—obtained from the employer
3. TTD rate—obtained from the applicable statute
4. Maximum and minimum TTD benefit—obtained from the applicable statute
5. Waiting period and retroactive period—obtained from the applicable statute
6. Return to work date, when applicable—obtained from the treating doctor, the employer, or the injured worker

The AWW is multiplied by the TTD rate to determine the benefit amount. The calculated benefit amount is then compared to the state minimum and maximum to determine if either applies. The disability period is calculated by counting the number of days the worker is unable to work. The waiting period is subtracted. The retroactive period is considered, if applicable.

The following hypothetical cases illustrate how TTD benefits are calculated.

CASE STUDY

TTD Calculation Involving a Waiting Period

Donald is thirty-seven years old and has been employed as a painter by Acme Decorating for five years. Donald earns $12 per hour and works a forty-hour week with occasional overtime. On August 12 at 3:00 PM as Donald was descending a ladder on the job site, his left foot slipped off the bottom rung, and he felt immediate pain in his left knee. By quitting time, the knee was swollen, and Donald had trouble walking. He reported the injury to his foreman, who suggested that he visit a nearby medical center for care. The medical center doctor diagnosed the injury as a strain and told Donald not to work until a reexamination in five days. On the second visit five days later, the doctor concluded that Donald's condition had not improved enough to allow him to use ladders. The disability continued for another five days. Having been seen by the doctor for the last time on August 22, Donald was released for full duty on August 23.

The following facts apply in calculating Donald's TTD benefit:

1. The injury date is August 12.
2. The AWW is $500, based on a thirteen-week pre-injury history (Donald worked some overtime).
3. The TTD compensation rate is 66⅔ percent of the AWW.
4. The maximum weekly TTD benefit is $473.
5. The minimum TTD benefit is $250.
6. The waiting period is 3 days, retroactive after 14 days.
7. The return to work date is August 23.

Following is the TTD benefit calculation:

$$\text{Weekly TTD benefit} = \text{AWW} \times \text{TTD compensation rate}$$
$$= \$500 \times 66.667\%$$
$$= \$333.33.$$

State maximum is not applicable.

State minimum is not applicable.

$$\text{Disability period} = \text{August 13 through August 22}$$
$$= 10 \text{ days.}$$

$$\text{Benefit period} = \text{Disability period} - \text{Waiting period}$$
$$= 10 \text{ days} - 3 \text{ days}$$
$$= 7 \text{ days.}$$

CASE STUDY

TTD Benefit Calculation for a Partial Week

Amy is a secretary for Apple Construction. She struck her right knee on an open desk drawer on February 5 at noon. Her knee became swollen and stiff, and by 4:00 PM she had difficulty walking. Amy saw her family doctor that evening. The doctor advised her to stay completely off her feet for a week and to return to his office for a release-to-work determination at that time. When Amy saw her doctor on February 12, the swelling was down, and she was released for work the next day, February 13.

The following facts apply in calculating Amy's TTD benefit:

1. Date of injury is February 5.

2. Amy is salaried at $350 per week; therefore, her AWW is $350.

3. The TTD compensation rate is 66⅔ percent of the AWW.

4. The maximum TTD benefit is $367.

5. The minimum TTD benefit is $200.

6. The waiting period is 3 days, retroactive after 14 days.

7. Return to work date is February 13.

Following is the TTD benefit calculation:

$$\text{Weekly TTD benefit} = \text{AWW} \times \text{TTD compensation rate}$$
$$= \$350 \times 66.667\%$$
$$= \$233.33.$$

State maximum is not applicable.

State minimum is not applicable.

$$\text{Disability period} = \text{February 6 through February 12}$$
$$= 7 \text{ days.}$$

$$\text{Benefit period} = \text{Disability period} - \text{Waiting period}$$
$$= 7 \text{ days} - 3 \text{ days}$$
$$= 4 \text{ days.}$$

$$\text{TTD benefit in this case} = \text{Benefit period as portion of week} \times \text{Weekly TTD benefit}$$
$$= \tfrac{4}{7} \text{ week} \times \$233.33$$
$$= \$133.33.$$

CASE STUDY

TTD Benefit Calculation With a Statutory Maximum and a Retroactive Period

Andrew Smith, a thirty-one-year-old electrician for Atlas Builders, was employed for six months, earning $16.50 per hour and working a forty-hour week at the time of his injury. On July 10 at 4:00 PM, Andrew tried to move a 150-pound spool of cable, slipped in mud, and twisted his back. He experienced pain and reported the injury to his boss, who instructed Andrew to see the company doctor immediately. The doctor saw Andrew on July 11, diagnosed back strain, advised him to stay out of work for three weeks, and sent him to physical therapy. At the end of three weeks, on July 31, Andrew returned to the doctor, reporting that he was better but still had pain in his back when bending. The doctor prescribed three more weeks of physical therapy and sent Andrew back to work full duty on August 21.

The following facts apply in calculating Andrew's TTD benefit:

1. Date of injury is July 10.

2. Andrew's AWW is $710, based on the available work history (he earned overtime).

3. The TTD compensation rate is 66⅔ percent of the AWW.

4. The maximum TTD benefit is $344.

5. The minimum TTD benefit is $200.

6. The waiting period is 7 days, retroactive after 21 days.

7. Return to work date is August 21.

Following is the TTD benefit calculation:

$$\text{Weekly TTD benefit} = \text{AWW} \times \text{TTD compensation rate}$$
$$= \$710 \times 66.667\%$$
$$= \$473.33.$$

State maximum of $344 applies.

State minimum is not applicable.

$$\text{Disability period} = \text{July 11 through August 20}$$
$$= 41 \text{ days.}$$

$$\text{Benefit period} = \text{Disability period} - \text{Waiting period}$$
$$= 41 \text{ days} - 0 \text{ days}$$
$$= 41 \text{ days.}$$

The waiting period does not apply because Andrew was disabled more than 21 days.

$$\text{TTD benefit in this case} = \text{Benefit period as portion of week} \times \text{Weekly TTD benefit}$$
$$= 5\tfrac{6}{7} \text{ week} \times \$344$$
$$= \$2,014.86.$$

Temporary Partial Disability (TPD) Benefits

Temporary partial disability wage loss benefits are a "bridge-the-gap" benefit compensating a disabled worker for the wage differential occurring when the worker returns to light work or reduced hours, resulting in a post-injury wage that is less than the pre-injury wage. The TPD compensation rate is a percentage of wage loss, calculated as a percentage of the difference between the worker's pre-injury AWW and wages upon return to work. The percentage used varies by state; therefore, adjusters should check the applicable statute for the proper percentage. TPD benefits, like TTD benefits, are stated as a percentage. For TPD benefits, the percentage is applied to the difference between the worker's pre-injury AWW and the worker's post-injury wage. TPD benefits, by definition, contemplate a return to regular duty when full healing occurs. Some factors common with TPD benefits also apply to TTD benefits: maximums and minimums, waiting periods, and, sometimes, retroactive periods.

Most doctors do not release a worker for full duty until they are certain that the patient has recovered 100 percent. However, a doctor may permit a return to part-time or light-duty employment. For a worker who sustains a hand injury, a doctor may approve one-handed work. For a worker with a back strain, a doctor may permit a return to work with restricted lifting for half days until the patient can resume full duty. Increasingly, employers support light duty for injured workers when possible. They have discovered that it is good business to accommodate a return to less than full duty to prevent a worker from falling into a "disability rut," to encourage job interest, to relieve the workload on co-workers, and to boost morale.

TPD Benefit Calculations—Cases

The same information needed to calculate TPD benefits is needed to calculate TTD benefits. In addition, the adjuster needs to know the difference between the worker's wage for regular duty and that for light duty. (The employer should supply wage information.) Instead of the TTD rate, the TPD rate is used. The following cases illustrate how to calculate TPD benefits in various situations.

CASE STUDY

Basic TPD Calculation

Walter Black suffered a left knee strain on August 12 and could not return to regular work until August 23. Walter was paid his regular wages for August 12. Suppose Walter's boss asked him to return to work answering the phone until he could resume full duty, and Walter's doctor approved this adjusted work effective August 16.

The following facts apply in calculating Walter's TPD benefit:

1. Date of injury is August 12.

2. Walter's AWW is $500.

3. The sit-down job pays $6 per hour, or $240 per week.

4. The TPD and TTD waiting periods are each 3 days.

5. The TPD compensation rate is 66⅔ percent of the wage loss.

6. Return to work date is August 16.

Following is the TPD benefit calculation:

$$\text{Wage loss} = \text{AWW} - \text{Adjusted wages}$$
$$= \$500 - \$240$$
$$= \$260.$$

$$\text{Weekly TPD benefit} = \text{Wage loss} \times \text{Compensation rate}$$
$$= \$260 \times 66.667\%$$
$$= \$173.33.$$

$$\text{Disability period} = \text{August 13 through August 22}$$
$$= 10 \text{ days}.$$

$$\text{Benefit period} = \text{Disability period} - \text{Waiting period}$$
$$= 10 \text{ days} - 3 \text{ days}$$
$$= 7 \text{ days}.$$

$$\text{TPD benefit in this case} = \text{Benefit period as portion of week} \times \text{Weekly TPD benefit}$$
$$= 1 \text{ week} \times \$173.33$$
$$= \$173.33.$$

CASE STUDY

TPD Calculation With a Lower TPD Compensation Rate and a Longer Disability Period

Joyce Harris is a twenty-five-year-old hostess for the Blue Star Restaurant, earning $10 per hour for a forty-hour week. Joyce slipped on a wet floor on November 15, twisting her right ankle. Joyce's doctor, whom she consulted the same day, diagnosed the injury as a sprain, wrapped the ankle, and instructed Joyce to use crutches and avoid putting her full weight on the ankle until her return office visit in two weeks. Joyce did not receive wages for November 15. When Joyce's manager was informed of her disability, he asked her to return to work as a cashier (a sitting job) during the dinner hour (four hours per day) until she could resume full duty. Joyce's doctor approved this arrangement. She was released for regular hostess work on November 29.

The following facts apply in calculating Joyce's TPD benefit:

1. Date of injury is November 15.

2. Joyce's AWW is for $400 per week, based on a 13-week pre-injury wage history.

3. The cashier position pays $10 per hour at 20 hours, or $200 per week.

4. The waiting period is 3 days.

5. The TPD compensation rate is 50 percent of wage loss.

6. Back to work date, full duties, is November 29.

Following is the TPD benefit calculation:

$$\text{Wage loss} = \text{AWW} - \text{Adjusted wages}$$
$$= \$400 - \$200$$
$$= \$200 \text{ per week.}$$

$$\text{Weekly TPD benefit} = \text{Wage loss} \times \text{Compensation rate}$$
$$= \$200 \times 50\%$$
$$= \$100.$$

$$\text{Disability period} = \text{November 15 through November 28}$$
$$= 14 \text{ days.}$$

$$\text{Benefit period} = \text{Disability period} - \text{Waiting period}$$
$$= 14 \text{ days} - 3 \text{ days}$$
$$= 11 \text{ days.}$$

$$\text{TPD benefit in this case} = \text{Benefit period as portion of week} \times \text{Weekly TPD benefit}$$
$$= 1\tfrac{4}{7} \text{ weeks} \times \$100$$
$$= \$157.14.$$

CASE STUDY

TPD Calculation of a Mixed Benefit, When Both TTD and TPD Benefits Are Payable

Monroe Office Repair employs Greg Miller as a serviceman. Greg is thirty years old, has been with Monroe for four years, and earns $15 per hour for a forty-hour week. On March 5, while attempting to move a copier that was positioned on an uneven floor, Greg strained his back. He finished his work for the day, called his office to report the injury when he got home, and visited the nearest hospital emergency room. The emergency room doctor diagnosed the injury as a low back strain, advised no work, and referred Greg to an orthopedist. After receiving this information from Greg, the Monroe manager asked Greg whether the doctor would permit light-duty shop work, paying $10 an hour, until he could return to full duty. Greg saw the orthopedist on March 12; the doctor approved light duty work beginning on March 24, cautioned Greg against heavy lifting, and scheduled a return visit for April 12. Greg was released for full duty effective April 13.

The following facts apply in calculating Greg's benefits:

1. Date of injury is March 5.

2. Greg's AWW is $600 based on a 13-week pre-injury wage history. The light duty wage is $400 ($10 per hour × 40 hours).

3. The TTD compensation rate is $66\frac{2}{3}$ percent of the AWW. The TPD compensation rate is $66\frac{2}{3}$ percent of the wage loss.

4. The maximum benefit is $420 per week.

5. The minimum benefit is $250.

6. The waiting period for both TTD and TPD is 3 days, retroactive after 14 days.

7. Return to work date, light duty, is March 24. Return to work, full duty, is April 13.

Following is the mixed compensation TTD benefit calculation:

First calculate the TTD benefit:

$$\text{Weekly TTD benefit} = \text{Wage loss} \times \text{Compensation rate}$$
$$= \$600 \times 66.667\%$$
$$= \$400.$$

$$\text{TTD disability period} = \text{March 6 through March 23}$$
$$= 18 \text{ days } (2\frac{4}{7} \text{ weeks}).$$

Waiting period does not apply to TTD or TPD because disability extended beyond 14 days.

$$\text{TTD benefit in this case} = \text{Benefit period as portion of a week} \times \text{Weekly TTD benefit}$$
$$= 2\frac{4}{7} \text{ weeks} \times \$400$$
$$= \$1,028.57.$$

Continued on next page.

Then calculate the TPD benefit:

$$\text{Wage loss} = \text{AWW} - \text{Adjusted wages}$$
$$= \$600 - \$400$$
$$= \$200 \text{ per week.}$$

$$\text{Weekly TPD benefit} = \text{Wage loss} \times \text{Compensation rate}$$
$$= \$200 \times 66.667\%$$
$$= \$133.33.$$

$$\text{TPD disability period} = \text{March 24 through April 12}$$
$$= 20 \text{ days}$$
$$= 2\tfrac{6}{7} \text{ weeks.}$$

Waiting period does not apply.

$$\text{TPD benefit in this case} = \text{Benefit period as portion of a week} \times \text{Weekly TPD benefit}$$
$$= 2\tfrac{6}{7} \text{ weeks} \times \$133.33$$
$$= \$380.94.$$

$$\text{Total benefit due} = \text{TTD benefit} + \text{TPD benefit}$$
$$= \$1,028.57 + \$380.94$$
$$= \$1,409.51.$$

Permanent Total Disability (PTD) Benefits

Although cases of permanent disability are a small minority of all disability cases, they account for a tremendous number of benefit dollars. Permanent disability can be total, in which case no work of any kind can be performed, or partial, in which case the worker is unable to perform certain tasks or jobs. This section discusses wage loss benefits payments for both kinds of permanent disability.

Permanent total disability (PTD)
A disability caused by a work-related injury or disease that renders a worker unable to return to gainful employment.

A disabled worker becomes eligible for **permanent total disability (PTD)** benefits when the worker is unable to return to gainful employment because of a work-related injury or disease. Some statutes use the term *suitable* gainful employment, that is, employment comparable with employment at the time of injury. For example, a disabled journeyman plumber who earned $20 per hour at the time of injury could, under some statutes, be found to be permanently disabled if the only job available is a security position paying $7 per hour.

The permanent total disability compensation rate is computed according to applicable statute; it is usually paid at the same percentage of the AWW as the TTD benefit. Maximums and minimums also apply and are typically the same as for TTD, with a few exceptions. Some states provide for an additional benefit for certain dependents, just as these states do with TTD benefits.

Presumption of Permanent Total Disability

All states consider some injuries to be so serious that permanent total disability is statutorily presumed; that is, the law deems a worker permanently totally disabled if his or her injury falls within a described category. Examples of permanent total disability include loss of vision in both eyes; loss, or loss of use, of both legs or both arms; and mental incapacity. Certain statutes permit rebuttal of the presumption if the worker finds new employment, but other statutes do not, even though a worker presumed to be permanently totally disabled actually returns to some type of employment.

Duration of Benefits

Permanent total disability benefits continue as long as the disability continues, usually for life, unless something changes that permits the individual to resume employment. Some states limit PTD benefits to a specified number of weeks or to a dollar amount. For example, a PTD provision can be limited to 500 weeks with exceptions for loss of both eyes, both arms, or both legs, or for mental incapacity, or it can have a dollar cap, such as $165,000.

Escalation of Benefits Over Time

Many states escalate PTD benefits over time. For example, some states provide an annual cost of living increase for PTD benefits. In a few states, this increase also applies to TTD benefits. The percentage of increase is determined and promulgated by the state administrative agency on a pre-scribed anniversary date and can be based on the original PTD rate each year, or it can be compounded. Compounding is more favorable to recipients because it applies a given percentage increase to the most recent level of benefits, not to the level of benefits in effect when the injury was first sustained, which might have been many years earlier. Escalation might not apply in some instances when a combination of benefits reaches a certain level of the pre-injury wage. For example, a statute might specify that a cost of living increase is not available to a worker if the combined PTD and Social Security disability benefits equal 80 percent of the pre-injury wage.

States that escalate benefits typically apply the most recent weekly maximum at the time of escalation each year. In other words, the PTD recipient is not restricted to the maximum in force at the time of the injury.

PTD Benefit Calculations—Cases

The method used to calculate PTD benefits is the same as the method used for TTD benefits. The following cases illustrate how to calculate PTD benefits in two situations.

CASE STUDY

PTD Calculation With an Annual Escalation That Is Not Compounded

Tom Taylor, a construction worker, sustained injury to both eyes when cement splashed on his face on the job site three years ago. After unsuccessful surgery on both eyes, Tom lost total vision and was awarded PTD.

The following facts apply in calculating Tom's PTD benefit:

1. Tom's AWW is $360.

2. The PTD compensation rate is 66⅔ percent of the AWW.

3. The maximum PTD benefit is $400 per week.

4. A cost of living (COL) increase that is not compounded applies. The second year COL increase is 3 percent and the third year COL is 2.5 percent.

Following is the PTD benefit calculation:

> Year 1 weekly PTD benefit = AWW × Weekly PTD compensation rate percentage
> = $360 × 66.667%
> = $240.

Year 2 weekly PTD benefit assumes a 3 percent cost of living increase.

> Cost of living increase = Year 1 PTD × Cost of living percent
> = $240 × 3%
> = $7.20.

> Year 2 weekly PTD benefit = Year 1 weekly PTD benefit
> + Cost of living increase
> = $240 + $7.20
> = $247.20.

Year 3 weekly PTD benefit assumes a 2.5 percent cost of living increase.

> Cost of living increase = Year 1 weekly PTD benefit × Cost of living percentage
> = $240 × 2.5%
> = $6.00.

> Year 3 weekly PTD benefit = Year 1 weekly PTD benefit + Year 2 cost of living increase
> + Year 3 cost of living increase
> = $240 + $7.20 + $6.00
> = $253.20.

Each year's increase is based on $240 and is added to the previous year's increase.

CASE STUDY

PTD Calculation With a Compounded Escalation

Robert Akins, a computer salesperson, was involved in an automobile accident on his way to visit a customer. Robert sustained a spinal cord injury resulting in paralysis below the waist. He was declared permanently totally disabled three years ago.

The following facts apply in calculating Robert's PTD benefit:

1. Robert's AWW is $600.

2. The PTD compensation rate is 66⅔ percent of the AWW.

3. The maximum PTD benefit is $500 per week.

4. The cost of living increase is compounded. The second year COL is 1.5 percent. The third year is 2 percent and the fourth year is 1.5 percent.

Following is the PTD benefit calculation:

Year 1 weekly PTD benefit $=$ AWW $\times$ Compensation rate
$$= \$600 \times 66.667\%$$
$$= \$400.$$

Year 2 weekly PTD benefit $=$ (First-year weekly PTD benefit $\times$ Cost of living adjustment)
    $+$ First year weekly PTD benefit
$$= (\$400 \times 1.5\%) + \$400$$
$$= \$6.00 + \$400$$
$$= \$406.$$

Year 3 weekly PTD benefit $=$ (Prior year PTD benefit $\times$ Cost of living increase)
    $+$ Prior year PTD benefit
$$= (\$406 \times 2\%) + \$406$$
$$= \$8.12 + \$406$$
$$= \$414.12.$$

Year 4 weekly PTD benefit $=$ (Prior year PTD benefit $\times$ Cost of living increase)
    $+$ Prior year PTD benefit
$$= (\$414.12 \times 1.5\%) + \$414.12$$
$$= \$6.21 + \$414.12$$
$$= \$420.33.$$

CASE STUDY

PTD With No Escalation and a Benefit Maximum

Hubert Tallman was employed as an electrician for Orange Electric for forty years before his injury. Two years ago, he received an electric shock, causing injury to both arms that prevented his return to work as an electrician. Hubert was sixty years old at the time of his injury. He underwent a program of vocational rehabilitation but could find no employment because of his lack of alternative work experience and his age. The workers' compensation administrative agency in Hubert's state awarded permanent total disability.

The following facts apply in calculating Hubert's PTD rate:

1. Hubert's AWW is $800.

2. The PTD rate is 66⅔ percent of the AWW.

3. The maximum PTD benefit is $450 per week.

4. Escalation of benefits does not apply.

Following is the PTD benefit calculation:

$$\text{Weekly PTD benefit} = \text{AWW} \times \text{Compensation rate}$$
$$= \$800 \times 66.667\%$$
$$= \$533.33.$$

However, the maximum benefit of $450 would apply.

Permanent Partial Disability (PPD) Benefits

Permanent partial disability (PPD)
A disability caused by a work-related injury or disease that is permanent in nature but partial in degree.

Wage loss benefits for **permanent partial disability (PPD)** cover disability that is permanent in nature but partial in degree. It is designed to compensate injured workers for diminished wages and/or residual disability to the injured part of the body. Statutes vary widely by state in specifying the methods of compensation for PPD. Most states compensate PPD for specified body parts according to a schedule that assigns a number of weeks of benefits to a body part. Body parts typically "scheduled" include the toe, foot, leg, thumb, finger, hand, arm, and eye. Loss of hearing is also compensated according to a schedule under many statutes. For disabilities not scheduled, such as a back injury that prevents a worker from returning to work at his or her pre-injury wage level, compensation might be based on loss of earning capacity. An injured worker cannot usually collect compensation both for disability to a scheduled body part and for loss of earnings from the same injury.

Statutes also provide compensation subject to a maximum dollar amount for permanent disfigurement, generally at the discretion of a workers' compensation administrative examiner. The examiner bases his or her opinion on the disfigurement's appearance, its location (exposed or unexposed area), and its effect on the worker's future employment. For example, a significant facial scar could influence a salesperson's employability and would be more highly compensated than a minor scar on the finger of a construction worker. Theoretically, PPD indemnifies for a possible decrease in future wages because of the disability. Benefits for loss of earning capacity are based on the decrease in post-injury income attributable to the work injury.

The degree of permanent partial disability is not measurable until the worker attains maximum medical improvement (MMI), that is, when it is apparent that no further recovery will occur. Because the worker might not attain MMI until sometime after returning to work, benefits awarded might begin at various times according to the applicable state law. For example, PPD might begin at the end of TTD disability or TPD disability, or when PPD disability is measured, or when MMI is attained. Therefore, the first payment of PPD benefits often includes an accrued amount or the entire amount due, depending on the amount of the award and the date the award orders benefits to begin. Payments might be ordered by way of an award by the state, or they might be voluntary on the employer's/insurer's part. For an award that was made in December for an injury that occurred the previous January, the entire award would be payable in December.

If an injured worker dies from a cause not related to the injury, any award outstanding at the time of death might be payable to eligible dependents or to a personal representative. This occurs when payments for a PPD award for a scheduled body part have not been completed at the time of the worker's death.

Benefits for Scheduled Injuries

As previously discussed, some state laws assign a specific number of weeks of benefits for loss of or loss of use of specific body parts. Injuries to any of the assigned body parts are called **scheduled injuries**. States vary in the number of weeks they assign for each body part.

Shoulders and hips can present problems in determining the benefits for scheduled injuries. The shoulder might be considered part of an arm or might be considered a nonscheduled part of the body; the same problem can arise with a hip injury. To resolve such problems, adjusters should rely on doctors to determine the site of disabilities under the applicable state statutes. An example of a PPD schedule is shown in Exhibit 4-2.

Scheduled injury
Injury to a specific body part for which a state law specifies the number of weeks of workers' compensation benefits to be paid for the body part's total loss or total loss of use.

EXHIBIT 4-2

Example of a Permanent Partial Disability Schedule

When the disability is partial in nature but permanent in duration, the compensation shall be 66⅔ percent of the worker's average weekly wages which shall be in addition to compensation for temporary total disability or temporary partial disability and shall be paid to the worker as follows:

(A) Arm lost—312 weeks' compensation;

(B) Leg lost—288 weeks' compensation;

(C) Hand lost—244 weeks' compensation;

(D) Foot lost—205 weeks' compensation;

(E) Eye lost—160 weeks' compensation;

(F) Thumb lost—75 weeks' compensation;

(G) First finger lost—46 weeks' compensation;

(H) Great toe lost—38 weeks' compensation;

(I) Toe other than great toe lost—16 weeks' compensation;

(J) Compensation for loss of hearing in one ear—52 weeks' compensation; 200 weeks for both ears.

(K) Compensation for an arm or a leg, if amputated at or above the elbow or the knee, shall be the same as for a loss of the arm or leg; but if amputated between the elbow and the wrist or the knee and the ankle, shall be the same as for loss of a hand or foot;

(L) Compensation for loss of two or more digits, or one or more phalanges of two or more digits, of a hand or foot, may be proportioned to the loss of use of the hand or foot occasioned thereby, but shall not exceed the compensation for loss of a hand or foot;

(M) Compensation for permanent total loss of use of a body part shall be the same as for loss of the body part.

As shown in Exhibit 4-2, PPD benefits are often stated in terms of a number of weeks' compensation. TTD benefits, for the time during which the person was unable to work at all, are generally handled in three primary ways:

1. In the majority of states, an injured worker would be allowed to keep both the TTD and the PPD benefits.

2. In some states, the insurer or employer would deduct TTD benefits from the benefits payable under the PPD schedule.

3. The remaining states allow a specified "healing period" during which TTD benefits are to be paid without any offset against PPD benefits. After the healing period has ended, the PPD benefits should start. If an injured worker receives TTD benefits for a period longer than the specified healing period, the TTD benefits paid after the end of the healing period would be deducted from the benefits payable under the PPD schedule.

To demonstrate these three possibilities, assume Joe, who works in the state subject to the schedule shown in Exhibit 4-2, has his arm amputated in a workplace accident. According to the schedule, Joe is entitled to received 312 weeks of compensation. This compensation would be paid at the same rate as any TTD disability benefits. Assume further that Joe was unable to perform any work for 12 weeks.

- In the majority of states, Joe could collect TTD benefits for the 12 weeks he was out of work, plus the 312 weeks of scheduled PPD benefits, for a total of 324 weeks of benefits.

- In some states, Joe would be entitled to receive only 312 weeks of benefits. If he had received 12 weeks of TTD benefits, the employer or insurer would be obligated to pay only 300 additional weeks of PPD benefits.

- In the remaining states, the worker is entitled to TTD benefits during a specified healing period. There are three possibilities, depending on the length of the healing period.

  1. If the healing period is 10 weeks, Joe would be entitled to 10 weeks of TTD benefits. Because he was out for 12 weeks and received TTD benefits for 12 weeks (2 more than the healing period), he would receive only 310 weeks of PPD benefits in addition to the 10 weeks of TTD (assuming that the TTD and PPD benefit levels are the same).

  2. If the healing period is 12 weeks, Joe would receive his TTD benefits for the 12 weeks he was out of work (and equal to the healing period) and then would receive, in addition, 312 weeks of PPD benefits.

  3. If the healing period is 24 weeks, Joe would receive his 12 weeks of TTD benefits and then his 312 weeks of PPD benefits. He would not be paid TTD benefits for the "unused" portion of the healing period.

To determine a PPD benefit, the injured worker must be evaluated by a doctor to rate the extent of the disability. This rating is expressed in terms of a percentage. For example, the inability to raise the arm above shoulder height might be considered a 50 percent disability while the inability to flex a ring finger might be only a 10 percent disability.

Scheduled PPD Benefit Calculations—Cases

Calculating the PPD benefits is slightly different than the three previous calculations because of the addition of the scheduled benefit. The following cases illustrate how to calculate PPD benefits in various situations.

CASE STUDY

Calculation of a PPD Benefit for the Loss of Use of a Scheduled Body Part

Mollie Burns is a forty-five-year-old salesperson for Famous Department Store. On December 12, she slipped on a wet tile floor, fell, and twisted her left foot, fracturing her left ankle. She received TTD benefits until her return to work on February 28. Mollie's doctor concluded she had reached maximum medical improvement on June 30. He rated the permanent disability for her ankle at 25 percent because of loss of motion and remaining stiffness. In Mollie's state, as in most, disability to the ankle is rated as disability to the foot. Therefore, Mollie's PPD benefit was for 25 percent of the foot.

The following facts apply in calculating Mollie's PPD benefit:

1. Mollie's AWW is $240.
2. PPD benefits begin at the end of TTD benefits.
3. The PPD rate is 66⅔ percent of the AWW.
4. The maximum PPD benefit is $300 per week.
5. The foot disability is assigned a benefit of 175 weeks.

Following is the PPD benefit calculation:

$$
\begin{aligned}
\text{Weekly PPD benefit} &= \text{AWW} \times \text{Compensation rate} \\
&= \$240 \times 66.667\% \\
&= \$160.
\end{aligned}
$$

$$
\begin{aligned}
\text{Duration of benefit} &= \text{Number of weeks specified in statute for the loss of use of a foot} \\
&\qquad \times \text{Percentage of disability} \\
&= 175 \text{ weeks} \times 25\% \\
&= 43.75 \text{ weeks.}
\end{aligned}
$$

$$
\begin{aligned}
\text{Total PPD benefits in this case} &= 43.75 \text{ weeks} \times \$160 \\
&= \$7,000, \text{payable at } \$160 \text{ per week beginning March 1.}
\end{aligned}
$$

CASE STUDY

Effect of a Disability Rating on the Amount of Benefits Received

Julia Redd is employed as an assembly-line worker for Bruno Industries, a tool manufacturer. She injured her right index finger on June 12 while cutting a piece of metal. Julia's injury was diagnosed as a laceration of a tendon. The tendon was repaired, and the finger was splinted. Julia was unable to work until August 1 and received TTD compensation through July 31. Julia continued to experience some soreness and restricted motion of the injured finger. Disability ratings were given by the treating doctor, Dr. Long, and by the employer's doctor, Dr. Petrie. Dr. Long rated Julia's finger injury as a 50 percent PPD, while Dr. Petrie rated it as a 40 percent PPD. The administrative officer in Julia's state split the ratings and awarded Julia a 45 percent PPD of the index finger.

The following facts apply in calculating Julia's PPD benefit:

1. Julia's AWW is $185.

2. PPD benefits begin at the end of TTD benefits.

3. The PPD rate is 66⅔ percent of the AWW.

4. The maximum PPD benefit is $300 per week.

5. The index finger disability is assigned a benefit of 40 weeks.

Following is the PPD benefit calculation:

$$\text{Weekly PPD benefit} = \text{AWW} \times \text{Compensation rate}$$
$$= \$185 \times 66.667\%$$
$$= \$123.33.$$

$$\text{Duration of benefit} = \text{Number of weeks scheduled in statute for loss of use of an index finger} \times \text{Compensation rate}$$
$$= 40 \text{ weeks} \times 45\%$$
$$= 18 \text{ weeks.}$$

$$\text{Total PPD benefits in this case} = 18 \text{ weeks} \times \$123.33$$
$$= \$2,219.94, \text{ payable at } \$123.33 \text{ per week beginning August 1.}$$

CASE STUDY

Calculation of a PPD Benefit When the Injury Results in a Permanent Scar

Emily Lee is a cook for Homewood Nursing Home. On January 5, hot grease splashed from a cooking utensil onto Emily's right forearm, causing a burn. Emily received treatment for the injury but did not lose any time from work because of it. The burned area healed but left some discoloration. Emily felt she was entitled to compensation for this disfigurement and asked for a hearing before her state workers' compensation administrative agency. The officer awarded Emily ten weeks of PPD benefits for the scar.

The following facts apply in calculating Emily's PPD benefit:

1. Emily's AWW is $350.

2. The PPD rate is 66⅔ percent of the AWW.

3. The maximum PPD benefit is $300 per week.

4. The statutory maximum dollar amount for disfigurement is $3,500.

5. PPD benefits begin at the end of TTD benefits.

6. The officer awarded 10 weeks of PPD for the scar.

Following is the PPD benefit calculation:

$$\text{Weekly PPD benefit} = \text{AWW} \times \text{Compensation rate}$$
$$= \$350 \times 66.667\%$$
$$= \$233.33.$$

$$\text{Total PPD benefits in this case} = 10 \text{ weeks} \times \$233.33$$
$$= \$2,333.30, \text{ payable at } \$233.33 \text{ per week beginning January 6.}$$

No TTD is paid because no time was lost.

Benefits for Nonscheduled Injuries

As previously mentioned, not every body part is assigned a scheduled amount of benefits. For injuries to nonscheduled body parts, the rating of the percentage of loss or loss of use rests with the administrative agency of the applicable state. In arriving at the disability rating, the administrative agency considers several factors, including the treating physician's opinion, any evaluating physician's opinion, the injury's appearance, and the injured worker's post-injury occupation and wages.

Disability ratings are commonly assigned according to prescribed guidelines, such as the American Medical Association's tables for rating. In rating a disability, the doctor can consider the injured body part's degree of motion, strength, and stability, as well as full or partial amputation, pain, and other criteria common to the particular injured body part. These considerations, when compared to an uninjured body part, provide a basis for rating. For example, assume an injured worker, Carol, has a 10 percent impairment of her body as a whole resulting from surgery on a herniated lumbar disc. Without the operation, Carol has an additional disability of 7 percent of the body. Using the appropriate tables, she has a 7 percent impairment for loss of back flexion and extension and a 2 percent impairment for loss of lateral bending. If she experiences stiffness, soreness, and loss of endurance, she faces the possibility of additional surgery and might be unable to perform the pre-injury job. These factors combine for an additional 20 percent impairment, giving Carol a total impairment of 46 percent of the body as a whole.

Rating is not precise even with the best guidelines because it is difficult to base a rating on an injured worker's description of symptoms, demonstration of movement, and like factors that could be understated or overstated by the worker. Consequently, the disability rating is often controversial. As previously mentioned, an administrative agency makes the final decision regarding the rating.

Like the TTD rate, the PPD rate changes periodically. It could be based on a percentage of the injured worker's AWW or on a percentage of the state AWW. The rate is not constant among states. In certain states, the rate changes with the degree of disability; that is, a higher rate is granted for a major or serious disability. Disability to certain body parts might be payable at a different rate from that payable for disabilities of other body parts. Maximums also differ by state. Because of these differences, adjusters should refer to the applicable statute for the proper number of weeks, applicable rate, and maximum benefits.

Mixed Benefit Calculations—Scheduled and Nonscheduled Benefit Cases

In practice, claims are often complicated by multiple injuries to different parts of the body. When one injury is a TTD and the other is a PPD, the calculations are fairly simple. Typically, the injured worker is paid TTD benefits until reaching maximum medical improvement. At that point, the worker is paid for any PPD. The calculations become more complicated when the worker suffers two PPDs to separate body parts, one scheduled and one nonscheduled. See the following case study.

CASE STUDY

How Mixed Disabilities Would Be Calculated in Most States

John, a forty-year-old welder, lost three fingers and injured his back in an accident. The injury to John's fingers is a scheduled disability. In his state, John could not normally collect for both his lost wages and the scheduled amount for the loss of his fingers. However, because he also suffered a back injury, he was paid TTD benefits while off work because of the back injury. Once John reached maximum medical improvement, he was given a 20 percent disability rating of his whole body because of the TTD for his back injury. This nonscheduled injury was combined with his scheduled injury for his TPD benefits.

Following is the PPD benefit calculation according to John's state statutes:

Scheduled Benefits:

Loss of first finger:	46 weeks
Loss of second finger:	30 weeks
Loss of third finger:	25 weeks
Total	101 weeks
PPD rate = $150	

101 weeks at $150/week = $15,150 for scheduled benefits.

Nonscheduled Benefits:

The whole body limit is 600 weeks. John was given a 20 percent PPD rating to the whole body, 120 additional weeks (20% × 600 weeks).

$$\text{Nonscheduled benefits} = \text{PPD rating to whole body} \times \text{Whole body limit}$$
$$= 120 \text{ weeks} \times \$150 \text{ a week}$$
$$= \$18,000.$$

$$\text{Combined PPD benefits in this case} = \text{Scheduled benefits} + \text{Nonscheduled benefits}$$
$$= \$15,150 + \$18,000$$
$$= \$33,150.$$

In this example, the two benefits were calculated separately. One complicating factor not included in the case is the trend for courts to "stack" disabilities to provide workers with higher benefits. Stacked benefits yield higher total benefits in states that increase the weekly benefit as the number of weeks increases. This approach gives greater benefits to injured workers with more serious injuries. For example, the weekly PPD benefit for 20 weeks might be $90 per week, but weekly PPD benefits for 120 weeks might be $150 per week, and $250 per week for 300 weeks. In John Lee's case, some courts might have stacked his 101 weeks of scheduled benefits and his

120 weeks of nonscheduled benefits for a total of 221 weeks. If the weekly benefit for 221 weeks were $225, then John would have received $49,725 (221 weeks × $225 per week). This amount is $16,575 more than if the weeks were not stacked.

Benefits Based on Loss of Earnings (LOE) Capacity

In many states, compensation for nonscheduled injuries is based on LOE capacity. **Loss of earning capacity** is a reduction in a workers' earning ability as a result of an injury. In the workers' compensation context, LOE is the loss resulting from the worker's return to post-injury employment at a lesser wage because of incapacity attributable to the injury. For example, if a construction worker who earns $15 per hour and who cannot return to construction work because of a back injury finds post-injury employment as a security person earning $8.50 per hour, then that worker has a loss of earnings capacity of $6.50 per hour because of his injury.

Loss of earnings capacity
The reduction in a worker's earning ability as a result of an injury.

Although the concept of LOE capacity is similar in all states offering this benefit, the basis for the amount differs. The basis for determining LOE capacity is either (1) actual economic loss or (2) a medically determined PPD impairment percentage that refers to disability of the body as a whole. **Actual economic loss** is the difference between pre-injury and post-injury earnings. In states not using actual economic loss, if the degree of medically determined impairment is 20 percent, the basis for the LOE capacity benefit is 20 percent of the worker's pre-injury AWW. In certain cases, this type of benefit might be payable in addition to benefits for disability to a scheduled body part.

Actual economic loss
For workers' compensation purposes, the difference between a worker's earnings before and after an injury.

Although it may be theoretically reasonable to provide LOE benefits based on a percentage of lost earnings because of a compensable injury, this approach can be problematic in practice. Differences in medical opinions about work restrictions (for example, lifting limits) create problems in establishing post-injury earnings, that is, the degree of loss. Work restrictions influence the kind of post-injury employment the impaired worker can gain and, therefore, the worker's earnings. Other problems can arise from controversy over job placement, personality conflicts with the rehabilitation counselor, disagreements about the kinds of jobs available, and the necessity for retraining. The job market at time of post-injury placement is another factor that can affect the loss of earnings capacity benefit. LOE capacity benefits are normally payable until actual earnings or earning ability changes.

LOE Capacity Benefit Calculations—Cases

The next case illustrates the use of LOE capacity as the basis for the PPD calculation.

CASE STUDY

Use of LOE Capacity in a PPD Calculation

Kent Green earned $18 per hour as a carpenter for Star Homes. Kent's state provides LOE capacity benefits for nonscheduled injuries based on actual economic loss. Kent injured his back lifting a scaffold on August 12 and was diagnosed with a herniated disc requiring surgery. Because carpentry is physically demanding, Kent's doctor advised him not to return to that employment after his back surgery. A rehabilitation counselor working with Kent found him a job, approved by his doctor, delivering building supplies. This driving job required no lifting or repetitive bending and paid $10 per hour. Kent started the new job on June 15 of the year after his injury.

The following facts apply in calculating Kent's LOE capacity benefits:

1. Kent's pre-injury AWW was $720.

2. Kent's post-injury AWW was $400.

3. The LOE capacity benefit is 66⅔ percent of the difference between his pre-injury and post-injury AWW.

4. The maximum LOE capacity benefit is $327 per week.

Following is the LOE capacity benefits calculation:

$$
\begin{aligned}
\text{Weekly benefit in this case} &= (\text{Pre-injury AWW} - \text{Post-injury AWW}) \times \text{LOE capacity benefit rate} \\
&= (\$720 - \$400) \times 66.667\% \\
&= \$320 \times 66.667\% \\
&= \$213.33 \text{ beginning June 15.}
\end{aligned}
$$

MEDICAL BENEFITS

Workers' compensation statutes provide for reasonable and necessary medical care to injured workers. This benefit entitles the worker to quality medical care, including sophisticated diagnostic testing, referral to the appropriate specialist, state-of-the-art treatment, and surgical procedures, as long as it is reasonable and necessary to treat the injury. (These requirements are discussed later in this chapter.) The scope of care is wide and can include the various types of care listed in the following box.

Types of Medical Care

- Initial doctor or emergency room visit
- Specialist referral
- Surgery
- Hospital care
- Diagnostic testing, for example, X-rays and CAT scans

- Nursing care
- Medications
- Physical therapy
- Occupational therapy
- Travel expense to and from the place of care
- Prosthetic devices, including artificial limbs, glasses, contact lenses, hearing aids, and dentures
- Repair or replacement of prosthetic devices when damaged in a compensable accident

Workers' compensation coverage provides primary medical coverage that includes every aspect of the necessary medical care. No other health insurance plan or coverage is usually necessary.

Medical Benefits Limitations

Although workers' compensation medical coverage is broad, it is not unlimited. All medical care must meet the following three conditions:

1. Be related to the injury
2. Be reasonable in amount given and amount charged
3. Be necessary to cure or relieve the worker's injury

Adjusters must have a great deal of knowledge about medicine and medical procedures to determine whether these conditions apply to specific cases.

As the medical field continues to expand, the injured worker benefits from new technologies. Many states now recognize practitioners whose care was disputed in the past. For example, some states have approved acupuncture treatments. However, the expansion of medical technology and care increases medical costs. To help contain the medical benefit cost, many states have adopted a medical fee schedule that establishes guidelines for charges for medical procedures. The medical provider is obligated to accept the allowed amount without seeking the balance from the worker. States with fee schedules also commonly provide a procedure to review medical fees.

Most states allow injured workers to choose their treating doctor; others restrict the choice to a list provided by the employer or by the state. If the worker frequently changes doctors without referral or without employer or administrative agency approval, the employer can request an opinion by a doctor of its own choosing.

To assure that treatment meets the conditions, the employer typically has the right to have the injured worker examined by the doctor of its choice. Requests for such medical examinations must be made at reasonable intervals and scheduled with physicians whose expertise applies to the type of injury involved. The examination location should be within a reasonable travel distance for the worker. If the worker objects to or fails to appear for the examination, the employer might request that the appropriate administrative agency become involved.

The injured worker becomes eligible for medical care benefits immediately following a compensable injury; no waiting period applies. The worker need not be disabled to receive medical care under workers' compensation. As long as the care is causally related to the injury or illness, medical benefits are provided for as long as necessary.

Medical Benefits—Cases

The following hypothetical cases illustrate workers' compensation medical benefits.

CASE STUDY

Types of Treatments Covered by Workers' Compensation

Joan Wilson works for Printers, Inc., as a secretary. She twisted her knee while getting up from her chair on July 15 at 10:00 AM. The knee immediately became painful and began to swell within an hour. When Joan reported the incident to her boss at 1:00 PM, he suggested she visit an industrial clinic in the next block. The doctor took X-rays, diagnosed a strain, prescribed medication and crutches, and suggested that Joan stay off her feet for three days and return to the clinic if there was no improvement. Joan's knee remained painful, and she was referred to a specialist, who performed diagnostic surgery and repaired a torn ligament. After a recuperative period, Joan was sent to therapy to strengthen her knee.

The medical benefit: All cost of all care is covered, including the cost of the visits to the industrial clinic and the specialist, the surgery, hospital stay, physical therapy, X-rays, medication, crutches, and travel expenses to the doctors' offices.

CASE STUDY

When Expenses Unrelated to the Injury Are Excluded

Scott Ames is employed as a laborer for Acme Decorating. On August 10 at 11:00 AM, his left eye became irritated. He was sent to a nearby clinic for care. The doctor removed a dirt particle from the left eye and referred Scott to an ophthalmologist for follow-up. The ophthalmologist performed an examination and prescribed corrective glasses in addition to examining Scott's left eye for remaining irritation. The doctor acknowledged that the need for corrective glasses had no relation to the injury.

The medical benefit: Clinic charges for initial care and ophthalmological care for the left eye irritation are covered under workers' compensation. Charges for the unrelated examination and for glasses are not covered.

REHABILITATION SERVICES BENEFITS

Under the workers' compensation system, rehabilitation services medically and vocationally assist the disabled worker. Medical rehabilitation includes supervising and coordinating care, counseling the disabled worker, providing emotional support, and assisting in adjusting the worker's lifestyle to accommodate the disability.

Vocational rehabilitation services, which help an injured worker to return to the work force, are an important part of the workers' compensation benefit program. Employers encourage rehabilitation efforts both to reduce the cost of paying open-ended TTD benefits and to promote the worker's well-being.

Rehabilitation services are provided in all states either mandatorily by statute or voluntarily by employers or insurers. In most states, employers and insurers bear the cost of such services. Some states have established a fund to cover all or a part of the expenses. Rehabilitation services are monitored by state administrative agencies.

Injured workers who are unable to return to their pre-injury employment are candidates for rehabilitation services. A worker might need one or more of the following four services:

1. Physical rehabilitation, which is a program of physical and occupational therapy to heal and/or strengthen the injured area
2. Modification of the pre-injury job to accommodate the disability, for example, providing a stool, raising or lowering the workstation, automating a machine, altering a foot pedal or button, or furnishing a truck with automatic drive
3. Assistance in applying for and finding a new job compatible with the disability
4. Retraining in a new career

Rehabilitation Process and Benefits

The rehabilitation process is conducted by counselors with a medical or a vocational background or both. The counselor could be employed by the state or by a private company. The counselor interviews the disabled worker for background information, including medical status, education, work history, skills, interests, and financial and family situations. The counselor may administer tests to determine academic level and vocational aptitude. The counselor works with the treating doctor to establish physical ability and to form a rehabilitation plan. The worker might be trained in preparing résumés, job-search techniques, and interviewing. If retraining is a viable option, the counselor assists the worker in choosing a new career and in exploring and applying to appropriate educational institutions for necessary training.

Rehabilitation is not always successful. Injured workers can develop negative attitudes, refuse to cooperate, or cooperate halfheartedly.

Sometimes no suitable employment can be found because of a poor job market, lack of marketable skills, age, or extent of disability. The earlier the process is begun, the better the result can be. A positive and structured program started early can keep a worker from falling into despair or from becoming apathetic or unnecessarily resigned to disability. Because rehabilitation is costly, a worker's failure to make a good faith effort to cooperate with the rehabilitation counselor could jeopardize the worker's TTD in most states.

Types and Duration of Benefits

Benefits can include the cost of the rehabilitation services, TTD compensation during rehabilitation, a specified maintenance allowance (board, lodging, and travel if services are given away from home), tuition, and the cost of books and supplies. The law of the applicable state must be consulted for the specific benefit provisions. Finally, the duration of rehabilitation benefits varies by state. Many states set a time limit on rehabilitation benefits. Rehabilitation services that are voluntarily provided normally continue until either the worker is placed in a job or the effort fails.

Rehabilitation Services Benefits—Cases

The following hypothetical cases illustrate the various types of costs covered by rehabilitation services benefits.

Costs Covered by Rehabilitation Service Benefits

Susan Sims, a twenty-eight-year-old machine operator for Molded Plastics, sprained her right ankle when she slipped at work. The sprain was severe. Susan could not return to work for Molded Plastics because she was unable to stand for the required eight hours. The employer had no modified employment available. Susan had some office experience but needed a refresher course in keyboarding to market her clerical skills. During rehabilitation, a counselor helped Susan enroll in a refresher keyboarding course. When Susan completed the course, the counselor helped Susan search for a job. Susan found a receptionist position in a law firm that was approved by her doctor. The rehabilitation services benefits included the following:

- TTD compensation, which continued until Susan's return to work
- Tuition and books for the keyboarding course
- Cost of the rehabilitation vendor's service

Bill Evans sustained a back injury while working on a construction job for Gene Brothers. After the necessary surgery, he could not return to construction work because of lifting and bending restrictions. Bill was forty-four years old at the time of injury and had worked in construction for twenty-six years. The rehabilitation counselor assigned to Bill's case worked

---

with his doctor and employer to place him in a supervisory capacity that would use his experience and accommodate his limitations. The rehabilitation services benefits included the following:

- TTD compensation, which continued during the placement process and until Bill's return to work

- The rehabilitation counselor's services

DEATH BENEFITS

Workers' compensation statutes allow benefits for dependent survivors of workers who are killed in a compensable accident or who die from a compensable injury or disease. This weekly benefit is designed to partially replace the financial support the deceased worker would have provided to those dependent on the worker. Certain states grant a lump sum in addition to weekly benefits. Those eligible for death benefits include the deceased worker's surviving spouse and minor children. In many states, others who depend financially on the deceased worker could be eligible for death benefits. The applicable statute should be carefully reviewed in all death cases to determine the criteria of eligibility for these benefits.

Funeral expenses are covered by statute, subject to a maximum. Many states provide for transportation of the body, sometimes subject to a maximum.

Amount and Duration of Benefits

The typical death benefit is $66^{2}/_{3}$ percent of the deceased worker's AWW, subject to a maximum and a minimum. If the only dependent is a spouse or a child, the percentage might be less, and it might change as the child reaches the age of majority or other statutory limitation. Many states escalate benefits in the same way as for PTD benefits. Others grant an additional benefit for a dependent child or dependent children.

Benefits payable to a surviving spouse typically cease upon remarriage, with a lump sum (for example, two years of benefits) awarded at that time. Some states limit survivorship benefits to a specified number of weeks or dollar amount. Benefits to children terminate at a certain age, usually eighteen, but may continue for an additional period while the child is enrolled in an approved school. Again, the law must be consulted because it might have provisions for special circumstances; for example, a mentally or physically incapacitated child or a disabled spouse.

Death Benefit Calculations—Cases

The following hypothetical cases illustrate death benefits.

CASE STUDY

This case illustrates a typical claim for death benefits.

Horace Means, forty-five, employed as an administrative manager for Peak Computers, died in an automobile accident when his car skidded on ice and ran off the road on his way to a business meeting. At the time of his death, Horace was salaried at $650 per week. Horace and his wife, Phyllis, had no dependent children. Phyllis remarried four years after his death.

The following facts apply in calculating Horace's benefits:

1.   The benefit rate is 66⅔ percent of the AWW.
2.   The maximum weekly death benefit is $450.
3.   Escalation of benefits is not permitted.
4.   At the time of remarriage, Horace's widow receives two years of benefits in a lump sum.

Following is the death benefit calculation:

$$\text{Weekly death benefit} = \text{AWW} \times \text{Compensation rate}$$
$$= \$650 \times 66.667\%$$
$$= \$433.33.$$

$$\text{Remarriage benefit} = 104 \text{ weeks (2 years)} \times \$433.33$$
$$= \$45,066.32, \text{payable at time of remarriage.}$$

CASE STUDY

This case illustrates the death benefit payable when there is a surviving spouse and children.

Edward Lind died at age twenty-five from massive internal injuries when he fell from a roof at a construction job. Edward was married to Helen and had two children, Edward, Jr., four years old, and Kelly, three years old. Edward's wage at the time of death was $12.50 per hour.

The following facts apply in calculating Edward's benefit:

1.   Edward's AWW was $570 (including overtime).
2.   The death benefit is 66⅔ percent of the AWW.
3.   The maximum weekly death benefit is $400.
4.   Escalation of benefits is permitted.
5.   The widow's benefit decreases to 50 percent of the AWW when the last child reaches age eighteen or age twenty-one if the child is attending an accredited school.

Following is the death benefit calculation:

$$\text{Weekly death benefit} = \text{AWW} \times \text{Compensation rate}$$
$$= \$570 \times 66.667\%$$
$$= \$380.$$

This benefit increases each year by a stated cost of living percentage compounded on the previous year's benefit. The widow's benefit decreases to 50 percent of Edward's AWW (escalated for time) when the last child is no longer eligible for benefits.

WORKERS' COMPENSATION COST FACTORS

Given the extent of the statutory benefits provided for injured workers, it is not surprising that workers' compensation is costly. Consequently, adjusters must understand the various factors that drive workers' compensation costs, so they can make cost-effective decisions when handling claims. The reminder of this chapter focuses on the various factors that affect workers' compensation costs.

Workers' compensation costs generally consist of loss adjustment expenses (LAE) and the costs of lost wages, medical treatment, rehabilitation services, and death benefits. Additionally, state-specific factors such as legislative, regulatory, and judicial factors; economic factors; and demographic factors can affect costs. Exhibit 4-3 shows the continuing acceleration of workers' compensation costs. This next section deals with loss adjustment expenses (LAE) and the most costly of all benefits, medical costs.

Loss Adjustment Expenses (LAE) Cost Factors

LAE costs are often overlooked as part of workers' compensation costs because they depend partly on how efficiently insurers operate and because they are a much smaller dollar amount than the cost of the actual benefits. LAE costs include items such as independent medical examination fees, medical cost containment fees, medical records expenses, legal fees, and bill auditing fees. Exhibit 4-4 shows workers' compensation net incurred LAE as a percentage of earned premium, and Exhibit 4-5 shows workers' compensation net incurred LAE as a percentage of net incurred losses.

LAE costs fluctuate depending on what the prevailing claim handling practices are. When insurers direct adjusters to use medical cost containment services on many, if not all, lost time claims, LAE costs rise. If insurers implement bill auditing procedures that require the use of an outside vendor rather than a staff nurse, LAE costs will rise. The point is that LAE costs should not be left out of the equation when considering the cost of workers' compensation.

EXHIBIT 4-3

The Rate of Change in Workers Compensation Costs Since 1995

Lost Time Claims

Indemnity Claim Cost (000s)

Annual Change 1991–1995:   **+0.3%**
Annual Change 1996–2002p: **+6.8%**

+1.0% –3.1% –2.8% +4.9% +1.7% +5.8% +5.7% +6.4% +7.3% +7.8% +7.7% +7.0%

1991 1992 1993 1994 1995 1996 1997 1998 1999 2000 2001 2002p

Accident Year

p Preliminary
Based on the states where NCCI provides ratemaking services
Analysis on 12/02/2002 using data through 12/31/2001, developed to ultimate; 2002 based on preliminary analysis
Excludes the effects of deductible policies
© 2003 NCCI Holdings, Inc.

EXHIBIT 4-4

Workers Compensation Net Incurred Loss Adjustment Expenses as a Percentage of Earned Premium

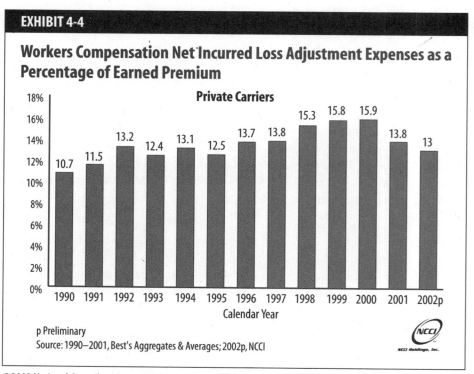

Private Carriers

10.7 11.5 13.2 12.4 13.1 12.5 13.7 13.8 15.3 15.8 15.9 13.8 13

1990 1991 1992 1993 1994 1995 1996 1997 1998 1999 2000 2001 2002p

Calendar Year

p Preliminary
Source: 1990–2001, Best's Aggregates & Averages; 2002p, NCCI

EXHIBIT 4-5

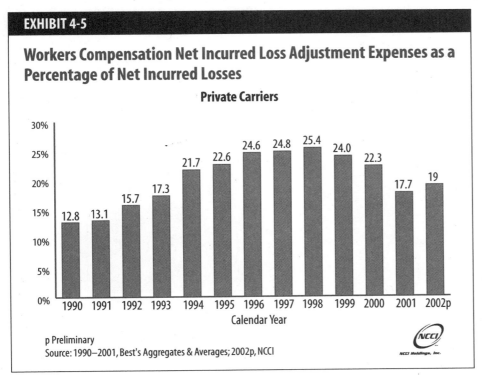

Workers Compensation Net Incurred Loss Adjustment Expenses as a Percentage of Net Incurred Losses

Private Carriers

Calendar Year	Value
1990	12.8
1991	13.1
1992	15.7
1993	17.3
1994	21.7
1995	22.6
1996	24.6
1997	24.8
1998	25.4
1999	24.0
2000	22.3
2001	17.7
2002p	19

p Preliminary
Source: 1990–2001, Best's Aggregates & Averages; 2002p, NCCI

Medical Cost Factors

The most significant cause of increased workers' compensation costs is high medical costs. Exhibit 4-6 shows the rate of increase from 1991 to 2002. Medical costs represent more than 50 percent of workers' compensation benefit costs. An increase or decrease in medical costs causes total benefit costs to increase or decrease to a much greater degree than does an increase or decrease in other benefit costs.

Medical costs increase faster than the general rate of inflation for the following reasons:

- Innovations in medical technology improve diagnostic and therapeutic equipment and treatment. However, these innovations are expensive. Additionally, doctors often use new technology even when traditional techniques are adequate. For example, magnetic resonance imaging (MRI) might be used to diagnose a fractured ankle even though an X-ray could be used less expensively.

- Hospital facilities and equipment are an enormous capital investment with high fixed overhead costs. If a hospital is not filled to capacity, those fixed costs must be paid by existing patients, increasing the per-patient cost.

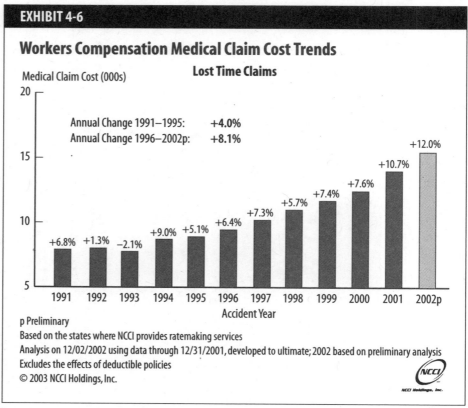

EXHIBIT 4-6

Workers Compensation Medical Claim Cost Trends

Lost Time Claims

Medical Claim Cost (000s)

Annual Change 1991–1995:   **+4.0%**
Annual Change 1996–2002p: **+8.1%**

+6.8% +1.3% –2.1% +9.0% +5.1% +6.4% +7.3% +5.7% +7.4% +7.6% +10.7% +12.0%

1991 1992 1993 1994 1995 1996 1997 1998 1999 2000 2001 2002p

Accident Year

p Preliminary
Based on the states where NCCI provides ratemaking services
Analysis on 12/02/2002 using data through 12/31/2001, developed to ultimate; 2002 based on preliminary analysis
Excludes the effects of deductible policies
© 2003 NCCI Holdings, Inc.

Recent changes in hospital payment methods have exacerbated workers' compensation cost problems. Under many managed care plans for group health insurance, the group health insurer pays hospitals an annual fixed sum based on the number of individuals insured under the group health plan. For example, a hospital might be paid $1,000 for each of the 100,000 people insured in the group health plan in exchange for an agreement to provide hospital care for patients in this group. In this type of arrangement, the less hospital care given, the more profitable the arrangement is for the hospital. However, fee-for-service reimbursement, as in workers' compensation, gives hospitals an incentive to provide these patients with more extensive care. This result is especially true for workers' compensation plans that have no expense caps or that have none of the mandatory discounts found in other group health insurance plans. Some hospitals might be tempted to shift the costs of treating patients with more limited coverage under group health insurance plans to patients covered by the less restrictive workers' compensation plans.

As a result of increasing per-patient costs, insurers have been directing patients away from inpatient hospitalization and to outpatient hospital services. Most insurers now require precertification (prior approval) for non-emergency in-hospital treatment.

Less cost control in workers' compensation leads to higher medical costs for workers' compensation insurers than for group health plans that set restrictions and that include patient cost-sharing requirements, such as deductibles and co-payments. For example, a patient with group health insurance might question a doctor's recommendation of five physical therapy sessions a week when the patient's insurance covers only three a week. An injured worker under workers' compensation, facing no out-of-pocket costs, is less likely to question the recommended number or frequency of the sessions.

Managed Care in Workers' Compensation

Managed care comprises programs, procedures, or practices designed to control medical care costs while ensuring the delivery of appropriate and timely medical care. For workers' compensation, with the stated goal of providing appropriate, cost-effective, and timely medical care, managed care might address medical costs in many ways. Workers' compensation systems might use a variety of managed care provider arrangements, discussed next, and plans to manage lost wages benefits through return-to-work programs, rehabilitation programs, case management, or emotional and social support systems for injured workers.

A broad range of managed care provider arrangements is available. Many are alternative fee arrangements, including the following, that give medical providers an incentive to manage the degree of medical services used:

- Preferred provider organizations (PPOs), which offer covered patients a network of health care providers who have agreed to certain cost-controlling measures

- Health maintenance organizations (HMOs), in which each patient has a primary care physician who controls all referrals

- Diagnostic related groups (DRGs), in which a diagnosis code is used to bill for hospital services and visits

Some of these arrangements use specific cost control measures, such as utilization review, a process that the insurer uses to determine whether specific health care services are necessary or appropriate; medical bill audits; and pre-certification, which requires that the insurer approve certain medical procedures and non-emergency hospital treatment in advance. Insurers have teams of medical providers, adjusters, case managers, and reviewers who perform utilization reviews, medical bill audits, and pre-certification reviews.

Adjusters might achieve mixed results from attempts to implement managed care. Studies indicate that managed care can reduce workers' compensation medical and lost wages benefits costs by 10 to 50 percent because of fewer treatments, lower prices, and less complex treatments.[1] In some

Managed care
Programs, procedures, or practices designed to control medical care costs while ensuring the delivery of appropriate and timely medical care.

cases, however, managed care does not result in reduced costs, for the following reasons:

- Preferred provider networks might not include the most qualified doctors for treating certain injuries, resulting in less effective treatments.
- Utilization review results vary dramatically, depending on the reviewer.
- Medical bill audits might focus on costs per treatment unit rather than on the number of treatments given.
- Case managers might not consider the psychological and emotional factors that prevent an injured worker from recovering.
- Labor unions might object to some aspects of managed care if the specifics of the program are not outlined in the labor contract and the use of managed care is seen as interfering with the union member's freedom to choose a doctor.

State Legislative Changes for Managed Care

Legislative efforts to provide relief from the cost problems of workers' compensation have required compromises among employers, labor unions, insurers, attorneys, and medical service providers. Examples of legislative medical cost controls include laws that decrease benefits and tighten eligibility standards; that initiate fee schedules and utilization review panels; and that allow employers to choose doctor panels for injured workers. Not all states have such legislation. However, adjusters must be familiar with the laws in each state in which they handle claims.

Legislative, Regulatory, and Judicial Cost Factors

For years, legislators, regulators, and judicial decisions have simultaneously expanded workers' compensation benefits and limited the premiums that insurers can charge. This section describes how benefits have changed, how regulatory approval affects workers' compensation insurance rates, and how legislators and regulators have attempted to make reforms. The section concludes with examples of legislative changes that affect workers' compensation costs.

Benefit Expansion

Legislative changes and judicial decisions have expanded medical and lost wages benefits by increasing the statutory benefit levels and broadly interpreting statutory benefits. Medical benefits are unlimited by statute; however, the scope of these benefits can be expanded when a legislative change or a judicial decision includes a previously excluded medical service or covers a condition not previously considered compensable. For example, a statutory change to cover experimental treatment or alternative therapies, such as acupuncture, massage, homeopathy, and naturopathy, would expand the scope of medical benefits.

Wage loss costs increase when statutory benefit levels increase, and these benefit costs often outpace inflation. Additionally, wage loss benefit costs often increase at a higher rate than the benefit amounts do. For example, a 5 percent increase in wage loss benefits might result in a 9 percent increase in wage loss benefit costs, for the following reasons:

- With higher benefits, workers might be tempted to extend the duration of disability, increasing loss severity.
- Workers might be tempted to engage in fraud, increasing loss frequency and severity.
- Workers might file claims that would previously have gone unreported, increasing loss frequency.
- Workers might choose to incur more risk on the job, increasing loss frequency.

Court decisions expand wage loss benefits when definitions of disability expand or when statutes are broadly interpreted. For example, a court might expand the occupational disease definition or interpret the compensable injury definition to include mental stress claims.

Regulatory Rate Delays and Denials

Regulators might delay or deny an insurer's workers' compensation insurance rate increase request because insurers and regulators disagree on the following:

- The validity of the insurer's data used to project the newly proposed rates
- The anticipated effects of changes in benefit levels
- The statistical methods used to project the newly proposed rates

Regulators might also be concerned about public pressure to maintain stable and affordable insurance premiums. Regulatory rate delays and denials might keep workers' compensation premiums artificially low while legislative and judicial changes expand benefit costs.

Federal Laws Affecting Workers' Compensation

The Americans with Disabilities Act (ADA) and the Family and Medical Leave Act (FMLA) have affected workers' compensation costs. The ADA protects workers with disabilities from discrimination in employment practices. FMLA gives twelve weeks of unpaid leave to workers with "serious health conditions." An injured worker could be covered by ADA or FMLA. The intricacies of these laws are beyond the scope of this text. However, adjusters should be aware that employers will incur additional costs when accommodating injured workers who are eligible for workers' compensation and who are also covered by ADA or FMLA. These accommodations, under ADA, generally entail creating a job environment to suit the injured worker. The twelve weeks of leave under FMLA could mean that an injured worker might not return to work as quickly as they otherwise would.

The Health Insurance Portability and Accountability Act (HIPAA) has a provision intended to protect a person's right to privacy about medical and personal health information. Essentially HIPAA curtails the sharing of medical and personal health information without the patient's specific written authorization. While workers' compensation insurers are not directly included in the scope of HIPAA, it is foreseeable that misunderstandings about HIPAA's application could occur. Doctors and other healthcare providers might withhold treatment records believing that HIPAA requires this and might be unwilling to release the information without a subpoena. This misunderstanding could lead to additional costs in obtaining the information needed to handle the workers' compensation claim.

Legislative and Regulatory Reforms That Have Reduced Costs

Although wage loss benefits have increased nationally, some states have decreased various benefits or increased them at less than the inflation rate. Other states have enacted the following measures:

- Limited the amount of vocational rehabilitation benefits.

- Limited the period that an injured worker can continue on TTD before converting to a PPD status, forcing a resolution of claims that would have lingered for years.

- Enacted anti-fraud legislation to deter injured workers from submitting fraudulent and inflated claims and monitored insurers' efforts to reduce the amount of money paid for such claims.

- Limited the amount doctors can charge for medical treatments for workers' compensation claims by tying charges to some stated percentage of the rates permitted by Medicare.

- Limited the selection of doctors for the initial treatment of injured workers. Nearly half of the states have enacted legislation permitting employers or their insurers to select the initial treating doctor for injured workers. In addition to reducing "doctor shopping" by injured workers, this provision permits the use of managed care techniques to curb unnecessary treatment and enables employers to better track the status of injured workers and help them return to work as soon as possible.

- Streamlined the adjudication process and instituted formal dispute resolution forums, often authorizing an ombudsman to assist workers, employers, and insurers in complying with state law. This reform has dramatically reduced attorney involvement and subsequently reduced costs without reducing the *net* benefit to injured workers.

Economic Cost Factors

The economy's demand for goods and services affects economic activity, industry mix, and interest rates. Each of those elements influences workers' compensation costs.

Economic Activity

The first economic factor that influences workers' compensation costs from the employer's perspective is the level of economic activity. It affects workers' compensation costs because workers' compensation insurance premiums are based on payroll, which increases with increased economic activity. Claims are also affected as workers work longer hours or as less experienced, more injury-prone workers join the work force.

As an example, increased economic activity could increase business-related vehicle traffic. Because truckers account for a large share of total workers' compensation insurance premiums and losses, more vehicle travel increases the number of motor vehicle accidents, thus increasing workers' compensation costs. Motor vehicle accidents are a leading cause of on-the-job fatalities.

A decrease in economic activity results in fewer workers exposed to injury. That lower exposure should have a positive effect on workers' compensation claims and costs. On the other hand, when economic activity decreases, employers might lay off workers or close plants. The remaining workers might strike if they are expected to produce as much as before the layoffs. Layoffs usually generate a significant number of claims and seem to make open claims worse. Not all such claims are attempts to defraud the insurer or the employer. The psychological stress of a strike or a job loss can sometimes lead to physical ailments.

It is a paradox that higher unemployment and increased employment both can lead to increased workers' compensation costs for the employer; the former because of greater incentive to report claims and the latter because of more workers exposed to hazards on the job. Ultimately, the degree to which increased unemployment or employment affects the loss ratio determines the final effect on workers' compensation costs.

Industry Mix

The second economic factor that affects an employer's workers' compensation costs is industry mix. For example, as more U.S. manufacturing jobs are transferred overseas, the number of workers in that employment category in the United States decreases. The mix of occupations affects workers' compensation costs because workers in some types of jobs are more likely to be injured than workers in other types of jobs. For example, construction or manufacturing workers are expected to generate more workers' compensation claims than service-sector workers. However, the increasing incidence of cumulative trauma and stress claims for service-sector workers is a cause of concern for employers and workers.

The nature of a business, as well as the industry mix, affects workers' compensation costs. Some businesses are more likely than others to experience workers' compensation cost increases. For example, high-technology businesses characterized by advanced use of computers, robotics, or antiseptically clean environments do not necessarily have safe work environments. Frequent video display terminal (VDT) use could increase eye strain. Long hours spent at a keyboard increase the likelihood of musculoskeletal discomfort. Stress-related disabilities also affect high-technology workers because they must deal with a rapid work pace, rapid change, and an impersonal atmosphere.

Another aspect high technology brings to the workplace is the opportunity for telecommuting. As more companies incorporate electronic communication into jobs, many more workers are able to do some or all of their work at home. The traditional rules used to determine when an accident "arises out of and in the course of employment" might no longer apply. Additionally, employers have less control over the variety of hazards that workers encounter in their home/work environment. The overall effect of telecommuting on the workers' compensation system is unknown.

Leased workers
Workers provided by a business, whose primary job is to provide such workers, to another business.

Industry mix has implications for the types of workers used. Some industries use more leased workers than others do. **Leased workers** are workers provided by one business, whose primary job is to provide such workers, to another business. The term "employee outsourcing" is also used to describe the practice of hiring leased workers.

Terms Used in Text

- Employment agencies—Companies that provide the leased workers
- Employers—Companies for which the leased workers perform work
- General employers—Companies that lease the workers *to* employers
- Special employers—Companies that lease the workers *from* these general employers

---

Leased workers can increase an employer's workers' compensation insurance premiums if the employment agency and employer both provide workers' compensation insurance. Leased workers can decrease workers' compensation insurance premiums if the employment agency purchases workers' compensation coverage for a lower rate than the employer does.

Leased workers are not necessarily temporary workers, because the lease contract between the employment agency and the employer can specify a permanent or an indefinite employment period. Employers are likely to use leased workers indefinitely to reduce administrative expenses, to reduce insurance and employee benefits costs, or to provide better employee benefits.

Depending on state statutes for workers' compensation benefits, leased workers might be considered the same as loaned workers. A loaned worker is a worker who is loaned by his or her employer to a third party. The employer is not in the business of leasing workers. An example of a loaned worker arrangement might be the rental of a crane and its operator by a third party. The crane operator's employer must provide workers' compensation benefits. However, usually lease contracts give the employment agency the right to hire, discipline, terminate, and set wages for leased workers. In that case, a court might determine that the third party and the employment agency are co-employers with joint and several liability for workers' compensation benefits. If the employment agency meets the criteria of control, consent, consideration, and other employment status criteria, then only the employment agency would be required to provide workers' compensation benefits. However, if the employment agency fails to provide those benefits, a court might find the employer legally liable for those benefits.

So that both the employment agency and the third party do not have to provide for workers' compensation benefits and to avoid coverage disputes, one party usually purchases workers' compensation insurance and adds the other party by endorsement. Adjusters should verify that the workers' compensation insurance has the correct endorsements to cover that situation.

Interest Rates

A third economic factor that affects an employer's workers' compensation costs is interest rates. Changes in interest rates affect how an employer chooses to use its money. If interest rates are high, an employer might choose to use more labor and spend less on new equipment and technology. The employer might also choose to decrease spending on safety. The opposite might be true if interest rates are low. Employers might purchase new equipment and machinery if financing is affordable and available.

Demographic Cost Factors

Demographics are the statistical characteristics of human populations. Age and geographic distribution are demographic factors affecting workers' compensation costs. The U.S. civilian labor force is growing older. Exhibit 4-7 shows how the percentage of workers in different age groups has changed and what the projections are for future years.

Demographics
The statistical characteristics of human populations.

Older workers tend to have fewer injuries than others, possibly because of greater on-the-job expertise and a higher regard for personal safety. However, older workers' injuries are often more severe, resulting in longer recovery periods. These workers also have a higher incidence of "nonspecific" diagnoses, in which a doctor has difficulty determining whether the condition is work-related or is an aggravation of a preexisting condition.

The Americans with Disabilities Act encourages employers to hire and retain workers with disabilities. However, those workers are statistically more likely to be injured on the job than workers without disabilities. For example, workers with hearing impairments are twice as likely, and vision-impaired workers are three times as likely, to suffer a workplace injury, than workers without such impairments. Arthritis raises the risk of work-related injury by 34 percent.[2]

EXHIBIT 4-7

Changes in Workforce Demographics

Age Range	1980	1990	1995	Projected 2005	1990–2005 Percent Change
16–19	9.4%	7.8%	7.7%	8.6%	0.8%
20–24	15.9	14.7	13.6	15.3	−0.6
25–34	29.3	36.0	34.2	30.5	−5.5
35–44	20.4	32.4	35.8	35.9	−3.7
45–54	16.9	20.2	25.2	34.5	14.3
55–64	11.9	11.5	11.9	17.8	6.3
65+	3.1	3.5	3.8	4.4	0.9

Compiled from U.S. Census Bureau, Statistical Abstract of the United States: 2002, p. 367.

In light of those statistics, employers should develop loss control programs and implement workplace accommodations to reduce the injury risk for disabled workers, and thereby reduce workers' compensation costs.

Certain areas of the United States have fewer workers' compensation claims than the rest of the country. The incidence of workers' compensation claims might be lower in such areas because of cultural norms. Another geographic influence on claims is the benefit levels provided by each state. In states with compensation benefit rates that are low compared to the cost of living, workers have less incentive to remain off work.

Other Cost Factors

Other factors affect the cost of workers' compensation insurance, such as the following:

- Moral hazards and fraud
- Loss control
- Litigation
- Acquired immune deficiency syndrome (AIDS)
- Underwriting cycles
- Disability rating determination
- Use of vocational rehabilitation
- Workplace violence

Moral Hazards and Fraud

Moral hazard is a condition that increases the likelihood that a person will intentionally cause or exaggerate a loss. Those characteristics also increase the likelihood of insurance fraud. Two types of fraud affect workers' compensation costs: premium fraud and claim fraud. **Premium fraud** occurs when employers intentionally misclassify workers or understate payroll to reduce premiums. The incentive for premium fraud increases if an employer has a cash flow problem. If premium fraud is not detected during audits, then it might be discovered when an adjuster determines that the injured worker's work duties do not fit any of the classifications listed on the workers' compensation policy. Because premium fraud reduces the workers' compensation premiums paid, the loss ratio worsens, and rates increase for all employers.

Premium fraud
An employer's intentional misclassification of workers or understatement of payroll to reduce its workers' compensation premium.

Premium Fraud Case

An employer classified its entire staff as office and clerical for the workers' compensation policy. However, worker injuries consisted of head and neck injuries in falls from roofs. A claim investigation revealed that the employer was a roofing contractor and that the workers were hired specifically to do roofing work. The premium fraud totaled $250,000.

According to the National Council on Compensation Insurance, claim fraud is involved to some degree in one out of every four claims. Claim fraud results in higher claim costs and higher loss adjustment expenses to combat fraud.

Claim fraud occurs in various ways for many reasons. The following examples illustrate the breadth of claim fraud in workers' compensation.

- A man hurts himself playing softball on Sunday. On Monday morning, he reports to his employer that he hurt himself at work.

- A worker legitimately injured at work exaggerates her complaints and malingers at home because she does not want to return to her job, which she considers boring.

- A worker who has exhausted his vacation and sick days fakes an injury so that he can have a few more "paid vacation days."

- A worker seeks excessive medical treatment to "build up" his liability claim against a third party.

- While on disability leave, an "injured" worker works at another job.

- A healthcare provider treats an injured worker more frequently than the injury requires.

- A healthcare provider continues to treat an injured worker even after the worker has reached maximum medical improvement.

- A healthcare provider exaggerates the extent of treatment provided to charge a higher rate (a practice known as upcoding).

- An attorney pays a doctor to give a higher disability rating than the worker's injury requires.

Loss Control

Loss control includes both activities to reduce the frequency of injuries and activities to reduce the severity of injuries after they occur. Therefore, managed care activities could be considered loss control to the extent that they reduce the cost of injuries. Insurers' loss control efforts increase loss adjustment expenses and general expenses but in return are expected to reduce medical and lost wages benefits costs. Employers' loss control efforts reduce workers' compensation losses and, consequently, workers' compensation premiums.

Litigation

Another factor contributing to an employer's workers' compensation costs is the frequency of litigation. Workers' compensation was designed to be a no-fault system under which injured workers exchanged the right to sue for common-law damages for the right to receive specified benefits from their employers. However, studies estimate that 5 to 10 percent of medical claims and 30 percent of lost wages claims involve attorneys. Attorney involvement increases average claim costs because of higher benefit awards and increased loss adjustment expense costs. Some states' statutes attempt to reduce such costs by using objective terms in their disability and compensability definitions and by placing limits on attorney fees.[3]

Acquired Immune Deficiency Syndrome (AIDS)

From the standpoint of workers' compensation, workers in healthcare professions, police, and emergency personnel are exposed to some risk of contracting human immune deficiency virus (HIV), which causes AIDS. Infection with an infectious disease, such as AIDS, that can be traced to a specific work-related incident qualifies as a covered injury. Treating AIDS is very expensive, adding to the cost of workers' compensation.

Workers responsible for first aid in the workplace might also be exposed to the virus. Co-workers fearful of AIDS patients might file stress-related claims. AIDS indirectly increases workers' compensation costs because hospitals and doctors try to recoup costs for uninsured AIDS patients by charging all other patients higher fees.[4]

Underwriting Cycles

Soft market
A highly competitive market for insurance, prompting insurers to lower rates.

Hard market
A market in which insurance is less available than normal, resulting in higher rates.

Workers' compensation costs can also be affected by insurance underwriting cycles. Coverage availability and price fluctuation depend on whether the insurance industry is in a soft or a hard market. A **soft market** exists when competition for insurance business is high and insurers lower rates to attract applicants. In a soft market, insurers might charge less in premiums than is required to pay for losses and expenses because the marketplace will not allow higher premiums. A **hard market** exists when insurance is less available and insurance rates are higher. In a hard market, insurers charge higher premiums that are more likely to cover losses, expenses, and a profit. Underwriting cycles can affect workers' compensation costs, although workers' compensation premium rates are not as easily raised or lowered as the premiums of other lines of business.

Disability Rating Determination

How a state determines the extent of a worker's disability affects lost wages benefits payments. PPD ratings vary widely by state, and workers with similar injuries or with the same evaluation from their treating doctor often have significantly different ratings. Factors such as the injured worker's age and education, as well as attorney involvement, influence the final rating.

Use of Vocational Rehabilitation

The use of vocational rehabilitation services to return disabled workers to the workforce might decrease the costs of some workers' compensation claims. Without vocational rehabilitation, many workers would be permanently removed from the work force and would continue collecting workers' compensation benefits for total disability.

Workplace Violence

Workers' compensation claims for injuries resulting from workplace violence are becoming more frequent and costly. Workplace violence is an increasing concern for employers and workers for the following reasons:

- The incidence of workplace violence is on the rise.
- Workplace violence claims often involve injuries to multiple body parts or to the head, neck, and spinal cord.
- Workplace violence injuries are twice as likely to result in PTD than are injuries from other causes.[5]

Workplace violence is considered any physical assault, threatening behavior, or verbal abuse occurring in a work setting. About 74 percent of workplace violence incidents involve verbal abuse during arguments or involve simple assaults, such as pushing and shoving, that do not lead to serious injuries. However, media attention often focuses on more sensational incidents, such as a disgruntled former worker's shooting spree. Homicide represents less than one percent of reported cases.[6]

Workplace violence
Any physical assault, threatening behavior, or verbal abuse occurring in a work setting.

With so many different factors affecting the cost of workers' compensation, it is easy to understand why methods of controlling these costs are such hotly debated issues. Many states struggle to find a balance between the need for comprehensive benefits and the cost to employers of supplying these benefits.

SUMMARY

Workers' compensation laws support disabled workers while they are unable to work by providing benefits for lost wages in the form of temporary total, temporary partial, permanent partial, or permanent total benefits. A worker who is temporarily unable to work or is temporarily able to work only on a limited basis receives temporary wage loss benefits. A worker with permanent disability, either total or partial, is entitled to benefits based on a schedule for the injured body part and/or to loss of earning capacity benefits. Temporary and permanent wage loss benefits are subject to minimum and maximum amounts. The benefits are calculated by multiplying the injured worker's average weekly wage by a percentage specified in the workers' compensation statute to arrive at the weekly benefit amount.

The duration of the benefit must also be calculated. The period of disability extends from the date of injury to the date the injured worker returns to work, if ever. Most workers' compensation statutes have provisions for a waiting period and for a retroactive period. The waiting period is the number of days after the injury before wage loss benefits begin. The retroactive period is the time from the date of injury to a specified date, after which benefits are retroactively paid to cover the waiting period.

In addition to lost wages, workers' compensation also pays for medical care and rehabilitation services. Medical benefits begin immediately following the injury and last as long as the need for care exists. Medical care must be related to the injury and must be reasonable in cost and frequency. To control medical and rehabilitation costs, workers' compensation statutes allow the employer to have the injured worker examined by an independent doctor and to direct an injured worker to a specific doctor for treatment. Rehabilitation services are provided to assist the injured worker in returning to work in a timely manner. The duration for rehabilitation benefits varies by state.

Death benefits are available to eligible dependent survivors of workers who die because of a compensable injury or illness. Death benefits are paid weekly, although some states include a lump sum payment as well. Funeral expenses are also included, subject to a maximum amount. Death benefits paid to a surviving spouse end when the spouse remarries. Death benefits to children usually terminate when the child reaches a certain age.

The trend is toward continued expansion of workers' compensation benefits, but at a pace slowed by sharply rising workers' compensation costs. Many factors affect workers' compensation costs. Adjusters can directly influence only a few of these factors, such as loss adjustment expense, use of rehabilitation services, and detection of fraud. The majority of the cost factors are external to the claims process and therefore beyond the control of the adjuster.

So far, this text has discussed workers' compensation as a requirement placed on employers by state and federal law. The next chapter discusses how employers can satisfy this requirement by purchasing insurance or participating in an approved alternative market.

CHAPTER NOTES

1. Mark J. Browne and Dan R. Anderson, "Managed Care in Workers Compensation," *1997–1998 Workers' Compensation Managed Care Sourcebook* (New York: Faulkner & Gray, Inc., 1997), pp. 14–15.

2. "Workers with Disabilities at Higher Risk for Injuries," *The Journal of Commerce*, December 30, 1997, p. 8A.

3. National Council on Compensation Insurance, "Attorneys Involved in Most High-Cost Workers Compensation Claims," *NCCI 1996 Issues Report*, p. 47.

4. "How to Deal with AIDS in the Workplace," *Workers Compensation Outlook*, April 1994, p. 2.

5. Martin H. Wolf, Dan Corro, and Chun Shyong, "The Who, When and How Much of Workplace Violence," *The Journal of Workers Compensation*, Spring 2000 (Vol. 9, No. 3), p. 28.

6. U.S. Department of Justice, "Violence in the Workplace, 1993–1999," Dec. 2001, www.ojp.usdoj.gov/bjs/abstract/vw99.htm (accessed March 31, 2004).

Chapter 5

Direct Your Learning

Workers' Compensation Insurance and Alternatives

After learning the content of this chapter, you should be able to:

■ Given a case involving a work-related injury to an employee, determine the coverage provided by the WC&EL policy.

  • Describe the coverage provided by the WC&EL policy for a claim made under Part One—Workers Compensation Insurance of the policy.

  • Describe the coverage provided by the WC&EL policy for a claim made under Part Two—Employers Liability Insurance of the policy.

  • Describe the exclusions in Part One—Workers Compensation Insurance of the policy.

  • Describe the exclusions found in Part Two—Employers Liability Insurance of the policy.

  • Explain the purposes of Parts 3, 4, 5, and 6 of a WC&EL policy.

■ Explain how, other than purchasing a WC&EL policy, an employer can meet its obligations to provide benefits to injured workers.

■ Describe the implications to the insurer and the claim adjuster of the use of alternatives to purchasing a WC&EL policy.

Develop Your Perspective

What are the main topics covered in the chapter?

An employer can use several methods to satisfy the statutory workers' compensation requirements. The Workers Compensation and Employers Liability Insurance Policy (WC&EL) is one method. This chapter describes the main provisions of the WC&EL. It also describes various alternatives to purchasing a WC&EL policy.

Identify the ways your state allows employers to meet workers' compensation obligations.

- Do employers purchase a WC&EL policy?
- Can employers purchase an alternative to the WC&EL policy?

Why is it important to learn about these topics?

Most workers' compensation adjusters will adjust losses under a WC&EL policy. The WC&EL is split into two parts, one that provides workers' compensation insurance and one that provides employers liability insurance. The distinction between Part One—Workers Compensation Insurance and Part Two—Employers Liability Insurance is important because the coverages differ. If a WC&EL policy alternative is selected by the insured, the adjuster will have to review the specific provisions of that alternative before investigating a claim.

Review the WC&EL policy in the appendix to Chapter 5.

- Find Part One—Workers Compensation Insurance and Part Two—Employers Liability Insurance.
- What does Part One insurance apply to?
- What does Part Two insurance apply to?

How can you use what you will learn?

Imagine you have received lawsuit papers from an insured alleging an injury to a worker.

- Is the alleged injury covered under Part One—Workers Compensation Insurance of the policy?
- Is the alleged injury covered under Part Two—Employers Liability Insurance of the policy?
- What is the insurer's duty to defend based on the allegations in the suit?

Chapter 5

Workers' Compensation Insurance and Alternatives

So far, this text has discussed the workers' compensation requirement that state and federal statutes place on employers. This chapter discusses the various methods that employers can use to meet their statutory requirements. The first method is the Workers Compensation and Employers Liability Insurance Policy (WC&EL).

Workers' compensation and workers' compensation insurance are so closely interrelated that many people think they are synonymous. However, workers' compensation insurance is but one method an employer can use to satisfy the requirements workers' compensation laws impose.

THE WORKERS COMPENSATION AND EMPLOYERS LIABILITY INSURANCE POLICY

Workers' compensation is compulsory for nearly all employments in almost every state. Even in those states that do not have compulsory workers' compensation, most employers have workers' compensation insurance to protect against the financial consequences of negligence suits.

The WC&EL insurance policy is among the most regulated of insurance policies. State workers' compensation statutes usually require certain insurance provisions and prohibit others. All states require either the insurance commissioner or the industrial commission to approve the policy. Although the provisions of every state workers' compensation statute differ, a standard WC&EL policy, with appropriate endorsements, is used in all states permitting private insurance. Some states with monopolistic funds allow the standard policy to be endorsed to provide protection only for the employers liability loss exposure.

The standard WC&EL policy in use since 1954 was developed through the collaboration of the insurers writing compensation coverage, committees of the National Council on Compensation Insurance (NCCI), the New York Compensation Rating Board, and various other independent and state rating bureaus. NCCI's most recent policy revision, called "easy read," was introduced in 1984. This policy combines two separate coverages:

1. *Workers' compensation* is governed entirely by the applicable state statutes. Its purpose is to pay whatever benefits are prescribed by statute.

2. *Employers liability* protects employers from the loss exposure of lawsuits brought by injured workers to recover money damages separate from claims for workers' compensation benefits. This protection is much like that provided under a commercial general liability policy because it also provides employers with legal defense coverage. The standard policy is designed so that employers liability coverage does not overlap with general liability coverage or with the workers' compensation coverage.

In states that allow employers to purchase compensation insurance from private insurers, one policy provides coverage for both workers' compensation and employers liability loss exposures. The policy contains uniform provisions even though workers' compensation benefits vary by state. The policy incorporates the workers' compensation statutes into the policy by reference. Note that Part One—Workers Compensation Insurance does not contain any exclusions.

Part One—Workers Compensation Insurance

Under Part One—Workers Compensation Insurance, the insurer agrees to pay promptly, when due, the benefits required of the employer by the workers' compensation statute. The policy refers to the workers' compensation statute as the compensation and occupational disease law of each state or territory named in Item 3.A. of the Information Page (declarations) and defines "state" as any state of the United States and the District of Columbia. The unendorsed policy refers only to state laws. No protection is provided against claims made under federal compensation laws, such as the Federal Employers' Liability Act and the U.S. Longshore and Harbor Workers Compensation Act. Coverage for such claims can be added by endorsement.

No policy limits apply to Part One—Workers Compensation Insurance. The insurer must assume whatever liability is prescribed for its insured by the applicable state statute. However, the absence of policy limits does not mean that benefits are unlimited. The kind and the extent of any benefits payable depend on the nature of the injury and the provisions of the applicable state statute. Also, because the policy restricts protection to that required by the statute or other laws listed or referred to in the policy, the information page must designate the state(s) in which all business locations or operations involving employee work loss exposures are or might be maintained.

Most state compensation laws are extraterritorial. A worker hired by an employer in State A might be injured on business in State B. That worker, depending on the laws or circumstances, might file a claim under the compensation laws of either State A or State B. If the Information Page of the employer's policy lists only State A, no insurance coverage would exist under this part of the policy for a claim filed under the laws of State B. See the Appendix of this chapter for a sample of the information page. The "other states" provision provides coverage for situations that present extraterritorial loss exposures.

The separate paragraphs of Part One—Workers Compensation Insurance are best understood by examining each separately. This section discusses each of the provisions, whose titles appear in italics.

How This Insurance Applies. Part One applies to bodily injury by accident during the policy period or to bodily injury by disease caused or aggravated by conditions of employment if the last day of the last exposure that causes or aggravates the disease occurs during the policy period. Coverage also applies regardless of when death has occurred as long as it has resulted from an otherwise covered bodily injury or disease.

We Will Pay. The insurer agrees to pay promptly, when due, the statutory benefits as required.

We Will Defend. The insurer agrees to defend at its expense any claim, proceeding, or suit against the insured for benefits payable. Although the policy expressly states that no duty exists to defend for claims that are not covered under the policy, this provision still continues to be litigated.

We Will Also Pay. In addition to the statutory benefits, the insurer also agrees to pay the following costs in the event of any claim, proceeding, or suit:

- Reasonable expenses incurred by the insured at the insurer's request, other than loss of earnings
- Premiums for bonds to release the insured's property from attachment to satisfy a judgment or court order and for appeal bonds within policy limits
- Litigation costs imposed on the insured
- All interest that has accrued on a judgment before the insurer pays the claim
- Any expenses that the insurer incurs

Other Insurance. If a claim, proceeding, or suit arises to which other insurance or self-insurance also applies, the most the insurer will pay under the policy is its share of damages. All shares are to be equal until the loss is paid. If any insurance or self-insurance is exhausted, the remaining insurance will contribute equally until the loss is paid.

Payments You Must Make. Workers' compensation insurance provisions specifically disclaim any payments in excess of those benefits provided by law, including any payments that might be required because of the following actions by an insured:

1. Serious or willful misconduct
2. Employment of a worker in violation of law
3. Failure to comply with any health or safety law or regulation
4. Discharge of or discrimination against any worker in violation of the workers' compensation statute

If the insurer makes any payments in excess of what is normally required by statute, the insured must reimburse the insurer promptly.

Recovery From Others. If any payment is made under the policy, the insurer assumes the insured's rights, as well as the rights of the worker who receives workers' compensation benefits, to recover from responsible third parties. Furthermore, the insured must take every precaution to protect the insurer's recovery (subrogation) rights and assist the insurer in exercising them. Recovery is accomplished through subrogation against the party responsible for the worker's injury. States differ on how the insurer can pursue the responsible third parties. Some states assign the injured worker's cause of action to the payer of the compensation. In other states, if the injured party does not sue the third party within a specified period, the payer of the compensation benefits may bring suit after that period has elapsed. Recognizing potential subrogation opportunities and understanding how to pursue subrogation properly are essential parts of an adjuster's job and are discussed in detail in a later chapter.

Statutory Provisions. The statutory provisions paragraph contains several statements required by law, including the following:

- The employer's notice of injury is deemed to be notice to the insurer as well.

- Neither bankruptcy nor insolvency of the employer or its estate relieves the insurer of its duties under workers' compensation insurance after an injury occurs.

- The insurer is contractually liable to any person entitled to the workers' compensation benefits as prescribed by statute.

- The policy conforms to the workers' compensation law that applies to the benefits, special taxes, funds, and assessments payable as required by law.

- Any terms of the insurance that conflict with the workers' compensation law are amended to conform to such law.

Part Two—Employers Liability Insurance

Part Two—Employers Liability Insurance of the WC&EL policy covers those situations in which an injured worker can sue the insured.

Statutory workers' compensation benefits are said to be the exclusive remedy that covered workers have against covered employers for work-related injury, disease, and death. Workers normally cannot reject the statutory benefits to which they are entitled after an injury or a disease and instead sue their employers to obtain higher awards at common law. Nor can workers accept the benefits and later decide to sue their employers for additional money damages.

However, there are ways workers or their families can circumvent the exclusive remedy of workers' compensation laws and bring tort suits for money damages.

The following eight situations in which the exclusive remedy of workers' compensation can be challenged are discussed in more detail later in this chapter:

1. The employer's intentional acts and willful misconduct
2. Family members' suits for loss of consortium
3. Dual capacity actions
4. Suits by employees of subsidiaries against parent companies
5. Third-party-over actions
6. The employer's failure to insure or set up qualified self-insurance plans
7. Claims filed under Title VII or the Americans with Disabilities Act (ADA)
8. Fellow worker actions

Employers liability insurance also protects employers against tort suits brought by injured workers who have rejected the compensation benefits under elective statutes, as well as suits brought by workers who are excluded from the acts by employment exemptions. Sometimes a worker's injury, disease, or death does not meet the coverage criteria, or the workers' compensation statute specifically permits (or is interpreted to permit) suits against employers by third parties, such as a worker's dependent.

The next section discusses specific policy provisions of Part Two—Employers Liability Insurance.

How This Insurance Applies. The employers liability insurance portion of the policy will pay benefits for injury, disease, or death that results from an accident during the policy period. The policy will also pay benefits for disease caused or aggravated by conditions of employment if the last day of the last exposure that causes or aggravates the disease occurs during the policy period. The injury, disease, or death must occur in a state listed on the policy.

We Will Pay. The insurer agrees to pay damages that the employer must legally pay because of injury, disease, or death sustained by workers and covered by employers liability insurance. Specifically included are damages involving third-party-over actions, care and loss of services, consequential injuries, and dual capacity actions, defined as follows:

• A *third-party-over action* arises when an injured worker sues and recovers from a negligent third party. The third party, in turn, sues the insured for at least partial recovery based on the insured's contributory or comparative negligence. For example, suppose a worker is injured while operating a vehicle that the insured, with knowledge of a safety defect, has allowed the worker to operate. The worker sues the vehicle manufacturer. The manufacturer then sues the insured because the insured was partially negligent in permitting the vehicle to be operated with a safety defect.

• *Care and loss of services* includes loss of affection and consortium.

• A *consequential injury* occurs when an occupational disease is transmitted by a worker to a spouse or family member. For example, a worker diagnosed with an occupational disease from a hazardous substance could transmit the disease when the substance is carried home on the employee's work clothes.

- *Dual capacity actions* deal with claims against the insured both in the capacity of an employer and in some other capacity. An example of dual capacity is an employer that is also the manufacturer of the product that has caused a worker's injury.

The fact that each of the four preceding loss exposures is specifically excluded under all commercial general liability policies and commercial auto policies makes employers liability insurance the only protection against such actions. When workers' compensation insurance is provided by a monopolistic state fund, employers need stopgap coverage to protect against their employers liability loss exposures. This stopgap coverage can be obtained by endorsing a standard WC&EL policy to exclude Part One—Workers Compensation Insurance and provide only Part Two—Employers Liability Insurance.

Exclusions. The WC&EL policy lists the following twelve exclusions:

1. Liability assumed under a contract
2. Punitive or exemplary damages that result from an injury to an illegal worker
3. Bodily injury to a knowingly employed illegal worker
4. Any obligation to pay workers' compensation
5. Any bodily injury or aggravation intentionally caused by the insured
6. Bodily injury that occurs outside the coverage territory
7. Damages arising out of employment practices
8. Bodily injury to any person subject to a federal workers' compensation law
9. Bodily injury to any person subject to the Federal Employers' Liability Act or similar federal laws
10. Bodily injury to a master or crew member of a vessel
11. Any fines or penalties for violating a federal or state law
12. Damages payable under the Migrant and Seasonal Agricultural Worker Protection Act

Exclusions 8 through 12 concern federal workers' compensation coverages. Exclusions 1 through 7 are more complicated to apply and are discussed in more detail here.

Exclusion 1, the contractual liability exclusion, eliminates coverage for liability the insured has assumed under any contract or agreement. Tort liability assumed under any contract or agreement, including liability toward a third party for a work-related injury (other than those covered under workers' compensation insurance), can be covered by a commercial general liability policy.

Agreements to assume others' tort liability to third parties are common. General contractors are often required to enter into such agreements with work project owners. Subcontractors also enter into such agreements with general contractors, often as a condition to obtaining the jobs. A work project owner is open to suit by the injured worker of a contractor (or subcontractor), particularly when the owner has contributed to the injury. To avoid adverse judgments and the inconvenience of lawsuits, owners frequently require contractors to agree contractually to handle any tort claims without involving them, regardless of the owner's negligence. Because such agreements can also be excluded under commercial general liability insurance, employers liability coverage must duplicate the exclusion.

However, an exception to the contractual liability exclusion exists. Employers liability coverage does extend to liability under any warranty that work performed by or on behalf of the insured will be done in a workmanlike manner. Such liability is not covered by the commercial general liability policy. Therefore, to avoid any gap in protection, employers liability covers this loss exposure.

Exclusion 2 is for punitive or exemplary damages. Workers' compensation statutes require employers to pay any punitive or exemplary damages assessed against them for violations of law. Under employers liability coverage, employers are denied coverage for any punitive or exemplary damages resulting from bodily injury, disease, or death to a worker in violation of the law.

Exclusion 3 is for employment in violation of law. Even in the absence of any punitive or exemplary damages, employers are still denied protection under employers liability coverage for a worker's injury, disease, or death if the worker was employed in violation of the law with the knowledge of the employer or its executive officers. Therefore, while the injured worker could sue the employer, Part Two—Employers Liability Insurance would not cover the employer.

Exclusion 4 is for obligations under workers' compensation laws. Employers liability coverage does not apply to any statutory benefit obligations imposed by workers' compensation, occupational disease, unemployment compensation, or disability benefits law or a similar law.

Exclusion 5 is for any bodily injury intentionally caused or aggravated by the employer.

Exclusion 6 is for injury, disease, or death occurring outside the United States and its territories and possessions. No coverage is provided for any claim or suit brought by others, such as foreign nationals. However, citizens or residents of the United States or Canada who are temporarily outside these countries are covered.

Exclusion 7 is for any damages arising out of employment practices such as the discharge of, coercion of, or discrimination against any worker in violation of law. These claims are more appropriately covered under Employment Practices Liability (EPL) policies available from a few insurers for an additional premium.

Controversy continues over the extent of this exclusion, especially regarding the insurer's duty to defend. Although the policy explicitly states that insurers have no duty to defend a claim, proceeding, or suit that the policy does not cover, several courts have ruled that "the duty to defend is broader than the duty to indemnify."[1] In addition, some states have laws controlling coverage required under insurance policies, which have been used to help employers recover defense costs in personal injury claims that might appear to be excluded. Some courts have held that the insurer has the duty to defend employers in claims that allege injury resulting from an employer's infliction of emotional distress (see box on duty to defend cases).

This exclusion continues to be controversial because the number of cases filed against employers every year remains high. Consequently, adjusters should carefully analyze the decision to deny a claim based on this exclusion and should consult with legal counsel. A thorough investigation often reveals that other exclusions and policy provisions apply to the claim. For example, many discrimination claims result from intentional acts, another policy exclusion. Also, an injury might not meet the definition of "bodily injury by accident" or might not have arisen "out of the course of employment," both requirements for coverage under this policy.

Duty to Defend Versus the Exclusion for Wrongful Discharge or Discrimination

In the case of *HDH Corp. v. Atlantic Charter Insurance Co.* (425 Mass. 433, 681 N.E.2d 847, 1997), a former employee of HDH Corp. claimed emotional distress and sued the company for sexual discrimination and wrongful termination. Because sexual discrimination and wrongful termination are excluded in the Employers' Liability Insurance Section of the WC&EL, the insurer did not defend HDH Corp. in the suit. The employee was eventually awarded $120,000. HDH Corp. then sued the insurer for this amount and its legal costs.

The lower court ruled in the insurer's favor. However, the appeals court reversed and remanded this decision (sent the case back to the lower court), in part stating that the claim for emotional distress caused by sexual discrimination might potentially have been covered by the WC&EL policy even though the employee filed the claim under the wrong legal principle.

The Supreme Judicial Court in Massachusetts reversed the appellate court's decision and held that the insurer had no duty to defend the employer because the employee had not preserved her common-law right of action by affirmatively rejecting the workers' compensation system as a means of recovery. The workers' compensation section of the policy limits defense and indemnity of the employer to claims for workers' compensation benefits, and the employers liability section excludes sexual discrimination and wrongful termination.

Part Two—Employers Liability Insurance exclusions 8 through 12 exclude coverage for bodily injury, disease, or death to persons subject to the

Longshore and Harbor Workers' Compensation Act, the Nonappropriated Fund Instrumentalities Act, the Outer Continental Shelf Lands Act, the Defense Base Act, the Federal Coal Mine Health and Safety Act of 1969, the Federal Employers' Liability Act, and the Migrant and Seasonal Agricultural Worker Protection Act; to a master or member of the crew of any vessel; or to persons subject to any other federal workers' compensation law. Fines and penalties for federal and state law violations are also excluded.

We Will Defend. This provision gives the insurer the right to investigate and settle any claim or suit against the insured for damages the policy covers, along with the duty to defend the insured. It specifically states that the insurer has no duty to defend any claim or suit not covered by the policy and no duty to continue a defense once the limit of liability has been paid.

We Will Also Pay. The insurer agrees to pay reasonable expenses incurred in defending a claim along with litigation costs imposed on the insured and any interest on a judgment.

Other Insurance. This provision states that if other insurance or self-insurance applies to the claim, the damages and expenses will be shared equally until the loss is paid, subject to applicable policy limits.

Limits of Liability. The policy is subject to specific limits of liability on the amount the insurer will pay. Three such limits of liability are specified in Item 3.B. of the Information Page. The first, the "bodily injury by accident—each accident" limit, is the maximum the insurer will pay for bodily injury or death to one or more employees in any one accident. The second and third limits are bodily injury by disease limits. The limit shown for "bodily injury by disease—policy limit" is the most the insurer will pay for all covered damages arising out of bodily injury by disease, regardless of the number of employees involved, whereas the limit shown for "bodily injury by disease—each employee" is the maximum amount payable to any one employee. The policy stipulates the following:

- A disease is not bodily injury by accident unless it results directly from bodily injury by accident.
- Bodily injury by disease excludes disease that results directly from a bodily injury by accident.

The rationale is to avoid any argument that an injury is attributable to both an accident and a disease. The two terms are mutually exclusive. The insurer has no contractual obligation to pay any claims for damages after it has paid the applicable limit of its liability under this provision.

Recovery from Others. This provision is the same in Part Two—Employers Liability Insurance as it was in Part One—Workers Compensation Insurance. The insurer has the right to recover payments from responsible third parties and the insured must cooperate in these efforts.

Actions Against Us. This provision is comparable to the suit provision of commercial general liability policies. It states that no right of action is permitted against the insurer under the insurance policy unless the insured has complied with all policy terms and the amount the employer owes has been determined with the insurer's consent or by actual trial and final judgment. This coverage does not allow lawsuits against the insurer for the purpose of determining the extent of the employer's liability.

Part Three—Other States Insurance

Part Three—Other States Insurance of the WC&EL policy applies to both Part One—Workers Compensation Insurance and Part Two—Employers Liability Insurance. The purpose of "other states insurance" is to provide coverage against those loss exposures that develop during the policy period in any state designated on the information page. The states in which an insured's operations are known to exist are designated in Item 3.A. If loss exposures *could* arise in other states, they should be listed in Item 3.C. However, monopolistic fund states in which workers' compensation insurance is available through the state government cannot be listed, and insurers that are not licensed to operate in all the states, such as regional insurers, cannot list states in which they are not permitted to operate. National insurers sometimes use standard wording that includes all nonmonopolistic fund states because no additional premium applies for listing a state in Item 3.C.

Part Four—Your Duties If Injury Occurs

The purpose of Part Four—Your Duties If Injury Occurs of the WC&EL policy is to explain the insured's duties in the event of injury. The first and most important duty is to inform the insurer at once if injury occurs that might be covered by the policy. The following are other duties of the insured under the policy:

- Provide immediate medical and other services that might be required by the workers' compensation law
- Give the insurer or its agent the names and addresses of the injured persons, as well as the names and addresses of any witnesses
- Promptly provide the insurer with all notices, demands, and legal papers related to the incident
- Cooperate and assist the insurer, as might be requested, in investigating, defending, or settling any claim, proceeding, or suit
- Do nothing after any injury that might interfere with or impair the insurer's right to recover from others
- Refrain from making any voluntary payments, assuming any obligations, or incurring any expenses except at the insured's own cost

Part Five—Premium

The purpose of this part of the WC&EL policy is to explain how the premium is developed. The WC&EL policy is subject to an agreement permitting the insurer to examine and audit all of the insured's records that relate to the policy. Such audits can be conducted within three years after the policy expires.

Part Six—Conditions

The purpose of Part Six—Conditions of the WC&EL policy is to describe the duties and obligations of both parties, the most significant of which concerns inspections.

Inspections. The insured agrees to permit the insurer to inspect the premises and operations covered by the policy. Insurer inspections are very important in workers' compensation insurance, to provide insurers not only with underwriting information but also with loss control information. This condition states that the inspections are not safety inspections; they relate only to the insurability of the workplace and the premium to be charged. The condition also states, however, that the insurer might give the insured the reports on the conditions its inspectors find as well as any recommended changes. Although these inspections can help the insured, the insurer attempts to clarify that it (1) does not have the duty to provide for the health and safety of the insured's employees or of the public and (2) does not warrant the workplace as being safe or legally compliant. These qualifying statements are considered necessary as a defense against any allegations that the insurer is responsible for unsafe working conditions that might result from the failure to perform an inspection or from an inadequate inspection.

Long Term Policy. This policy condition provides that if the policy period is longer than one year and sixteen days, the policy provisions will apply as if a new policy had been issued on each annual anniversary date.

Transfer of Your Rights and Duties. This condition states that the insured's rights and duties under the policy cannot be transferred without the insurer's written consent.

Cancellation. This condition gives the insured or the insurer the ability to cancel the policy only upon written notice to the other party. If the insured is canceling the policy, the notice must contain an effective date. If the insurer is canceling the policy, the insurer must give the insured ten days' notice of the cancellation date.

Sole Representative. Because a business entity can take various forms, such as sole proprietorship, partnership, or corporation, or several entities might be insured by one policy, this condition specifies that the first named insured listed in Item 1 of the Information Page will act on behalf of all insureds.

As previously mentioned, employers can use several methods to meet their obligations under workers' compensation statutes. The remainder of this chapter discusses these methods.

ALTERNATIVES TO PURCHASING A WC&EL POLICY

In the past, standard WC&EL policies provided most workers' compensation benefits. However, because of cost and the characteristics of standard policies, WC&EL alternatives offer other means of providing workers' compensation benefits. For example, an employer might choose to purchase a product other than a standard WC&EL or might choose a different method of funding to meet its obligations to its injured workers. Those products and funding mechanisms constitute the alternatives to purchasing a WC&EL policy and include the following:

- Self-insurance
- Nonsubscriber workers' compensation plans
- Fronting arrangements
- Large deductible plans
- Captive insurers
- Finite risk insurance

Self-Insurance

Self-insurance

In a workers' compensation context, the employer's planned assumption of and financing of the workers' compensation and employers liability loss exposure.

Self-insurance in the workers' compensation context is an employer's planned assumption and financing of workers' compensation and employers liability loss exposures. It requires formal plans for financing estimated losses. Almost all states allow employers to retain these loss exposures if they can demonstrate the financial capacity to do so. Strict financial requirements effectively prohibit all but the largest employers from self-insuring.

Self-insurance group (SIG)

A group of several employers that forms a not-for-profit association or corporation to which they pay premiums for self-insurance purposes.

A **self-insurance group (SIG)** consists of several similar employers that have formed a not-for-profit association or corporation to which they pay premiums. The premiums earn investment income until they are needed to fund losses. If funds are not used, they are returned to the SIG members. However, if large losses exceed the funds available to pay for them, the members could be assessed additional amounts to cover those losses.[2]

Nonsubscriber Workers' Compensation Plans

Most states require that the employer provide statutory workers' compensation benefits. One exception allows the employer to opt out of the workers' compensation statutory requirements. Another exception allows an employer to provide equal or greater benefits by some means other than by workers' compensation insurance.

Two states—Texas and New Jersey—allow an employer to elect not to be bound by workers' compensation statutes. Because the employer is not required to provide benefits to an injured worker, the employer loses the exclusive remedy protection of workers' compensation and is exposed to tort liability from injured workers. About a dozen states allow an employer to provide workers' compensation benefits by purchasing some product other than a standard workers' compensation policy. The product must provide equivalent benefits that are at least equal to those required by the workers' compensation statute. Some combination of group health insurance and wage loss benefits or twenty-four-hour coverage might be considered equivalent benefits.

Fronting Arrangements

In a **fronting arrangement**, one entity transfers the financial consequences of the workers' compensation and employers liability loss exposures to an insurer with the agreement that the entity will indemnify the insurer for most or all of the losses paid. The entity pays a fronting fee to the insurer for the services provided. For example, Corporation A wants to retain its workers' compensation loss exposure but must secure an insurance policy for regulatory reasons or for certificates of insurance. Insurer B writes a Workers Compensation and Employers Liability Insurance policy for Corporation A. Insurer B issues the policy but includes an endorsement stating that Corporation A will indemnify Insurer B for any losses paid.

Fronting arrangement
An agreement whereby one entity transfers financial consequences of loss exposure to an insurer with the agreement that the entity will indemnify the insurer for most or all of the losses paid.

Large Deductible Plans

In a **large deductible plan**, the employer purchases workers' compensation insurance with a deductible of at least $100,000 and often $250,000 or more. The insurer provides administrative and claim services, and the employer reimburses the insurer for any losses under the deductible. More than forty states currently allow a large deductible plan.

Large deductible plan
A workers' compensation plan with a deductible of at least $100,000 for which the insurer provides administrative and claim services and the employer reimburses the insurer for any losses under the deductible.

Captive Insurers

A **captive insurer** is an insurer formed as a subsidiary of its parent company, organization, or group, that provides all or part of the insurance of its parent company. The owner hopes to lower costs or obtain insurance that is not available in the voluntary market. For example, a large employer could choose to form its own captive insurer to write its workers' compensation coverage. The captive insurer might transfer some of the financial consequences for its loss exposures to the employer in a fronting arrangement.

Captive insurer
An insurer formed as a subsidiary of a parent company, organization, or group that provides all or part of the insurance of its parent company or companies.

Finite Risk Insurance

Finite risk insurance is often thought of as a blend of self-insurance and guaranteed cost insurance. These policies run for multiyear periods, and the insurer returns a portion of the premium if it makes a profit. A finite risk plan usually covers an insured's high-severity losses for several years under a single contract. Finite risk insurance plans are usually custom-tailored to an insured's needs. These plans usually have the following characteristics:

- The limits of coverage apply on an aggregate basis.
- The term of coverage is for multiple years and is noncancelable.
- The premium is often 50 percent or more of the policy limit.
- The insurer shares profit with the insured.

Finite risk insurance can be used in conjunction with a self-insured workers' compensation program to help employers manage premium and losses. Assuming favorable financial accounting treatment, finite risk plans can smooth out over time the effect of large losses on the employer's net income. Finite risk insurance will also help an employer avoid large swings in premium caused by losses.

Implications for the Insurer and the Claim Adjuster

Alternatives to the WC&EL policy pose competitive challenges for insurers and claim adjusters but can also offer opportunities. Employers that use an alternative to the WC&EL policy must select and manage service providers and supervise the service provider's claim handling.

As more employers choose alternatives to the WC&EL, insurers might find themselves writing fewer policies and losing market share. If administrative costs remain constant while fewer policies are sold, costs per policy are higher.

Another challenge is that insurers might be left with less desirable insureds. An employer that chooses an alternative to the WC&EL policy is likely to have a lower-than-average loss experience and greater case reserves. As those employers shift to alternatives, insurers are left with employers that have average or higher-than-average loss experience. As insurers' loss ratios increase because of that shift, insurance rates must increase.

To remain competitive in the face of these challenges, insurers must provide more and better services and reduce costs. To reduce costs, they might consider reducing staff, including claim adjusters, a move that could result in overworking remaining staff and reducing the quality of claim handling. Insurers might also consider increasing premiums, making employers who use the WC&EL pay more. Alternatively, if insurers decide to lower premiums to be competitive, they might jeopardize their financial positions.

The pressure to provide more services and to provide them more efficiently could force insurers with a small percentage of workers' compensation premiums to stop offering WC&EL insurance. The resulting unavailability of WC&EL insurance could harm insurers, employers, and producers.

Alternatives to WC&EL policies present the following opportunities to the insurer and the claim adjuster:

- Claims must still be handled.
- Services could be unbundled.
- Closer relationships with employers might develop.

Regardless of the mechanism chosen to fund workers' compensation benefits, adjusters must still investigate and pay or deny claims, whether they work for an insurer, a third-party administrator, or the employer. For some WC&EL policy alternatives, such as large deductible plans, the insurer continues to provide claim services with its claim staff, thereby decreasing the need to reduce claim staff.

When a traditional insurer sells a WC&EL policy, the insurer sells a package of services, including claim handling, premium auditing, loss control, reporting for regulators and the employer, and defense services. If an employer chooses a WC&EL policy alternative, not all of these services may be included. Insurers can offer unbundled services, allowing the employer to choose which services it needs without purchasing the entire package of services provided with a WC&EL policy. That opportunity might provide additional revenue for the insurer and offset some of the threats from WC&EL alternatives.

Some WC&EL alternatives, such as large deductible plans, can increase an employer's interest in the outcome of claims because the employer pays a large share of claim payments. Although the insurer handles the loss, the employer reimburses the insurer for any losses under its deductible. Therefore, the insurer and the employer develop a closer relationship that encourages loss control.

SUMMARY

Employers can meet their statutory obligation to provide workers' compensation benefits through several methods, including the WC&EL policy. The WC&EL policy provides coverage for the statutory benefits required by the states the insured has designated on the policy's Information Page. It also covers the insured for claims made by a third party as a result of damages paid to the injured worker by the third party.

If the claim arises under Part One—Workers Compensation Insurance of the policy, the limits of insurance are mandated by statute. If the claim arises under Part Two—Employers Liability Insurance of the policy, specific policy limits are stated on the Information Page.

The workers' compensation and employers liability parts of the policy contain similar provisions:

- Duty to defend
- Other insurance
- Recovery from others

Part One—Workers Compensation Insurance contains no exclusions or policy limits because the insurer must assume whatever liability is prescribed for employers in the applicable state statute. Part Two—Workers Compensation Insurance contains the following twelve exclusions:

1. Liability assumed under a contract
2. Punitive or exemplary damages that result from an injury to an illegal worker
3. Bodily injury to a knowingly employed illegal worker
4. Any obligation to pay workers' compensation
5. Any bodily injury or aggravation intentionally caused by the insured
6. Bodily injury that occurs outside the coverage territory
7. Damages arising out of employment practices
8. Bodily injury to any person subject to a federal workers' compensation law

9. Bodily injury to any person subject to the Federal Employers' Liability Act or similar federal laws

10. Bodily injury to a master or crew member of a vessel

11. Any fines or penalties for violating a federal or state law

12. Damages payable under the Migrant and Seasonal Agricultural Worker Protection Act

Finally, the policy has several parts that apply to both the workers' compensation and employers liability coverages:

- Part Three—Other States Insurance

- Part Four—Your Duty If Injury Occurs

- Part Five—Premium

- Part Six—Conditions

The employer can choose alternatives to the WC&EL policy. These alternatives include:

- Self-insurance

- Nonsubscriber workers' compensation plans

- Fronting arrangements

- Large deductible plans

- Captive insurers

- Finite risk insurance

These alternatives present challenges and opportunities for the insurer and adjuster. When an employer chooses an alternative, the employer must also choose, manage, and supervise service providers for claim handling and other needs.

Regardless of whether the adjuster works for the insurer or for a third-party administrator the basic adjustment practices for a workers' compensation claim remain the same. Adjusting workers' compensation losses is the focus of the next chapter.

CHAPTER NOTES

1. *Gray v. Zurich Insurance Co.*, 65 Cal.2d 263 (1966), and *Travelers Insurance Co. v. Lesher*, 187 Cal. App. 3d (1986).

2. Roberta Reynes, "Do-it-Yourself Workers' Comp," *Nation's Business*, April 1995, pp. 26–28.

Appendix

NCCI's Workers Compensation and Employers Liability Insurance Policy

With the exception of maritime employers, almost all employers must obtain workers' compensation insurance or qualify as a self-insurer under the applicable state workers compensation statute. Except in the few states that require workers' compensation insurance to be bought from the state government, most workers' compensation insurance is provided in connection with employers' liability insurance in a single policy.

The most commonly used workers' compensation and employers liability policy is that of the National Council on Compensation Insurance, reprinted here. The workers' compensation portion of the policy covers the insured's obligations for occupational injury and disease under the relevant workers' compensation law(s). The employers liability portion of the policy covers common-law suits against the employer that arise out of employee injury or disease. By endorsement, the policy can be extended to cover obligations under other statutes, such as the Federal Longshore and Harbor Workers Compensation Act.

WORKERS COMPENSATION AND EMPLOYERS LIABILITY INSURANCE POLICY

INFORMATION PAGE

Insurer:

```
┌─────────────────────────────────────────────┐
│        P O L I C Y   N O .                    │
│ │ │ │ │ │ │ │ │ │ │ │ │ │ │ │ │ │ │ │ │ │ │ │ │
└─────────────────────────────────────────────┘
```

1.   **The Insured:**   AMR Corporation   ___ Individual   ___ Partnership
     Mailing address: 2000 Industrial Highway   _X_ Corporation or   _____
                            Workingtown, PA 19000

Other workplaces not shown above:

2.   **The policy period is from**   10/1/03   **to**   10/1/04   **at the insured's mailing address.**

3.   **A.   Workers Compensation Insurance:** Part One of the policy applies to the Workers Compensation Law of the states listed here: PA

     B.   Employers Liability Insurance: Part Two of the policy applies to work in each state listed in Item 3.A. The limits of our liability under Part Two are:

Bodily Injury by Accident	$ 100,000	each accident
Bodily Injury by Disease	$ 500,000	policy limit
Bodily Injury by Disease	$ 100,000	each employee

     C.   Other States Insurance: Part Three of the policy applies to the states, if any, listed here:

          All except those listed in Item 3A and ME, ND, OH, WA, WV, WY and OR

     D.   This policy includes these endorsements and schedules:

          See Schedule

4.   The premium for this policy will be determined by our Manuals of Rules, Classifications, Rates and Rating Plans. All information required below is subject to verification and change by audit.

Classifications	Code No.	Premium Basis Total Estimated Annual Remuneration	Rate Per $100 of Remuneration	Estimated Annual Premium
Sheet Metal Shop	0454	300,000	11.53	34,590
Clerical Office	0953	275,000	.49	1,348
		Experience Modification of 1.382 Applied		13,728
		Estimated Premium Discount		(4,869)

Total Estimated Annual Premium $ 44,797

Minimum Premium $ 1,273   **Expense Constant $**   140

Countersigned by _____ A. M. Abel _____
                                 (authorized representative)

WC 00 00 01 A
© 1987 National Council on Compensation Insurance.

WORKERS COMPENSATION AND EMPLOYERS LIABILITY INSURANCE POLICY   **WC 00 00 00 A**

1st Reprint   Effective April 1, 1992   **Standard**

WORKERS COMPENSATION AND EMPLOYERS LIABILITY INSURANCE POLICY

In return for the payment of the premium and subject to all terms of this policy, we agree with you as follows:

GENERAL SECTION

A. The Policy

This policy includes at its effective date the Information Page and all endorsements and schedules listed there. It is a contract of insurance between you (the employer named in Item 1 of the Information Page) and us (the insurer named on the Information Page). The only agreements relating to this insurance are stated in this policy. The terms of this policy may not be changed or waived except by endorsement issued by us to be part of this policy.

B. Who Is Insured

You are insured if you are an employer named in Item 1 of the Information Page. If that employer is a partnership, and if you are one of its partners, you are insured, but only in your capacity as an employer of the partnership's employees.

C. Workers Compensation Law

Workers Compensation Law means the workers or workmen's compensation law and occupational disease law of each state or territory named in Item 3.A. of the Information Page. It includes any amendments to that law which are in effect during the policy period. It does not include any federal workers or workmen's compensation law, any federal occupational disease law or the provisions of any law that provide nonoccupational disability benefits.

D. State

State means any state of the United States of America, and the District of Columbia.

E. Locations

This policy covers all of your workplaces listed in Items 1 or 4 of the Information Page; and it covers all other workplaces in Item 3.A. states unless you have other insurance or are self-insured for such workplaces.

PART ONE
WORKERS COMPENSATION INSURANCE

A. How This Insurance Applies

This workers compensation insurance applies to bodily injury by accident or bodily injury by disease. Bodily injury includes resulting death.

1. Bodily injury by accident must occur during the policy period.
2. Bodily injury by disease must be caused or aggravated by the conditions of your employment. The employee's last day of last exposure to the conditions causing or aggravating such bodily injury by disease must occur during the policy period.

B. We Will Pay

We will pay promptly when due the benefits required of you by the workers compensation law.

C. We Will Defend

We have the right and duty to defend at our expense any claim, proceeding or suit against you for benefits payable by this insurance. We have the right to investigate and settle these claims, proceedings or suits.

We have no duty to defend a claim, proceeding or suit that is not covered by this insurance.

D. We Will Also Pay

We will also pay these costs, in addition to other amounts payable under this insurance, as part of any claim, proceeding or suit we defend:

1. reasonable expenses incurred at our request, but not loss of earnings;
2. premiums for bonds to release attachments and for appeal bonds in bond amounts up to the amount payable under this insurance;
3. litigation costs taxed against you;
4. interest on a judgment as required by law until we offer the amount due under this insurance; and
5. expenses we incur.

E. Other Insurance

We will not pay more than our share of benefits and costs covered by this insurance and other

WC 00 00 00 A   **WORKERS COMPENSATION AND EMPLOYERS LIABILITY INSURANCE POLICY**

<u>**Standard**</u>   Effective April 1, 1992   **1st Reprint**

insurance or self-insurance. Subject to any limits of liability that may apply, all shares will be equal until the loss is paid. If any insurance or self-insurance is exhausted, the shares of all remaining insurance will be equal until the loss is paid.

F. Payments You Must Make

You are responsible for any payments in excess of the benefits regularly provided by the workers compensation law including those required because:

1. of your serious and willful misconduct;
2. you knowingly employ an employee in violation of law;
3. you fail to comply with a health or safety law or regulation; or
4. you discharge, coerce or otherwise discriminate against any employee in violation of the workers compensation law.

If we make any payments in excess of the benefits regularly provided by the workers compensation law on your behalf, you will reimburse us promptly.

G. Recovery From Others

We have your rights, and the rights of persons entitled to the benefits of this insurance, to recover our payments from anyone liable for the injury. You will do everything necessary to protect those rights for us and to help us enforce them.

H. Statutory Provisions

These statements apply where they are required by law.

1. As between an injured worker and us, we have notice of the injury when you have notice.
2. Your default or the bankruptcy or insolvency of you or your estate will not relieve us of our duties under this insurance after an injury occurs.
3. We are directly and primarily liable to any person entitled to the benefits payable by this insurance. Those persons may enforce our duties; so may an agency authorized by law. Enforcement may be against us or against you and us.
4. Jurisdiction over you is jurisdiction over us for purposes of the workers compensation law. We are bound by decisions against you under that law, subject to the provisions of this policy that are not in conflict with that law.
5. This insurance conforms to the parts of the workers compensation law that apply to:

a. benefits payable by this insurance;

b. special taxes, payments into security or other special funds, and assessments payable by us under that law.

6. Terms of this insurance that conflict with the workers compensation law are changed by this statement to conform to that law.

Nothing in these paragraphs relieves you of your duties under this policy.

**PART TWO
EMPLOYERS LIABILITY INSURANCE**

A. How This Insurance Applies

This employers liability insurance applies to bodily injury by accident or bodily injury by disease. Bodily injury includes resulting death.

1. The bodily injury must arise out of and in the course of the injured employee's employment by you.
2. The employment must be necessary or incidental to your work in a state or territory listed in Item 3.A. of the Information Page.
3. Bodily injury by accident must occur during the policy period.
4. Bodily injury by disease must be caused or aggravated by the conditions of your employment. The employee's last day of last exposure to the conditions causing or aggravating such bodily injury by disease must occur during the policy period.
5. If you are sued, the original suit and any related legal actions for damages for bodily injury by accident or by disease must be brought in the United States of America, its territories or possessions, or Canada.

B. We Will Pay

We will pay all sums you legally must pay as damages because of bodily injury to your employees, provided the bodily injury is covered by this Employers Liability Insurance.

The damages we will pay, where recovery is permitted by law, include damages:

1. for which you are liable to a third party by reason of a claim or suit against you by that third party to recover the damages claimed against such third party as a result of injury to your employee;

WORKERS COMPENSATION AND EMPLOYERS LIABILITY INSURANCE POLICY   **WC 00 00 00 A**

1st Reprint   Effective April 1, 1992   **Standard**

2. for care and loss of services; and

3. for consequential bodily injury to a spouse, child, parent, brother or sister of the injured employee;

provided that these damages are the direct consequence of bodily injury that arises out of and in the course of the injured employee's employment by you; and

4. because of bodily injury to your employee that arises out of and in the course of employment, claimed against you in a capacity other than as employer

C. Exclusions

This insurance does not cover:

1. liability assumed under a contract. This exclusion does not apply to a warranty that your work will be done in a workmanlike manner;

2. punitive or exemplary damages because of bodily injury to an employee employed in violation of law;

3. bodily injury to an employee while employed in violation of law with your actual knowledge or the actual knowledge of any of your executive officers;

4. any obligation imposed by a workers compensation, occupational disease, unemployment compensation, or disability benefits law, or any similar law;

5. bodily injury intentionally caused or aggravated by you;

6. bodily injury occurring outside the United States of America, its territories or possessions, and Canada. This exclusion does not apply to bodily injury to a citizen or resident of the United States of America or Canada who is temporarily outside these countries;

7. damages arising out of coercion, criticism, demotion, evaluation, reassignment, discipline, defamation, harassment, humiliation, discrimination against or termination of any employee, or any personnel practices, policies, acts or omissions;

8. bodily injury to any person in work subject to the Longshore and Harbor Workers' Compensation Act (33 USC Sections 901–950), the Nonappropriated Fund Instrumentalities Act (5 USC Sections 8171–8173), the Outer Continental Shelf Lands Act (43 USC Sections 1331–1356), the Defense Base Act (42 USC Sections 1651–1654), the Federal Coal Mine Health and Safety Act of 1969 (30 USC Sections 901–942), any other federal workers or workmen's compensation law or other federal occupational disease law, or any amendments to these laws;

9. bodily injury to any person in work subject to the Federal Employers' Liability Act (45 USC Sections 51–60), any other federal laws obligating an employer to pay damages to an employee due to bodily injury arising out of or in the course of employment, or any amendments to those laws;

10. bodily injury to a master or member of the crew of any vessel;

11. fines or penalties imposed for violation of federal or state law; and

12. damages payable under the Migrant and Seasonal Agricultural Worker Protection Act (29 USC Sections 1801–1872) and under any other federal law awarding damages for violation of those laws or regulations issued thereunder, and any amendments to those laws.

D. We Will Defend

We have the right and duty to defend, at our expense, any claim, proceeding or suit against you for damages payable by this insurance. We have the right to investigate and settle these claims, proceedings and suits.

We have no duty to defend a claim, proceeding or suit that is not covered by this insurance. We have no duty to defend or continue defending after we have paid our applicable limit of liability under this insurance.

E. We Will Also Pay

We will also pay these costs, in addition to other amounts payable under this insurance, as part of any claim, proceeding, or suit we defend:

1. reasonable expenses incurred at our request, but not loss of earnings;

2. premiums for bonds to release attachments and for appeal bonds in bond amounts up to the limit of our liability under this insurance;

3. litigation costs taxed against you;

4. interest on a judgment as required by law until we offer the amount due under this insurance; and

5. expenses we incur.

WC 00 00 00 A   **WORKERS COMPENSATION AND EMPLOYERS LIABILITY INSURANCE POLICY**

<u>**Standard**</u>   Effective April 1, 1992   **1st Reprint**

F. Other Insurance

We will not pay more than our share of damages and costs covered by this insurance and other insurance or self-insurance. Subject to any limits of liability that apply, all shares will be equal until the loss is paid. If any insurance or self-insurance is exhausted, the shares of all remaining insurance and self-insurance will be equal until the loss is paid.

G. Limits of Liability

Our liability to pay for damages is limited. Our limits of liability are shown in Item 3.B. of the Information Page. They apply as explained below.

1. Bodily Injury by Accident. The limit shown for "bodily injury by accident—each accident" is the most we will pay for all damages covered by this insurance because of bodily injury to one or more employees in any one accident.

   A disease is not bodily injury by accident unless it results directly from bodily injury by accident.

2. Bodily Injury by Disease. The limit shown for "bodily injury by disease—policy limit" is the most we will pay for all damages covered by this insurance and arising out of bodily injury by disease, regardless of the number of employees who sustain bodily injury by disease. The limit shown for "bodily injury by disease—each employee" is the most we will pay for all damages because of bodily injury by disease to any one employee.

   Bodily injury by disease does not include disease that results directly from a bodily injury by accident.

3. We will not pay any claims for damages after we have paid the applicable limit of our liability under this insurance.

H. Recovery From Others

We have your rights to recover our payment from anyone liable for an injury covered by this insurance. You will do everything necessary to protect those rights for us and to help us enforce them.

I. Actions Against Us

There will be no right of action against us under this insurance unless:

1. You have complied with all the terms of this policy; and

2. The amount you owe has been determined with our consent or by actual trial and final judgment.

This insurance does not give anyone the right to add us as a defendant in an action against you to determine your liability. The bankruptcy or insolvency of you or your estate will not relieve us of our obligations under this Part.

PART THREE
OTHER STATES INSURANCE

A. How This Insurance Applies

1. This other states insurance applies only if one or more states are shown in Item 3.C. of the Information Page.

2. If you begin work in any one of those states after the effective date of this policy and are not insured or are not self-insured for such work, all provisions of the policy will apply as though that state were listed in Item 3.A. of the Information Page.

3. We will reimburse you for the benefits required by the workers compensation law of that state if we are not permitted to pay the benefits directly to persons entitled to them.

4. If you have work on the effective date of this policy in any state not listed in Item 3.A. of the Information Page, coverage will not be afforded for that state unless we are notified within thirty days.

B. Notice

Tell us at once if you begin work in any state listed in Item 3.C. of the Information Page.

PART FOUR
YOUR DUTIES IF INJURY OCCURS

Tell us at once if injury occurs that may be covered by this policy. Your other duties are listed here.

1. Provide for immediate medical and other services required by the workers compensation law.

2. Give us or our agent the names and addresses of the injured persons and of witnesses, and other information we may need.

WORKERS COMPENSATION AND EMPLOYERS LIABILITY INSURANCE POLICY   **WC 00 00 00 A**

<u>**1st Reprint**</u>   Effective April 1, 1992   **Standard**

3. Promptly give us all notices, demands and legal papers related to the injury, claim, proceeding or suit.

4. Cooperate with us and assist us, as we may request, in the investigation, settlement or defense of any claim, proceeding or suit.

5. Do nothing after an injury occurs that would interfere with our right to recover from others.

6. Do not voluntarily make payments, assume obligations or incur expenses, except at your own cost.

PART FIVE—PREMIUM

A. **Our Manuals**

All premium for this policy will be determined by our manuals of rules, rates, rating plans and classifications. We may change our manuals and apply the changes to this policy if authorized by law or a governmental agency regulating this insurance.

B. **Classifications**

Item 4 of the Information Page shows the rate and premium basis for certain business or work classifications. These classifications were assigned based on an estimate of the exposures you would have during the policy period. If your actual exposures are not properly described by those classifications, we will assign proper classifications, rates and premium basis by endorsement to this policy.

C. **Remuneration**

Premium for each work classification is determined by multiplying a rate times a premium basis. Remuneration is the most common premium basis. This premium basis includes payroll and all other remuneration paid or payable during the policy period for the services of:

1. all your officers and employees engaged in work covered by this policy; and

2. all other persons engaged in work that could make us liable under Part One (Workers Compensation Insurance) of this policy. If you do not have payroll records for these persons, the contract price for their services and materials may be used as the premium basis. This paragraph 2 will not apply if you give us proof that the employers of these persons lawfully secured their workers compensation obligations.

D. **Premium Payments**

You will pay all premium when due. You will pay the premium even if part or all of a workers compensation law is not valid.

E. **Final Premium**

The premium shown on the Information Page, schedules, and endorsements is an estimate. The final premium will be determined after this policy ends by using the actual, not the estimated, premium basis and the proper classifications and rates that lawfully apply to the business and work covered by this policy. If the final premium is more than the premium you paid to us, you must pay us the balance. If it is less, we will refund the balance to you. The final premium will not be less than the highest minimum premium for the classifications covered by this policy.

If this policy is canceled, final premium will be determined in the following way unless our manuals provide otherwise:

1. If we cancel, final premium will be calculated pro rata based on the time this policy was in force. Final premium will not be less than the pro rata share of the minimum premium.

2. If you cancel, final premium will be more than pro rata; it will be based on the time this policy was in force, and increased by our short-rate cancelation table and procedure. Final premium will not be less than the minimum premium.

F. **Records**

You will keep records of information needed to compute premium. You will provide us with copies of those records when we ask for them.

G. **Audit**

You will let us examine and audit all your records that relate to this policy. These records include ledgers, journals, registers, vouchers, contracts, tax reports, payroll and disbursement records, and programs for storing and retrieving data. We may conduct the audits during regular business hours during the policy period and within three years after the policy period ends. Information developed by audit will be used to determine final premium. Insurance rate service organizations have the same rights we have under this provision.

WC 00 00 00 A   **WORKERS COMPENSATION AND EMPLOYERS LIABILITY INSURANCE POLICY**

Standard   Effective April 1, 1992   **1st Reprint**

PART SIX – CONDITIONS

A. Inspection

We have the right, but are not obliged to inspect your workplaces at any time. Our inspections are not safety inspections. They relate only to the insurability of the workplaces and the premiums to be charged. We may give you reports on the conditions we find. We may also recommend changes. While they may help reduce losses, we do not undertake to perform the duty of any person to provide for the health or safety of your employees or the public. We do not warrant that your workplaces are safe or healthful or that they comply with laws, regulations, codes or standards. Insurance rate service organizations have the same rights we have under this provision.

B. Long Term Policy

If the policy period is longer than one year and sixteen days, all provisions of this policy will apply as though a new policy were issued on each annual anniversary that this policy is in force.

C. Transfer of Your Rights and Duties

Your rights or duties under this policy may not be transferred without our written consent.

If you die and we receive notice within thirty days after your death, we will cover your legal representative as insured.

D. Cancelation

1. You may cancel this policy. You must mail or deliver advance written notice to us stating when the cancelation is to take effect.

2. We may cancel this policy. We must mail or deliver to you not less than ten days advance written notice stating when the cancelation is to take effect. Mailing that notice to you at your mailing address shown in Item 1 of the Information Page will be sufficient to prove notice.

3. The policy period will end on the day and hour stated in the cancelation notice.

4. Any of these provisions that conflict with a law that controls the cancelation of the insurance in this policy is changed by this statement to comply with the law.

E. Sole Representative

The insured first named in Item 1 of the Information Page will act on behalf of all insureds to change this policy, receive return premium, and give or receive notice of cancelation.

Chapter 6

Direct Your Learning

Workers' Compensation Claim Administration

After learning the content of this chapter, you should be able to:

■ List the four types of notice of injury in the workers' compensation system and the requirements for each.

■ Explain how to determine coverage for a workers' compensation claim.

■ Given a case, explain how workers' compensation reserves are set.

■ Describe the factors that affect workers' compensation reserves and the pitfalls adjusters should avoid in setting reserves.

■ Given a case, explain how to conduct an investigation of a workers' compensation claim.

■ Describe the procedures and issues involved in paying and managing workers' compensation claims.

■ Explain why and how state second injury funds operate.

■ Describe the issues relating to procedures insurers follow in terminating workers' compensation benefits.

■ Describe the procedures for denying a workers' compensation claim.

■ Explain how a disputed workers' compensation claim can be settled.

■ Describe the ramifications if an unlicensed adjuster is found to be handling claims in a state that requires licensing.

■ Explain how and why penalties may be assessed for mishandling claims.

■ Describe a workers' compensation adjuster's role in loss control and workplace safety.

Develop Your Perspective

What are the main topics covered in the chapter?

This chapter discusses workers' compensation claim issues such as notice, compensability, amount of benefits, investigation of the accident or injury, and medical treatment rendered.

Consider your responsibilities as an injured worker to give notice of your injury to your employer.

- What types of notice are acceptable?
- Why is prompt notice important to a workers' compensation claim?

Why is it important to learn about these topics?

Workers' compensation adjusters must determine compensability and the amount of benefits to be paid. To determine compensability, the adjuster must investigate the notice given to the employer, the circumstances of the accident or injury, and the medical treatment being rendered. The adjuster uses all this information to set reserves, pay benefits, and bring the claim to an ultimate conclusion.

Consider a possible workers' compensation loss in your company.

- If a worker hurts her back while putting paper in the copier, what questions might the workers' compensation adjuster ask?
- What action(s) might the adjuster take based on the answers to these questions?

How can you use what you will learn?

Analyze a closed workers' compensation claim.

- What investigation was completed before the claim was accepted or denied?
- How did the adjuster assess the cost of this claim and set the reserve?
- How was the claim ultimately resolved?

Chapter 6

Workers' Compensation Claim Administration

This chapter discusses the processes and procedures adjusters use in handling workers' compensation claims. Many of the procedures within each phase of the process are set out in the state workers' compensation statute. Many other important procedures are the responsibility of and are initiated by insurers, third-party administrators (TPAs), and the adjusters who handle claims for them.

To accomplish their purpose of providing a timely remedy for work-related injuries, workers' compensation laws specify the process for handling a claim, starting with notice of injury. Upon receipt of a notice of loss, insurers make a determination of coverage. Insurers that use third-party or independent adjusters often perform preliminary investigations of coverage before assigning out claims. This process will often eliminate non-covered claims before they are assigned to outside adjusters.

After a claim is assigned, the adjuster makes an initial case assessment and sets reserves based on the known facts. The compensability of a claim and the nature and extent of the disability are investigated simultaneously. Traditionally, the adjuster performs both investigations, but in some companies, the adjuster investigates the compensability issues, and a medical case manager addresses medical treatment and disability issues.

The claim process also includes payment or denial of benefits, termination of benefits, appeal of contested claims, and settlement. Adjusters should know the specific legal requirements involved in each phase of the claim process for the state(s) in which they handle claims. Exhibit 6-1 illustrates the claim process.

NOTICE OF INJURY REQUIREMENTS

Promptness in claim handling is emphasized in the workers' compensation claim process, starting with the initial notice of the injury. The four kinds of notice are (1) notice from the worker to the employer, (2) notice from the worker to the state workers' compensation agency, (3) notice from the employer to the state workers' compensation agency, and (4) notice from the employer/insured to the insurer. The first three are required by statute. The fourth is required by the WC&EL policy. The notices and their requirements are explained next.

EXHIBIT 6-1

The Claim Process

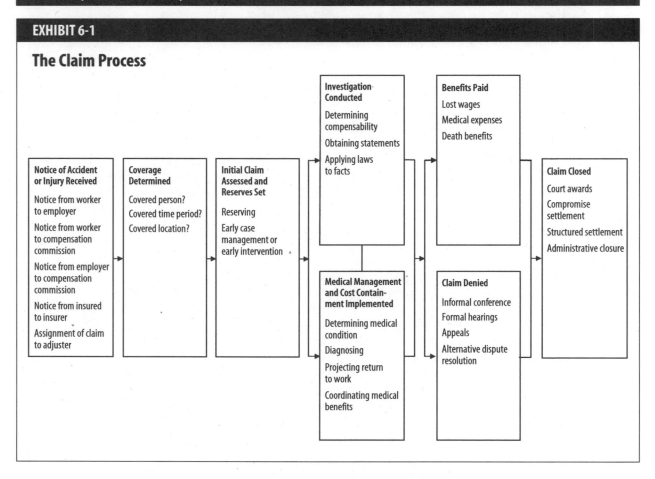

Notice of Accident or Injury Received

Notice from worker to employer

Notice from worker to compensation commission

Notice from employer to compensation commission

Notice from insured to insurer

Assignment of claim to adjuster

Coverage Determined

Covered person?

Covered time period?

Covered location?

Initial Claim Assessed and Reserves Set

Reserving

Early case management or early intervention

Investigation Conducted

Determining compensability

Obtaining statements

Applying laws to facts

Medical Management and Cost Containment Implemented

Determining medical condition

Diagnosing

Projecting return to work

Coordinating medical benefits

Benefits Paid

Lost wages

Medical expenses

Death benefits

Claim Denied

Informal conference

Formal hearings

Appeals

Alternative dispute resolution

Claim Closed

Court awards

Compromise settlement

Structured settlement

Administrative closure

Notice From Worker to Employer

Because the workers' compensation system requires prompt claim payments, every state specifies a time limit in which the notice of accident or injury must be given. Thirty days is the most common period, although some statutes require notice "immediately," "forthwith," or "as soon as practicable." Others allow as long as ninety days.

Notice of the accident or injury need not be in writing. Oral notice from the worker to the employer is sufficient. In some cases, constructive notice, such as an employer's witnessing a slip and fall, is sufficient. Virtually no compensation commission will deny benefits simply because the injured worker's notice was unwritten.

No legal requirement mandates that an injured worker's accident or injury be witnessed. An absence of witnesses might be one indication among many that a claim should be closely investigated. However, that fact alone does not defeat a claim.

Although statutes emphasize timely notice, a delay in notice is unlikely to be a sufficient reason to deny a workers' compensation claim. Most workers' compensation statutes permit late notices of injury when the delay is excusable. Other circumstances under which compensation boards might tolerate late notification, or even lack of notification, include the following:

- The injured worker was not initially aware of the injury's severity, extent, or prognosis.
- The employer had actual or constructive notice of the accident or injury. **Actual notice** occurs when a worker directly informs the supervisor of the injury. **Constructive notice** occurs when the employer is deemed to know of the injury, even without direct notification, such as when a supervisor observes a worker's injury. The worker's failure to give formal notice does not allow the employer to avoid playing a claim.
- The symptoms of the occupational disease did not manifest themselves until some time after the exposure had occurred.

The absence of prompt notice does not necessarily prejudice the employer's or its insurer's ability to investigate or defend against the claim. Prejudice means that the employer's or the insurer's ability to investigate or defend against the claim has been hampered. For instance, a delay in notice would prejudice a case when key witnesses are no longer available or are unable to accurately recall the circumstances leading to the injury because of the passage of time or because evidence has been destroyed. It is not necessarily the duration of the delay but the effect that the delay has on the employer's or insurer's investigation and on its subsequent ability to defend against the claim that constitutes prejudice.

Actual notice
In workers' compensation, an injured worker's verbal or written notification to an employer of the injury or of the accident causing it.

Constructive notice
In workers' compensation, notification that is inferred because the employer knows or has reason to know the accident or injury has occurred.

Notice From Worker to Compensation Commission

Many state laws require the worker to notify the workers' compensation commission of the accident or injury, although the commission might receive such notice from the employer. Compensation commissions are usually flexible about the form of such notice from the worker. A handwritten note can suffice.

Notice From Employer to Compensation Commission

Employers give notice to compensation commissions by filing an "employer's first report" as required by statute. States supply forms for this purpose. The adjuster should carefully review the wording of the employer's first report. In some states, the report is considered an admission against interest (a statement that may be adverse to the utterer's position) and is therefore admissible in court as proof of its contents. Consequently, an employer who writes the employer's first report stating that the accident happened might be later estopped from asserting that the accident had never occurred. Any inconsistencies found in the employer's first report should be investigated before the report is submitted.

Most states require an employer's first report within a prescribed number of days after the accident. Failure to do so can subject the employer to fines or penalties. Some states allow the insurer or the third-party administrator to make this filing on behalf of the employer.

Notice From Insured to Insurer

Workers' compensation policies require the insured/employer to provide prompt, if not immediate, notice of injury to the insurer. The National Council on Compensation Insurance (NCCI) standard Workers Compensation and Employers Liability Insurance Policy (WC&EL) states: "Tell us at once if injury occurs that may be covered by this policy."[1] Because "at once" is not quantified, courts can determine what is a reasonable time. Usually, to deny coverage because of late notice, the insurer must prove that its ability to investigate or defend the workers' compensation claim was prejudiced. Adjusters trying to deny coverage based on late notice must have strong grounds for doing so.

The notice of claim for the accident or injury must contain the following information:

- Injured worker's name, address, social security number, and phone number
- Employer's name, address, and contact information
- Injured worker's wage information
- Injury information including the date, time, and place of injury, names of any witnesses, name and address of the treating doctor, and a description of how the injury occurred

PRELIMINARY POLICY REVIEW

To determine coverage, the adjuster must review the notice of injury for items relating to the WC&EL policy. Most states require that relevant policy information be included on claim notice forms. When an insurer opens a claim, the related policy information should be attached to the file for the adjuster to review. The adjuster must compare the insurer's policy information to the details provided on the notice of injury form.

The date of injury must fall within the policy's coverage dates. The adjuster should notify the policy underwriter when an injury date falls outside the coverage period. Most injuries occurring outside the coverage period are not covered, with a few exceptions. An example of an exception would be when a policy is in negotiation during a lapse in coverage.

The notice of injury form should indicate the primary insured location as well as the accident location. The preliminary coverage review should verify that the accident location is listed on the policy. An employer might have coverage during the time of the injury but might not have all locations insured. If the worker was injured at a location not listed on the policy, the adjuster should contact the underwriter to make sure the claim file has current information about covered locations.

The injured worker's employment status affects coverage, for example, as previously mentioned, WC&EL policies do not normally cover independent contractors. Adjusters should always confirm the injured worker's employment status with the employer. Employers normally notify adjusters of questionable employment relationships. In many policies, especially for small businesses, the owners are excluded from workers' compensation coverage. Because notice of injury forms do not usually indicate whether an injured worker is the business's owner, adjusters should check the policy owner's name. If questions remain concerning the injured worker's employment status, the adjuster should seek the advice of counsel before making a determination.

In most cases, adjusters can determine coverage simply by reading the WC&EL policy. In some cases, however, they may need more information and may take the statement of the employer, the injured worker, or the producer to clarify a coverage issue.

Following are some examples of situations that should alert the adjuster to the need for further investigation during a coverage review:

- Insured's prejudicial delay in reporting a claim to the insurer
- Injury to an out-of-state worker
- Material misrepresentation of the type of loss exposure (for example, an insured who completed the insurance application as a fireworks retailer is found to be manufacturing fireworks).
- Injured worker's failure to cooperate with the insurer in investigating or defending the claim
- Suspected collusion between the employer and the injured worker to obtain workers' compensation benefits when payment is unwarranted

When an adjuster is faced with a coverage question, the considerations for workers' compensation claims are no different from those for handling a coverage problem for any other insurance policy. The adjuster must be careful to avoid actions that would cause the insurer to lose its rights to coverage defenses. Such actions include waiver, a voluntary relinquishment of a right; and estoppel, a bar to asserting a right. To avoid waiver and estoppel, the adjuster should send a reservation of rights letter to the employer specifically stating the insurer's intention to preserve its rights to coverage defenses or should obtain a signed nonwaiver agreement from the employer. When coverage questions remain, judicial resolution can come in the form of a declaratory judgment, a court's determination about whether coverage exists.

INITIAL ASSESSMENT AND RESERVING

Once a claim is assigned, the adjuster must estimate the claim's cost and set this amount as a reserve. **Reserves** are amounts shown as liabilities on an insurer's financial statements that represent how much is expected to be paid on all existing but not yet settled claims. A reserve on an individual case is an

Reserves
The liabilities on an insurer's financial records that represent the amount it expects to pay on all existing but not yet settled claims.

amount the insurer sets aside to cover the claim's ultimate cost. (Reserves for incurred but not reported [IBNR] losses are set separately and are projected by actuaries to estimate the financial effect of losses that have occurred but have not yet been reported to the insurer.) Reserving—assessing the claim's ultimate value based on known facts—occurs as part of a claim's early assessment. Reserves are subject to change as more information is obtained throughout the claim process. Reserving procedures differ by insurer. Some insurers set standard initial reserves immediately upon receipt of a notice of injury. Other insurers set a seven- or fourteen-day deadline for investigating a claim and determining a reserve amount.

Adjusters handling workers' compensation claims must be thoroughly familiar with proper reserve practices. Underreserving or overreserving can damage an insurer's financial condition. **Underreserving**—setting case reserves that fall short of a claim's actual costs—is a major cause of insurer insolvency, particularly if it has been a continuing practice. **Overreserving**—setting reserves higher than actual claim costs—misrepresents an insurer's balance sheets, restricts its ability to write new business, and leads to excessive insurance rates.

> **Underreserving**
> The practice of setting case reserves that fall short of the actual claim costs.

> **Overreserving**
> The practice of setting case reserves too high to avoid underreserving and stair-stepping.

Accurate loss reserves are also important to insureds because they affect policy premiums. For example, many insureds have workers' compensation coverage under a prospective experience rating plan or a paid loss retrospective rating plan (paid loss retro plan). Prospective experience rating plans base policyholders' premiums in a current policy period on the losses incurred in the previous experience periods, usually three years excluding the most recent year. Misstated reserves for losses during the experience period affect an insured's premium in the current policy period. Paid loss retro plans base the premiums for the current policy period on losses incurred during the current policy period. The insured pays a deposit premium at the beginning of the policy period; then, at the close of the policy period, the premium is adjusted to reflect the insured's actual loss experience. Because incurred losses include reserves, not just amounts actually paid, the adjuster's reserve decisions can directly affect a policyholder's budget.

Reserving Factors

Workers' compensation claims fall into three categories:

1. Medical only, for which some medical treatment is provided but no time is lost from work
2. Lost time claims, for which medical treatment and rehabilitation are provided and time is lost from work
3. Fatalities

Whether handling medical-only claims or lost-time claims, the adjuster must have an analytical method for setting reserves. Workers' compensation reserves are typically separated into three components: (1) wage loss, (2) medical costs and case management, and (3) other expenses. Wage loss reserves are for lost-time benefits. Medical reserves are for medical and case management expenses. Other expense reserves include private surveillance firm expenses, medical record expenses, legal fees for defense attorneys, and court reporter fees. Other expense reserves have not always been reserved separately; however, with the increase in litigation costs, most insurers now require a separate reserve that can be tracked independently from wage loss and medical payments. Reserving for fatalities is a slightly different process and is discussed separately. The following is a list of the factors affecting reserves.

Factors Affecting Reserves

- Nature and extent of disability
- Preexisting medical conditions
- Anticipated medical costs
- Amount of average weekly wage
- Attorney involvement
- Defense attorney
- Claim history of the injured worker
- Realistic assessments of the likelihood of winning contested claims
- Venue or state
- Injured worker's age
- Injured worker's occupation
- Availability of transitional employment
- Injured worker's employability, re-employability, or trainability
- Union status
- Motivation of injured worker
- Possibility of subrogation

Workers' compensation reserves are usually based on the facts of an individual case and the following factors:

- *Nature and extent of injury.* Generally, a soft tissue injury (usually an injury to ligaments, tendons, or muscles) is reserved for a lower amount than a fracture. A widespread burn might be reserved at a higher amount than a fracture. The diagnosis, from the medical reports, should give the adjuster some guidance about the expected number of weeks of disability. Tables and guidebooks that set out the typical disability time for various injuries are available to adjusters.

- *Preexisting medical conditions.* Conditions such as diabetes and high blood pressure can complicate (and increase the cost of) treatment of a work-related injury.

- *Anticipated medical costs.* Costs for the emergency room, ambulance, treating physician, any specialists/consultants, X-rays, surgery, hospitalization, lab work, medication, physical therapy, and nursing services should be included.

- *Amount of average weekly wage.* Because the weekly wage loss rate is a function of the average weekly wage, the higher the injured worker's compensation rate, the higher the reserve.

- *Injured worker's attorney involvement.* An attorney's involvement can mean a higher reserve for several reasons. Injured workers represented by attorneys might have a greater incentive to remain out of work, thereby increasing the cost of the claim. Communicating with the worker and scheduling independent medical exams (IMEs) can become more complex because any communications with the injured worker must be done through the attorney.

- *Defense attorney involvement.* If the insurer must retain an attorney to deal with contested issues, the adjuster must factor in legal and defense fees, often identified as a separate reserve for "other expenses."

- *Injured worker's claim history.* A claim by a worker who has had previous compensation claims can be expected to require higher reserves than a claim by a worker who has never been hurt on the job, other factors being equal.

- *Realistic predictions for winning contested claims.* No matter how serious the injury, if the employer/insurer has an airtight defense and the injured worker's claim is implausible, that information should be factored into the reserve. However, such cases are extremely rare. Compensation boards deny very few claims outright. For that reason, some insurers' policies dictate reserving on the basis of "injury exposure" alone, without considering any possibilities of successfully denying compensability.

- *Venue or state.* States workers' compensation benefit maximums vary, and state compensation boards' approaches to denying claims also vary. Adjusters must consider these differences in benefits and in rates of denial when setting reserves.

- *Injured worker's age.* Generally, the younger the worker, the better the chance for a faster medical recovery and return to work and, therefore, the lower the reserves. A fracture of a weight-bearing bone might heal well in a young person but result in a serious disability for a sixty-two-year-old. Disc surgery on an older worker eighteen months from retirement might yield a longer TTD period than the same injury to a twenty-five-year-old salesperson. Conversely, a catastrophic injury, such as paralysis, to a young person can be extremely expensive and require higher reserves if the injured person survives the full work life expectancy.

- *Injured worker's occupation.* An orthopedic injury for a carpenter might require a higher reserve than the same injury for an office worker. Some adjusters believe that management-level workers identify more with company goals and are more motivated to return to work than are hourly workers, thus requiring lower reserves for the same type of injury. Office workers might have more job opportunities than tradespersons, calling for lower reserves.

- *Availability of transitional employment.* **Transitional employment** provides injured workers with job duties they can perform before returning to full employment. Transitional employment is considered part of the recovery process. Workers can return to work sooner if transitional employment is available, rather than waiting until they are sufficiently recovered to return to full employment. The availability of transitional employment, which varies with employers, is a moderating factor in establishing reserves.

- *Injured worker's employability, re-employability, or trainability.* Because of factors such as age, attitude, and education, some people are more likely than others to be able to learn new skills and change the type of work they do. These factors must be considered when setting reserves.

- *Union status.* Union rules might forbid transitional employment, and reserve estimates should be made accordingly.

- *Motivation.* The injured worker's motivation to return to work (or the employer's motivation to have the injured worker return) is a subjective factor. Many adjusters are able to identify situations in which motivation might be a problem; for example, a dissatisfied worker might seek to use workers' compensation as an escape from a job, or an employer might want to get rid of a troublesome worker. Because motivational problems can complicate a claim, they should be considered when setting reserves.

- *Subrogation.* If it appears that some or all of the workers' compensation benefits will be recovered from a responsible third party, these offsets can be reflected in the reserves. Some insurers do not factor the potential recovery into their reserves, preferring to reserve for the amount that will actually be paid out in benefits.

Transitional employment
The job duties an injured worker can perform before a return to full employment.

Reserving for Fatalities

For fatality claims, not all of the preceding factors, such as employability and transitional employment issues, are relevant. For fatality claims, however, the adjuster must consider the following additional factors:

- *Marital status.* Most workers' compensation statutes offer specific wage loss benefits to a deceased's survivors and consider dependency in determining survivors' entitlement to death benefits. The more dependents, the higher the reserve; for example the reserve for a single person with no dependents is lower than that for a married person with three children. The adjuster should consider the state's regulations about death benefits and should check birth and death certificates and court records or get a statement from survivors to clarify survivors' dependency status.

- *Surviving spouse's life expectancy.* Some states pay death benefits to a surviving spouse for life, others pay benefits for a set period, such as

500 weeks. In either case, the surviving spouse's life expectancy and state of health affect the reserve. The death benefit reserve for a thirty-three-year-old in good health would normally be higher than for a sixty-eight-year-old with chronic obstructive pulmonary disease. However, in states that terminate death benefits upon the surviving spouse's remarriage, the spouse's chances of remarriage should also be a factor in setting reserves.

Reserving Methods

Reserving methods include the individual case method, the formula method, and the round-table method. The **individual case method** is the most common. It is usually done with the aid of a worksheet and reevaluated at six-month intervals or when circumstances change. Adjusters complete the worksheet and set the reserve, considering the factors previously discussed along with their experience in similar cases. Individual case reserving is subjective and more of an art than a science. The strength of this method is that the adjuster considers the many factors that affect each case's value and tailors each reserve to the specific claim. The disadvantage of this method is that it is subjective, so reserves can vary widely by adjuster. It can also be time-consuming to examine all of the individual reserve factors.

Individual case method
A method an adjuster uses to set workers' compensation claim reserves based on the facts of the claim and the adjuster's experience with similar claims.

Adjusters use worksheets like the one illustrated in Exhibit 6-2 to calculate workers' compensation reserves and to review them periodically. Insurers use a variety of worksheets, most of them computer-generated.

Formula reserves expedite the setting of initial reserves. With the **formula method**, a mathematical formula is used to set reserves. A formula might, for example, set a back surgery case reserve at the weekly compensation rate multiplied by the average number of weeks for recovery from surgery. Similarly, an arm fracture might be reserved at the TTD rate multiplied by a predesignated number of weeks, usually the average number of weeks for a fracture to heal. Another formula could be based on a ratio of medical cost to wage loss on a claim, for example, setting wage loss reserves at 90 to 100 percent of the medical reserve. The weakness of the formula method is that it fails to account for differences from claim to claim and can, therefore, be arbitrary. The strengths of the formula method are that it is quicker to learn, to teach, and to apply than the individual case method, and it can be computer-generated. Because it is less subjective, results vary little among adjusters for claims with similar factors. However, formulas vary by insurer and by software application.

Formula method
A method an adjuster uses to set workers' compensation claim reserves by applying a formula to assign an injury a specific number of weeks of benefits and multiplying the number of weeks by the weekly compensation rate.

The **round-table method**, or claim committee method, involves two or more adjusters, who each evaluate a claim file and suggest a reserve. Ideally, none should initially know the amounts the others have set. The adjusters discuss their reserve amounts and either reach a consensus reserve amount or compute an average of all the amounts. Because this technique is so time-consuming, it is used only for the most serious workers' compensation claims. Its strength lies in the exchange of knowledge among team members, who have differing experiences and areas of expertise.

Round-table method
A method for setting workers' compensation claim reserves by which two or more adjusters evaluate the claim and reach a consensus on the reserve amount.

EXHIBIT 6-2

Workers' Compensation Reserve Worksheet

INJURY CLAIM OF _____   ☐ Initial ☐ Revised _____
                                                                                                            (Date)

GENERAL FACTORS: Date of Injury _____   Jurisdiction _____

☐ Medical Only   ☐ Lost Time   ☐ Death, Permanent Total Disability

Cause of Injury: _____   Subrogation: ☐ Yes   ☐ No

Nature of Injury: _____

Attorney Representation: ☐ Yes   ☐ No _____

ANTICIPATED MEDICAL TREATMENT: ☐ Approved

    Principal Treating Physician: _____   ☐ Not Approved

    TYPE OF MEDICAL:

    Emergency Room Costs $ _____

    Ambulance $ _____

    Treating Physician $ _____

    Specialist, Consultant $ _____

    X-Rays, Radiologist $ _____

    Surgery $ _____

    Hospitalization (_____ days @ $ _____) $ _____

    Other Hospital Fees $ _____

    Laboratory Costs $ _____

    Drugs, Medical Supplies $ _____

    Physical Therapy $ _____

    Other Medical Costs (_____) $ _____ $ _____
                Subtotal

FUNERAL BENEFITS: $ _____ $ _____

TOTAL MEDICAL RESERVE WITHOUT CONSIDERATION OF SUBROGATION OR CONTRIBUTION $ _____

Less Anticipated Subrogation Recovery or Contribution   – $ _____

                    TOTAL ESTIMATED MEDICAL RESERVE $ ═══════════

DISABILITY:

Required Compensation Rate: $ _____   Week   ☐ Applicable   ☐ Not Applicable

Anticipated Disability Period: _____   Weeks Total Disability

Anticipated Disability Period: _____   Weeks Partial Disability

Waiting Period: ☐ Applicable   ☐ Not Applicable

Anticipated Disability Benefits Due: $ _____

PERMANENCY:

Nature of Disability: _____

Award Basis: Part of Body: _____   Percent of Body: _____ %

Anticipated Scheduled Award: Cash $ _____   No. Weeks: _____ × _____ $ _____

Vocational Costs $ _____   Attorney Fee: _____ $ _____

                                   SUBTOTAL $ _____

Continued on next page.

DEATH BENEFITS:

No. Dependents _____   Age(s) of Dependent Children _____

Age of Surviving Spouse _____   Surviving Spouse's Life Expectancy _____

Maximum Award/Cost $ _____

TOTAL INDEMNITY RESERVE WITHOUT CONSIDERATION OF SUBROGATION OR CONTRIBUTION $ _____

Less Anticipated Subrogation Recovery or Contribution   − $ _____

                                                            TOTAL ESTIMATED INDEMNITY RESERVE $ ================

OTHER COSTS:

Defense $ _____   Other $ _____   Explain: _____

                                                            TOTAL ESTIMATED EXPENSE RESERVE $ ================

Completed By _____   Approved By _____
                                        (Date)   (Date)

THIS WORKSHEET IS INTENDED TO BE USED ONLY AS A TOOL FOR PROJECTING MAXIMUM RESERVE EXPOSURE AND SHOULD NOT BE USED AS THE FINAL CLAIM EVALUATION OR AUTHORIZATION FOR SETTLEMENT PURPOSES.

Adjusters' claim reserve decisions are not necessarily final. They are subject to revision as the facts of the claim develop, and they are subject to review by claim supervisors. On an aggregate basis, claim managers monitor reserve trends within their offices or departments. Corporate management assesses reserve trends on a companywide basis. Therefore, checks and balances exist within insurer organizational structures to monitor reserve adequacy and accuracy.

Reserves are typically dynamic. Many factors can change throughout the life of a claim and can prompt reserve revisions. Claim departments need management controls to ensure that reserves are not only accurately set initially but also regularly reviewed. Periodic review of reserves is crucial to avoid the common pitfalls that harm a company's financial condition, as discussed next.

Reserving Pitfalls

Three common reserving pitfalls are underreserving, stair-stepping, and over-reserving. Adjusters can avoid these pitfalls by reviewing the claim reserves each time new information surfaces and by checking to ensure that reserves posted are appropriate for the known facts every time they work on the claim.

Underreserving, that is, setting reserves that fall short of the actual claim costs, can be caused by unforeseeable claim developments or by an adjuster's inexperience or inattention. Optimism about a when a worker will return to duty or about the likelihood of winning a contested claim or lack of time to analyze case reserves sufficiently can produce an unrealistically low reserve amount. Failing to correct understated reserves promptly when discovered can adversely affect an insurer's profitability and financial condition.

Adjusters should also avoid **stair-stepping** reserves, the practice of initially reserving a claim inadequately and then updating the reserves continually. The adjuster, instead of establishing a sufficient reserve based on the realistic value of the claim, sets only enough reserve to cover costs for the immediate future. Then, when payments meet or exceed the established reserve, the figure is increased for another round of payments. The problem with stair-stepping is that the true value of the claim does not become evident to senior claim management until perhaps years after the initial reserve was set, meaning that cost-control procedures that might have helped to reduce the overall loss exposure were never considered. Furthermore, stair-stepping can mislead the insurer into delaying a report to a reinsurer or, in a serious liability claim, in delaying notification of the policyholder of a potential excess loss situation.

Stair-stepping
The practice of making incremental increases in claim reserves without any significant change in the facts of the claim.

Few initial reserves on claims that are open for more than a few weeks remain accurate over the long run unless the loss is reserved for policy limits. Therefore, most claim reserves must be reevaluated as additional information about the loss is received. This reevaluation can occur often enough that the claim appears to be stair-stepped. However, reevaluation is quite different from stair-stepping, and the evaluation should more accurately represent both positive and negative loss factors.

Overreserving, setting an unrealistically high reserve, is a way to avoid under-reserving and stair-stepping, but it distorts an insurer's financial picture. With inaccurately high reserves, the insurer's net income and net worth both appear smaller than they are. In response, the insurer might be reluctant to write new business and might raise premiums unnecessarily. Overreserving also skews loss development analysis.

INVESTIGATING COVERAGE AND COMPENSABILITY ISSUES AND MEDICAL ISSUES

After an adjuster receives notice of an injury and confirms coverage by reviewing the policy, the investigation process begins. The extent to which a claim should be investigated depends on the claim's potential severity and the accident's circumstances. Adjusters should avoid over-investigating minor claims and under-investigating major ones.

Investigation issues fall into two broad categories: (1) coverage and compensability issues and (2) medical issues. This section discusses investigation of both types of issues as well as the additional issues that arise in investigating claims involving automobile accidents, fatalities, and products liability.

In addition to being covered, a claim must be compensable. To investigate coverage and compensability in workers' compensation, an adjuster must determine whether an injury occurred in the course and scope of employment. The concept of whether a claim "arises out of and in the course of employment" have been previously discussed. Most work-related injuries are clearly related to the job, but when the relationship is unclear, a thorough investigation of all related facts is required. Adjusters may take statements from the involved parties and might also conduct an on-site investigation.

Statements and Scene Investigation

To determine coverage and compensability in claims involving lost time from work, an effective investigation should include (1) statements from the injured worker, the employer, and any witnesses; (2) a visit to the accident location; (3) information about prior injuries and accidents; (4) investigation of the worker's post-accident activities; and (5) medical investigation. In some cases, such as most medical only or no-lost-time claims, statements are not needed. Some insurers require statements only for claims that involve specific disabilities of a defined level of severity or injury (for example, hernia, disc surgery, and amputation). Other insurers require statements whenever the facts surrounding an injury are questionable.

When conducting interviews, the adjuster must seek information about what occurred before, during, and after the injury. Determining what occurred before an injury helps the adjuster construct the chain of events that led to the accident. With this information, the adjuster might broaden the investigation to include activities of the injured person and witnesses before the accident, preexisting medical conditions, and previous claim activity. In some cases, what a person was doing the night before, or days before, could be relevant. For example, if the adjuster suspects that the injured worker's intoxication caused the accident, the adjuster should determine what the injured worker was doing before the accident. If a worker has had a heart attack at work, the adjuster might seek to determine whether the worker had any related symptoms days before. If an injury is reported on a Monday morning, the adjuster might inquire about activities that occurred over the weekend that might have caused the injury. Much of this information can be obtained while visiting the accident scene and interviewing witnesses.

Before interviewing an injured worker, the adjuster should determine if the worker is represented by an attorney. If the worker has retained counsel, the adjuster should contact the attorney to arrange an interview of the worker. When conducting an interview, the adjuster should ask the worker to describe his or her specific job duties and activities. This information helps the adjuster estimate the likely extent of the disability in relation to the job. A worker who must lift twenty-pound packages all day might require a longer period of disability before returning to work from a back injury than someone with the same injury who drives a forklift and only occasionally does heavy lifting. The worker should also provide related details about the job, such as wages, hours, and additional compensation. The adjuster should ask detailed questions and request detailed responses so that someone reading or hearing the statement can visualize what the injured worker is describing. A sample of an injured worker's statement outline, with annotations, can be found in Appendix A.

After taking the worker's statement, the adjuster should obtain a signed release from the worker for medical and wage information. The authorization should contain language stating that it complies with the requirements of the Health Insurance Portability and Accountability Act (HIPAA).

An investigation might include (1) statements from co-workers who witnessed the accident; (2) a statement from the immediate supervisor about the worker's job duties, length of employment, and the supervisor's opinions about the claim; and (3) a copy of the worker's personnel file with the initial employment application, any pre-employment physical report (if the appropriate authorization has been given), copies of any previous workers' compensation claims, information about any disciplinary action, employment history, and the wage statement.

For claims of questionable compensability or those with a potential for subrogation, the adjuster should conduct a witness investigation, that is, take statements from co-workers or others who witnessed the injury. Such statements can help (1) determine whether an injury occurred and, if so, whether it was work-related; (2) determine the cause of an injury; and (3) confirm or rule out the accident's connection to the workers' compensation claim.

Witnesses, co-workers, and supervisors should be asked to describe what they know or what they saw, not what they were told or later heard. Supervisors often have valuable information about the worker's work history and habits. Many questionable claims arise after a worker has been disciplined or reprimanded at work. Typical questions for interviewing witnesses and employers/supervisors are listed in Appendix A. The list is a guideline and is not all-inclusive. Some questions are appropriate only when the claim raises suspicions.

Appendix B provides a list of possible indicators of workers' compensation fraud. Although most claims are legitimate, fraudulent claims cost insurers billions of dollars, costs that are passed on to consumers in the form of premiums. A thorough investigation of the claim is the best defense against fraud. The presence of even several of these indicators does not necessarily indicate fraud, but it does indicate the need for additional investigation. These indicators should help adjusters organize their investigative time by isolating claims that suggest the possibility of fraud.

Adjusters who suspect fraud should involve their Special Investigation Unit (SIU) in the investigation as early as possible. The SIU investigator assists the adjuster in the fraud investigation and prepares the reports required by the state and various fraud bureaus.

Prior Injury and Accident Investigation

Whether or not a claim is suspected of being fraudulent, investigating prior injuries and accidents can provide information that can be used to challenge the credibility of a worker who has denied prior accidents or injuries, can suggest other sources of exposure to occupational disease and other causes of the injury, and can help establish second injury fund relief (explained later in this chapter). The following sources of information about prior injuries or accidents are available to the adjuster:

- Index bureaus, to which insurers and self-insureds can subscribe, furnish on request printouts of any prior claims an injured worker has filed.
- The local workers' compensation commission might be able to confirm whether any claims are on file for a particular injured worker.
- Motor vehicle records might provide evidence of prior auto accidents and injury claims.

Post-Accident Activity Investigation

The adjuster's investigative responsibilities do not end when compensation benefits are awarded. Although a claim is accepted as compensable, the adjuster might be able to demonstrate that the injured worker is not prevented from working. Medical evidence is important to prove the extent of the disability (see later discussion about medical investigation). Nonmedical evidence might show that the worker's injuries are not as severe as they appear to the treating physician. For example, evidence that the worker is employed elsewhere or has been engaging in vigorous physical activities can defeat a disability claim.

Adjusters can use several tactics to investigate a worker's post-accident activities, including observing the person for the purpose of confirming the credibility of the worker's statements and medical reports claiming disability. In an activity check, the adjuster or investigator visits the worker's neighborhood and questions neighbors about the worker's general level of physical activity. Investigators should candidly identify their interests and never misrepresent their identity to the neighbors. They should also refrain from making any remarks impugning the injured worker's integrity.

If the claim warrants the expense, a professional investigator or private surveillance team should be hired. Many surveillance firms have specially equipped vans for staking out a house or a neighborhood. They try to obtain photos or videotapes to document an injured worker's ability to perform physical activity, such as lifting, bending, walking, yard work, home repair, or athletic activity.

An adjuster, in consultation with the SIU investigator, should consider retaining an outside surveillance firm when possible fraud indicators such as the following are encountered:

- Inconclusive medical opinions in which physicians can provide only subjective medical findings
- Difficulty contacting a worker whose disability would most likely keep him or her at home
- The worker's frequent cancellation of appointments with physicians, other practitioners, and the adjuster

- A longer duration of recovery for the type of injury as compared to recovery guidelines and the experience of others with similar injuries
- Premature involvement of the worker's attorney in the claim
- Information from co-workers or anonymous sources that the injured worker is active
- Observation of the injured worker performing restricted activities

The adjuster should establish a plan and budget with the surveillance firm. Open-ended assignments invite problems. The investigator should be given a certain number of hours or a dollar threshold as a control point. The adjuster should also help to establish a plan and divulge any suspicions, tips, or leads from the employer.

Medical Investigation

The nature and extent of an injury affect its disability assessment or rating. Adjusters should not wait until all of the compensability facts are gathered before investigating the claim's medical aspects. As illustrated in Exhibit 6-1, the medical investigation can be conducted concurrently with the accident investigation. Some medical investigations are conducted by nurses, case managers, or medical claim expediters. Many insurers use nurses to review new claims to initiate immediate medical case management.

The medical investigation can begin upon receipt of a signed medical authorization from the injured worker. Medical and wage authorization forms should be sent to the injured worker for signature as soon as practicable after notice of injury. The medical authorization releases the medical reports and records needed to evaluate the claim. Such records can reveal preexisting medical problems and can aid in auditing medical expenses for appropriateness and billing accuracy.

Medical records help determine whether all or part of an alleged work injury is preexisting. For example, a thirty-seven-year-old pressman alleges a shoulder injury that occurred when he lifted an ink roller off a large press. Medical reports confirm a rotator cuff tear. Records received later from the injured worker's group medical insurer indicate that the worker was treated for injury to the same shoulder after competing in a karate competition two years earlier.

A preexisting injury does not preclude compensation for a claim. If the preexisting injury was aggravated by a work-related accident, then workers' compensation should owe for the time required to return the person to the condition preceding the most recent injury.

Current Medical Providers

As soon as possible, the adjuster or medical case manager should contact the medical provider who first treated the worker for the injury as well as any subsequent providers. The adjuster or case manager should request a diagnosis and prognosis and should request that all medical reports and bills relating to the specific injury be sent to the adjuster. In workers' compensation claims, a medical release is not normally required to obtain medical reports relating to the current injury. However, because of the uncertainty about complying with HIPAA, it is prudent to obtain one.

The prompt request for medical records and bills has several advantages:

- It helps the adjuster assess compensability by comparing what the injured worker reported to the physician against what the worker reported to the adjuster.

- It helps establish the existence and extent of disability. The medical report can confirm a report of on-the-job injury, but it might also indicate that the injured worker is able to return to work immediately.

- It expedites payment. The sooner the adjuster gets the bills, the sooner they can be processed for payment. Prompt payment enhances goodwill and demonstrates a well-managed file. In some instances, it can decrease the injured worker's perception that an attorney is needed.

Medical History

The injured worker's statement or personnel file might contain information about the worker's medical history. The adjuster can request additional medical history from the worker, with the appropriate authorization. Medical history can help the adjuster decide whether an alleged job injury is, or might have arisen from, a preexisting condition.

If a preexisting condition has been aggravated by a job-related injury, then workers' compensation should owe for the time required to return the injured person to pre-injury condition. For example, does a worker with a back injury have a history of backache, or does a worker with a hernia have a history of a preexisting hernia? Has the worker submitted a group health or disability claim form, checking the box "Unrelated to Employment"? Does the personnel application omit a history of shoulder problems when medical records reveal previous shoulder surgery? For serious injuries, a thorough medical history might be needed to determine the worker's right to benefits or to limit the insurer's exposure.

One medical history investigative issue involves what is commonly called the "Monday morning syndrome." This type of claim involves an injury that occurred outside of work but that was reported as being work-related. The term refers to claims involving injuries that occur over the weekend and that are reported to the employer on Monday morning as work-related injuries. The following case illustrates this type of claim.

The worker alleged that he fell and injured his back at work. The medical investigation revealed that the worker had been admitted to a hospital while on vacation. He had injured his back lifting heavy bales of hay at his son's farm. Compensation was denied.[2]

Special investigations are required for the following three types of claims:

1. Auto accident
2. Fatality
3. Products liability

Auto Accident Investigation

For auto accidents, evidence the adjuster should obtain includes statements from all drivers and witnesses, the police accident report, photos and a diagram of the accident scene, and statements from tow-truck crews or paramedic services. This evidence can be useful not only for determining compensability but also for establishing (or defending) a subrogation claim.

The adjuster must confirm or rule out that the injured worker was operating the car within the scope of employment. If the injury occurred while the worker was within the scope of employment, the adjuster should search for subrogation possibilities. In investigating the scope of employment issue, the adjuster should ask questions such as the following:

- Was it a company car? If not, did the worker own the car?
- How often and for what purpose did the worker drive the car?
- Did the worker's job description involve travel by car?
- Where was the last stop made by the worker?
- Where was the next destination?
- Was the worker reimbursed for mileage?
- Was the worker on a travel expense account?
- Did the worker have a company credit card or debit card for gas or other travel expenses?
- Did the worker's supervisor confirm that the worker was operating the car within the scope of employment?
- Was there any evidence of drinking, intoxication, or drug impairment?
- Was there any evidence that the car was used for a personal errand instead of for a job purpose?
- Was the car marked by a sign or otherwise identified as belonging to the employer?
- Who paid title, taxes, tags, and insurance for the car—the worker or the employer?

In determining the scope of employment, the adjuster might find it helpful to take a map of the area and mark or highlight the employer's location, the accident location, and the worker's destination.

Fatality Investigation

The following information should be obtained in investigating any fatality claim:

1. *Death certificate.* A death certificate is normally a matter of public record. Death certificates usually indicate the cause of death, dependency information, whether the death was work-related, and whether an autopsy was performed.

2. *Autopsy report.* An autopsy report is also usually a public record. The pathologist performing the autopsy dictates a detailed report, which can provide further clues about the cause of death and the injured worker's general health.

3. *Toxicology report.* A toxicology report usually accompanies an autopsy. The pathologist runs a routine blood test on the deceased to detect traces of alcohol and drugs. In states in which intoxication or drug impairment is a claim defense, this report could be important in establishing or ruling out such a defense.

4. *Marriage records or divorce decrees.* Such records, from the courthouse, may confirm dependency status. Copies of birth certificates of children claiming dependency might also be needed.

5. *Obituary.* A newspaper obituary can include dependency information. The adjuster should compare the newspaper report to the information the survivors have provided about dependency status.

6. *Articles.* Newspaper articles about the accident can provide valuable investigative leads.

7. *Policy reports.* Any police investigation into the death can provide details about how the death occurred.

Products Liability Investigation

Any injury caused by a product raises additional investigative issues. Without prejudging the manufacturer or retailer, the adjuster should investigate whether there was a defect in design, manufacture, or warning, or a breach of warranty in all cases in which a product contributed to the worker's injury. Identifying product defects that have caused the worker's injury might indicate the manufacturer's liability. The adjuster could seek subrogation from the manufacturer to offset the employer's insurer's financial loss from workers' compensation. (Subrogation is discussed in the next chapter.) Products liability claims are legally and technically complex and might involve different considerations for a retailer than for a manufacturer.

When investigating a products liability claim, the adjuster should ensure the *preservation of evidence* by asking the employer to take a machine or other evidence out of commission until experts can examine it. If the employer is reluctant to cooperate with such a request, the adjuster can seek assistance from underwriting or claim management. The adjuster should not allow the product or product pieces to be destroyed or discarded. An employer's failure to preserve evidence can result in a spoliation of evidence claim against the employer or its insurer. **Spoliation of evidence** is the destruction or significant alteration of physical evidence. An employer or insurer who loses or discards evidence can prejudice the worker's ability to pursue a claim against a responsible third party, and the employer or insurer would lose the opportunity for subrogation.

Spoliation of evidence
The destruction or significant alteration of physical evidence.

An injured worker who files a spoliation tort claim against an employer must prove all of the following seven requirements:

1. Existence of a potential civil action
2. Legal or contractual duty to preserve evidence relevant to that action
3. Destruction of evidence
4. Significant impairment of the ability to prove the potential civil action
5. Causal connection between the evidence's destruction and the inability to prove a lawsuit
6. Significant possibility of success of the potential civil action if the evidence were available
7. Damages

Generally, there is no duty to preserve evidence. In fact, most spoliation actions are dismissed because the defendant owed no such duty to the plaintiff. Courts dismiss claims if the result would be an "unwarranted intrusion on the property rights of a person who lawfully disposes of his or her own property."[3] However, courts have ruled that a duty to preserve evidence can arise under any of the following circumstances:

1. The spoliator (person who has destroyed or significantly altered the evidence) has voluntarily undertaken the responsibility to preserve the evidence, and a person has reasonably relied on the spoliator to his or her detriment.
2. The spoliator has entered into an agreement to preserve the evidence.
3. The spoliator was specifically requested to preserve the evidence.
4. A contract, statute, regulation, or some other special circumstance or relationship has created a duty to preserve the evidence.

The duty to preserve evidence exists under any of these circumstances if a reasonable person in the defendant's position should have foreseen that the evidence was material to a potential civil action. In other words, the scope of the duty to preserve evidence is not boundless. A "potential spoliator need do only what is reasonable under the circumstances."[4]

In spoliation cases, the insurer or other third party administering the injury claim is not considered an agent of the employer and is not held culpable for spoliation unless it actually takes possession of the evidence and destroys or alters it.[5] Courts do not allow employers who have spoiled evidence to use the exclusive remedy as a defense. Further, no coverage exists for this cause of loss, even under the employer's commercial general liability or commercial property policy.

PROVIDING BENEFITS

After determining coverage and compensability, the adjuster accepts or denies the claim. Compensation laws specify procedures for paying and denying claims. Although state procedures vary, they have certain common features. Each state statute must address the same types of questions: How are payments made and terminated? What forms and procedures are required in providing benefits? How does medical management affect payments?

Claim Payment

Procedures for paying compensable claims are straightforward. The insurer accepts the claim, leading to the payment of wage loss, medical, or death benefits, as previously discussed. A single agency within state government usually oversees the administration of workers' compensation. In some states, the agency is a board within the state Department of Labor. Some common titles for such state boards are Industrial Commission, Workers' Compensation Commission, and Industrial Accident Board. These boards promulgate regulations for applying the workers' compensation statutes. State boards are responsible for administering the workers' compensation law in a manner consistent with that state's legislative history and the law's intent.

Adjusters must know the procedural requirements of the states in which they adjust or supervise claims. At a minimum, they should have a copy of the state workers' compensation statute and administrative rules and should be familiar with them. Supplemental material, including circulars from the workers' compensation commission, opinions of the commission, periodic updates, and newsletters from the legal community, might also be available.

Generally, when an adjuster accepts a claim, wage loss payments are made until the injured worker (1) returns to work or (2) has reached maximum medical improvement (MMI). When one of these events occurs, the adjuster must resolve the claim with the worker and/or file the required form with the workers' compensation commission and pay any final medical bills. In some cases, payment for medical care might continue beyond the time wage loss payments end. Some states require that a claim remain open as long as the worker needs and is entitled to medical care for the disability. Other states require the medical claim remain open for life, absent a final settlement. However, once the adjuster rules out permanent disability or makes a settlement, the claim can be closed. Procedures become more involved in disputed claims, as discussed in a subsequent section of this chapter.

Filing Systems

In a state that has a "filing system" of handling benefit payment, the adjuster submits one form when workers' compensation benefit payments begin and another when they end. The adjuster needs neither the injured worker's signature on the forms nor the worker's explicit consent to the terms or cessation of payment. The two forms have different names in various states. Adjusters must familiarize themselves with the nomenclature of the forms used in the states in which they handle claims. Exhibit 6-3 shows a form that can be used to open, pay, or deny a claim.

Agreement Systems

In a state using an "agreement system" of handling benefit payment, the adjuster must obtain the injured worker's signature on the forms officially signifying acceptance or termination of compensation payments. Some states call the form signifying employer/insurer acceptance of a claim a memorandum of agreement. The adjuster files the completed agreement with the state workers' compensation commission, which then issues an award.

Obtaining the injured worker's signature on the form ending compensation can sometimes pose a problem. The form ending payments, which some states call an agreed statement of fact, states that the worker returned to work or was able to return to work on a specific date. The worker might not agree that payments should stop. If the worker refuses to sign the form, the adjuster must meet specific and rigorous requirements to stop payments. Often, the employer/insurer must file an application for a hearing. The employer/insurer might have to continue payments to the worker while awaiting a hearing date and decision.

Payment Time Limits

All state laws have time limits within which the employer/insurer must start payments, commonly fourteen days from the date compensation becomes due or fourteen days from the accident date. Adjusters handling workers' compensation must be familiar with their state requirements. Regardless of the time limit, the act of payment is key. Failure to start or continue payments on a timely basis as required by statute might invoke penalties against the insurer. Penalties vary by state and can be as much as 20 percent of an award. In some states, an adjuster can issue a *pro forma denial* within the time limit for payment, pending a complete investigation. The pro forma denial facilitates the completion of the investigation. It does not necessarily mean the claim will ultimately be denied.

Payment Codes

In workers' compensation claims, benefit payments are coded by the type of injury and the general circumstances of the claim. Those codes are put in the database of the National Council on Compensation Insurance (NCCI) or the state's compensation bureau to help track claim injury trends and develop workers' compensation insurance rates. The codes are also passed along to loss control departments and to the insured. Claim data entered into a claim processing system is used to help identify claim problem areas and address them with risk control measures.

EXHIBIT 6-3

Form to Open, Pay, or Deny a Claim

TEXAS WORKERS' COMPENSATION COMMISSION
7551 Metro Center Drive, Suite 100
Austin, Texas 78744

TWCC # _____

Carrier's Claim # _____

PAYMENT OF COMPENSATION OR NOTICE OF REFUSED/DISPUTED CLAIM

1. MARK ✎ TYPE OF BENEFIT	3. Employee's Name and Mailing Address	10. Name and Mailing Address of Insurance Carrier
☐ Certify benefits will be paid as accrued Art. 8308-5.21		
☐ Temporary Income Benefits	4. Social Security Number 5. Date of Injury	11. Address of Insurance Carrier Claims Office
☐ Impairment Income Benefits		
☐ Supplemental Income Benefits	6. County of Injury	12. Insurance Carrier Representative and Phone No.
Lifetime Income Benefits ☐ Initial Payment ☐ Annual Increase	7. Nature of Injury	13. Professional License No.
☐ Death Benefits ☐ Correction to Previous Filing	8. Employer's Name and Mailing Address	14. Insurance Carrier's First Written Notice of Injury Received on
2. Date of this Notice:	9. Federal Tax I.D. No.	15. Name and Title of Person Notifying Insurance Carrier

COMPLETE APPROPRIATE SECTION BELOW

INITIAL PAYMENT A-1	TERMINATION A-2	REDUCTION/RESUMPTION A-
16. Date of Lost Time Began	25. Reason for Termination	34. Date of Resumed or Reduced
17. Date of Payment		35. Date of Payment
18. Amount of Payment $	26. Date of Last Payment 27. Rate Paid $	36. Amount of Payment $
19. For No. of Weeks 20. Rate of Comp. $	28. Intermittent Periods of Lost Time From Work	37. No. of Weeks
21. From 22. To		38. From 39. To

23. Remarks
*If fatal injury name & Address of Beneficiary (ies)

COMPENSATION PAID

29. From	30. To
31. Weeks	32. Days

33. Total Amount	
Indemnity	$
Medical Impairment Income Benefits	$
Lump Sum	$

40. Payment Resumed or Reduced

☐ Temporary Income Benefits
☐ Impairment Income Benefits
☐ Supplemental Income Benefits

41. Average	Weekly Wage	42. Hourly Wage
Prior to Injury	$.	$
Following Injury	¢	¢

24. Payment mailed or delivered to:

Notice of Refused Or Disputed Claim

PAYMENT REFUSED OR DISPUTED FOR THE FOLLOWING REASON(S): (ART. 8308-5.21 (B), (C))

43.

MEDICAL PAYMENT DISPUTES (Art. 8308-4.68(d)): If an Insurance Carrier disputes the amount of payment for medical services or the entitlement to payment for medical services or the entitlement to payment for medical services, the carrier must report its position on Form TWCC-62 REPORT OF MEDICAL PAYMENT DISPUTE.

A COPY OF THIS FORM WAS MAILED TO   ☐ CLAIMANT   ☐ CLAIMANT'S REPRESENTATIVE _____

(date)

Commission Date Stamp Here

Interim TWCC-21 (2/91)

TEXAS WORKERS COMPENSATION COMMISSION

Interim Form TWCC-21
(Payment of Compensation
or Notice of Refused/Disputed Claim)

Not later than the 7th day after the date on which the insurance carrier receives written notice of an injury, the carrier shall: (1) begin payment of benefits, or (2) notify the TWCC and the injured employee, in writing, of its refusal to pay, and of the employee's right to request a benefit review conference, and (3) how to obtain additional information from TWCC.

Interim Form TWCC-21 should be used to accomplish these requirements. An insurance carrier who fails to either begin compensation or file Interim Form TWCC-21, within this 7-day period, may receive a Class B Administrative Violation. Initiation of compensation does not prevent the carrier from investigating and subsequently denying the claim during the 60-day period following receipt of written notice of the injury. The carrier must specify the reason for refusal of compensation.

Interim Form TWCC-21 should also be used by the carrier to indicate the intent to begin benefits when compensable time begins to accrue, or medical payments are due (Art. 8308-4.22 and 8308-4.68).

This form should be used by the carrier when transitioning from payment of one type of benefits to another. A carrier should attach a payment summary for frequent adjustments when filling in block 40.

The Interim Form TWCC-21 is a 3-part form and is considered filed when personally delivered or postmarked. Send TWCC's copy to the **field office handling the claim**.

[Art. 8308-4.22, Accrual of Rights to Income Benefits; Art.8308-4.23, Temporary Income Benefits; Art.8308-4.26, Impairment Income Benefits; Art.8308-4.28, Supplemental Income Benefits; Art. 8308-4.31, Lifetime Income Benefits; Art. 8308-4.41, Death Benefits; Art. 8308-4.68, Payment of Health Care Provider; Art. 8308-5.21, Initiation of Compensation Insurance; Carrier's Refusal; Rule 124.1, Written Notice of Injury Defined; 1224.2, Notice of Initiation of Compensation; 124.4, Notice of Reduction or Termination of Compensation; 124.6, Notice of Refused or Disputed Claim]

Interim TWCC-21 (2/91)   TEXAS WORKERS COMPENSATION COMMISSION

Medical Management of Claims

Having determined coverage and compensability, the adjuster must determine the amount and type of medical treatment and rehabilitation the injured worker requires. This determination is made through medical management. **Medical management** involves directing and coordinating the efforts of healthcare providers to meet the needs of the worker and the insurer. Medical management can be performed by adjusters, nurse case managers, and managed care organizations. Its goal is to avoid undertreating or overtreating an injured worker. One important tool of medical management in workers' compensation cases is the choice of a physician or physician panels.

Medical management
Directing and coordinating a healthcare provider's efforts to meet the needs of the injured worker and the employer.

Choice of Physician or Physician Panels

Approximately half the states give employers the right to choose either the treating physician or a panel of physicians that injured workers must initially use.[6] Workers must go to the designated physician or a physician on the panel for a period ranging from ten to ninety days after the injury, depending on the state. After that period, many states allow injured workers to choose their own physicians. Adjusters should become familiar with the law in their states to preserve employers' rights. If the employer fails to exercise the right to choose a treating physician or panel of physicians, the adjuster's ability to manage claims might be impaired.

The employer's right to choose the physician can be a key factor affecting the length of disability. Physicians who, as a practice, tend to diagnose injuries as more severe than other doctors might can increase medical costs, prolong treatments, lengthen an injured worker's time away from work, and rate disabilities as permanent that might be temporary. All of these factors increase claim costs. Effective medical management can reduce and sometimes eliminate these excess costs. On the other hand, some physicians might classify only the severely injured as disabled or they might prematurely release a worker to return to work, increasing the likelihood of aggravating the original injury.

Physician Panels

For effective claim management, employers and insurers compile lists of recommended physicians and facilities, usually providing a choice within each medical specialty. Some states allow employers to limit the worker's choice of physicians to practitioners on the panel. The most frequently consulted specialists are orthopedists, neurologists, and neurosurgeons. Panel physicians should be impartial, dispassionate, and board certified, and they should be accessible for phone calls and inquiries. They should write prompt, thorough, clear, and unequivocal reports and should be comfortable testifying in court.

Employers that provide panels should educate workers about procedures for and benefits of using such panels. If an injured worker, unaware of the physician panel, sees another physician first, it can be difficult to persuade the worker to change to a physician on the panel.

Commonly, an employer or insurer contracts with a managed care organization (MCO) that selects and maintains the physician panel. The MCO selects physicians based on their experience with occupational health and their understanding of return-to-work issues and negotiates the fee schedules. The MCO has case managers who monitor the treatment of injured workers and who review providers' medical bills for proper coding and compliance with billing guidelines. Case managers communicate with the medical providers on behalf of the employer or insurer. With their knowledge of medical management and return-to-work strategies, case managers can complement adjusters' knowledge of compensability and claim administration issues.

Managed Care Techniques and Tools

Workers' compensation managed care seeks to deliver high quality healthcare efficiently and to return the injured worker to work as soon as possible, thus saving significant costs for employers/insurers. To handle claims effectively, adjusters must understand the basics of managed care and be conversant with the professionals who practice managed care techniques. Effective managed care in workers' compensation integrates the following three techniques:

1. Utilization management
2. Disability management
3. Fee management

Utilization management monitors and controls the types, duration, and intensity of medical treatments. Independent medical exams (IMEs) and physician peers' retrospective reviews of the treatment are two examples of utilization management tools. **Disability management** involves providing rehabilitation and arranging transitional employment to help return the injured worker to work. **Fee management** includes negotiating discounted provider fees, developing billing guidelines, and auditing medical bills to ensure accuracy. The adjuster's role in implementing these tools varies by insurer. At a minimum, adjusters must be able to explain to the injured worker the general procedures of managed care and to help employers understand the need for transitional work duty.

Obtaining Medical Information

Adjusters need information from physicians and must find effective ways to obtain it. Calling the physician at the outset of a claim helps the adjuster or case manager establish a relationship. Case managers can assist the adjuster with obtaining much of the needed medical information.

Many insurers and self-insureds form teams with nurse case managers to obtain medical information. Nurses, by virtue of their educational background,

Utilization management
Monitoring and controlling the types, duration, and intensity of medical treatments in an effort to control costs.

Disability management
Managing an injured worker's rehabilitation and arranging for transitional work in an effort to return the worker to full work duties as soon as possible and to control costs.

Fee management
Controlling healthcare provider fees by negotiating discounts, developing billing guidelines, and auditing medical bills.

communicate effectively with healthcare providers and can identify important medical issues. This team approach allows adjusters to focus their time and attention on investigating compensability issues and other claim administrative matters, such as apportionment and the involvement of second injury funds.

Apportionment

Adjusters frequently deal with compensation claims for an injury to a worker with a preexisting injury. The amount of compensation for the second injury depends on state statutes. Some states allow insurers to apportion the loss between the two injuries. Other states have second injury funds to handle claims for these types of injuries.

Apportionment
Assigning to an injured worker's current employer only the portion of the worker's permanent disability that occurred while in the current employment.

Apportionment applies to claims involving workers who have previously suffered permanent injuries. **Apportionment** makes an employer responsible only for the portion of a worker's disability that results from an injury that has occurred while the worker was working for the employer. Apportionment significantly limits the cost of a claim and favors the employer. For example, assume a worker has already lost sight in one eye and then loses sight in the other eye because of a work-related accident. Under strict apportionment, the employer is responsible only for the loss of one eye, even though the worker is totally blind. In practice, apportionment is complicated because it is often difficult to medically establish a preexisting condition and to assign percentages of disability to the preexisting condition and to the second injury. This type of apportionment should not be confused with the apportionment of benefits that occurs when two concurrent employers share responsibility for the same injury to a worker.

Nonapportionment of the loss is more common. With nonapportionment, the employer pays benefits for the combined disability that results when a second injury merges with a preexisting disability. In the previous example, the employer would be responsible for the resulting combined disability (total blindness). Nonapportionment is costly to employers and discourages them from hiring workers with preexisting disabilities because a new injury combined with a preexisting disability could produce an overall disability much greater than would normally be the case. Holding employers responsible for the greater disability creates a disincentive to hire the disabled. To help remedy this problem, second injury funds were created.

Second Injury Funds

Second injury funds
State-controlled funds that contribute compensation for workers who have preexisting conditions and who suffer work-related "second" injuries.

Second injury funds are state-controlled funds that contribute compensation for workers with preexisting conditions who suffer subsequent work-related injuries. Second injury funds help to minimize employer reluctance to hire disabled workers by providing a financial safety net for employers. An increasing number of states are eliminating second injury funds because the Americans with Disabilities Act (ADA) now gives employers an incentive to hire disabled workers. The ADA requires employers to make reasonable accommodations to workers with disabilities. However, unlike second injury funds, the ADA does not compensate employers or their insurers for the increased cost of disabilities resulting from preexisting disabilities.

Though provisions vary, the second injury fund limits the employer's liability when an injured worker suffers a combined total disability that is greater than what would have resulted solely from the second injury. The second injury funds pay benefits in addition to those that an employer would owe from the *second injury alone* and are usually financed with premium taxes and special assessments in death cases involving no dependents. The second injury fund usually applies to permanent injuries and, in some states, only to permanent *total* injuries. About half of the states cover only specified injuries. The U.S. Chamber of Commerce *Analysis of Workers' Compensation Laws* provides up-to-date information on which states have second injury funds.

The following case illustrates the importance of determining whether an injury is covered by the second injury fund.

Importance of Determining Second Injury Fund Coverage

When the injured worker started work with his employer, he had a 35 percent permanent partial disability to his right foot because of a previous injury. While working as a welder for his new employer, he suffered a 20 percent permanent partial disability to his neck. The new employer's insurer paid the worker benefits and then filed for reimbursement from the state's second injury fund, stating that the neck injury, when merged with the foot injury, caused a greater disability than the injured worker would have had from the second injury alone. The claim for reimbursement was denied because the insurer could not prove that the preexisting foot injury caused an increase in disability beyond that related to the second injury alone.[7]

Second Injury Fund Operation

Most state second injury funds pay the difference between compensation payable for the second injury alone and that for the total disability. However, some statutes limit the employer's liability to payment for a set time, for example, 104 weeks. Beyond that period, the second injury fund compensates the injured worker and might even reimburse the employer for any payments it has already made in excess of 104 weeks. Once the adjuster has identified a covered injury and has determined how the second injury fund applies, the adjuster must seek contribution from the second injury fund.

Obtaining Second Injury Fund Relief

Using second injury funds is important in managing workers' compensation claims and limiting the insurer's loss exposure. The adjuster's time spent in documenting a case for second injury fund relief can save the employer or insurer many thousands of dollars—with no hardship to the injured worker. Limiting the employer's responsibility to 104 weeks of compensation might initially seem inconsequential. However, in some severe cases, it represents considerable savings.

Second injury funds typically impose the following three requirements:

1. The injured worker has a prior disability.
2. The employer has knowledge of the preexisting disability.
3. The combination of the preexisting disability and the current injury produce a greater disability overall.

First, the adjuster must document a preexisting disability by researching an injured worker's medical history. The original injury or condition need not be work-related for the second injury to be covered by a second injury fund. When taking the worker's statement, the adjuster should ask about prior injuries, treatments, accidents, and hospitalizations. The adjuster should obtain a signed medical authorization form and identify family physicians to request complete copies of medical charts. Union health records, personnel files, and group health files might contain information on preexisting conditions or disabilities. Previous employers might be useful sources of information. Index bureaus and local compensation commissions could also produce evidence of prior claims and disabilities.

Second, the adjuster must prove that the employer knew of the preexisting condition or disability. Pre-employment physicals or medical questionnaires can provide such proof, as can testimony from co-workers or supervisors about an injured worker's physical limitations. Some states hold that an employer has constructive knowledge of a preexisting condition as long as the information is available to the employer. For example, the employer might know about a worker's physical limitations because the limitation is obvious, such as for a worker who wears glasses. In such cases, the adjuster need show only that medical evidence indicating the prior disability existed and was available to the employer.

Third, the adjuster must demonstrate that a combination of the preexisting condition and the recent injury has produced an overall greater disability. This proof requires a physician, either the treating physician or an independent medical examination (IME) physician, to allocate the percentage of permanent partial disability respectively attributable to the two injuries or conditions. When using an IME, the adjuster must provide all relevant medical records and must clearly communicate the medical issue that must be addressed.

TERMINATION OF BENEFITS

Terminating benefits when the worker has recovered and returned to work normally proceeds without difficulty. However, termination can be challenging when the worker does not agree that benefits should end. The decision to terminate benefits should not be taken lightly or made arbitrarily. Many state commissions impose penalties against the insurer if they do not agree with the adjuster's reason for termination. Adjusters must be familiar with the state procedural requirements for terminating benefits.

Each state has statutes defining the justifications for terminating benefits. Establishing a justification might require medical opinions or other evidence, such as photographs or videotapes, to show that a worker is more active than the claimed disability would allow, or documentation to show that the worker has returned to employment with another employer. Adjusters should not rely solely on co-workers' opinions to terminate benefits. The following case illustrates a dispute over termination of benefits.

Dispute Over Termination of Benefits

A worker was placed on disability after a knee injury prevented him from returning to work as a carpenter. However, the worker had training and experience as a computer operator. The state law allowed for termination of benefits when a worker's earning power was restored. Because the worker's knee injury did not prevent him from working as a computer operator, his benefits were terminated. The worker appealed, but the court upheld the decision because he had the training and education to work as a computer operator and because his physician testified that he was medically able to do computer work. [8]

ADJUDICATION OF DISPUTES

Most workers' compensation claims are routinely investigated, adjusted, and paid. For some claims, however, the injured worker's entitlement to compensation might be questionable. When an adjuster denies a claim outright, most states require the insurer to notify the injured worker in writing giving reason for the denial within a specified time. Many states require the adjuster to submit a denial form to the appropriate state agency for approval before denying the claim. The agency might then invite the injured worker to file for a hearing before approving or disapproving the denial.

A common situation leading to claim adjudication (a hearing to decide the claim) occurs when the adjuster initially views a claim as compensable and issues payments, then later finds grounds for contesting continued payments. These termination of benefits situations can arise for several reasons, including the following:

- An independent examining physician determines that the injured worker is able to return to work.
- The adjuster discovers that the injured worker is employed elsewhere while collecting workers' compensation benefits.
- The adjuster discovers, through surveillance or other means, that the injured worker is engaged in physical activity that would prove the worker's ability to work.

Forums

Workers' compensation claim disputes can be adjudicated in different forums and usually have several stages, ranging from informal conferences to formal state appeal courts. The methods of adjudication become more costly and time consuming, have stricter rules of evidence, and have more formal procedures as the judicial system becomes more involved. The role of state courts varies by state (see the following box). The types of adjudication discussed in this section are informal conferences, formal hearings, full commission appeals, and appeals to state courts.

Role of Courts

In a few states, the state courts, rather than a workers' compensation commission or board, have the original jurisdiction or authority to adjudicate workers' compensation claims. This role is different from the court's appellate (appeals) role, which is discussed next. In those few states, the courts handle matters that are handled by a commissioner or hearing officer in other states.

Informal Conferences

In many states, the first stage in adjudication is an informal conference. At this stage, the adjuster represents the employer/insurer. Some adjusters, often called hearing examiners, specialize in presenting cases at informal conferences. The employer can send an attorney or both an adjuster and an attorney to the conference. The injured worker is usually present with an attorney. A representative of the commission supervises the conference, which seeks to (1) identify items of agreement, (2) isolate areas of contention, and (3) encourage low-level, informal dispute resolution.

In these conferences, each side informally presents its position. Commissions do not observe strict rules of evidence. The adjuster might have a chance to question the injured worker. A commission representative might make a recommendation at the conference or might issue one within a certain number of days. Recommendations are appealable to the next adjudication stage, which is usually a formal hearing. An appeal can be initiated by either the injured worker or the employer/insurer.

Formal Hearings

For formal hearings, the insured should be represented by an attorney. Although rules of evidence are more relaxed than they are in a civil trial, the setting and procedures are not as casual as in the informal conference. A formal hearing resembles a trial before a single commissioner. Results normally come weeks after the hearing. Hearing rulings, while binding, are often appealable, depending on the state statute.

Full Commission Appeals

In some states, employers can appeal a formal hearing ruling to the full commission. This process involves filing briefs that include a statement of facts and an analysis of the applicable laws. One criticism of full commission review is that the full commission might be reluctant to overrule one of its members. In many states, the appeals board within the commission is a body separate from the hearing officers.

State Court Appeals

Both injured workers and employers can appeal compensation decisions to state appeals courts. A state appellate court's decision to hear a case is completely discretionary. In some states, decisions can be appealed for one of two reasons: (1) an alleged error of law or (2) an alleged error of fact. In about half the states, only errors of law are grounds for appeal.

Alleged errors of law include questions related to the interpretation of a legal issue. Workers' compensation appeals must involve fundamental interpretation of the workers' compensation law or an issue of state constitutionality. For example, does an injury resulting from usual activities like walking up and down steps constitute an accidental injury within the meaning of the compensation law? Must a slip, twist, fall, or unusual exertion accompany lifting for such lifting to be compensable?

Alleged errors of fact arise over whether the commission correctly determined some element of verifiable truth, including circumstances of the accident or medical issues. For example, a witness testifies that the worker fell from a ladder and injured her back. A witness for the employer says that no such fall occurred. The two sets of testimony are mutually exclusive and raise a legitimate question about the facts of the case. In states in which only alleged errors of law can be appealed, the commission's determination about which witness to believe is not appealable.

Because the stakes and expenses rise with each appeal level, an adjuster should consider the costs of an appeal. What, objectively, are the odds of success? How much money is at stake? Will the compensation award be precedent-setting if unchallenged? In many states, the losing employer/insurer must pay the injured worker, pending an appeal, and these costs should be considered.

Rules of Evidence in Workers' Compensation Hearings

Unlike civil trials, workers' compensation hearings have fairly informal and relaxed rules of evidence. Commissioners can allow hearsay testimony and other evidence that would be inadmissible in court. Medical reports can be admissible evidence in lieu of having the physician physically present. Most states allow any evidence to be admitted but require that the ultimate findings rest on some evidence that would be admissible in civil courts.

Use of Statements and Reports

An adjuster might use an injured worker's signed or recorded statement to impeach the worker's testimony at a compensation hearing. This possibility underscores the importance of the adjuster's investigative statements. Medical reports, police reports, and surveillance photos and videotapes may also be allowed without having the doctor, police officer, or investigator testify.

Burden of Proof

In most states, the injured worker has the minimal burden of proof to show that he or she sustained an accidental injury arising out of and in the course of employment. This is not a rigorous standard. A worker's uncorroborated testimony can establish a *prima facie* case (a case in which sufficient evidence exists to support the party's conclusion) of compensability. Once the injured worker meets this burden of proof, the burden shifts to the employer/insurer to show why the worker's injury is not compensable.

Presumptions

In most states, hearing commissioners presume that a claim falls under the workers' compensation act and that the worker sustained an accidental injury arising out of and in the course of employment. This presumption effectively places the burden of disproving the claim on the employer/insurer even though the legal burden of proof remains on the injured worker. This presumption is consistent with the liberal interpretation of workers' compensation laws. Legislative histories of state laws reflect the intent to develop a compassionate system of payment for injured workers. In some states, the law explicitly requires commissioners to resolve any reasonable disputes in the worker's favor. In New York, for example, various presumptions are created by statute: that the claim is covered, that sufficient notice was given, and that the injury did not result from the worker's willful wrongdoing. These presumptions make claim denial and defense more challenging for the employer/insurer/adjuster. To win a workers' compensation case, the employer must have a stronger and more convincing case than the worker.

Attorney Fees

The award of the injured worker's attorney fees is generally subject to statutory limits and to the commission's approval. Upon any award of compensation following a hearing, the commission can be expected to approve an attorney's fee. The fee of the injured worker's attorney is generally restricted to no more than 25 percent of the award. Each state has its own rules regarding the payment of the injured worker's attorney fees. Attorney fees generally come out of the award to the worker, but in some states they may be in addition to the sum awarded.

Adjuster's Role in Adjudication

Many states allow adjusters to act on behalf of the employer/insurer instead of attorneys. These adjusters are highly trained, experienced professionals who can successfully present their position in most workers' compensation disputes. Most complicated cases, however, require an attorney.

When defense attorneys are involved, adjusters should, nevertheless, attend workers' compensation hearings regularly. Although not allowed to question witnesses, the adjuster, because of his or her familiarity with the case, might be able to assist the defense attorney with background information and with observations about testimony. Adjusters usually do not testify in hearings, although occasionally they receive subpoenas, which require them to testify, usually concerning a statement from a witness.

The adjuster should continue to be involved once a disputed workers' compensation case enters litigation, in part to monitor the progress of the case. Some insurers have litigation management guidelines the adjuster can use to monitor the defense attorney's participation and effectiveness in the case. The adjuster can control litigation costs, to an extent, by ensuring that the attorney's work (at an hourly fee) does not overlap with the adjuster's work. Adjusters should investigate claims, take statements, locate witnesses, set up IMEs, obtain medical records, and, in some cases, attend formal conferences, reserving the attorney's time for filing pleading and motions, evaluating the case, and trying it.

Alternative Dispute Resolution

Some states use alternative dispute resolution (ADR) for disputed workers' compensation claims. ADR is a method of resolving disputes without referring them to courts or administrative agencies. ADR provides out-of-court settlements with the advantages of economy, greater speed of resolution, less hostility between parties, and some degree of privacy. The two most common types of alternative dispute resolution are arbitration and mediation.

Arbitration

Arbitration involves submitting a disagreement to a private body for a decision that is usually final and binding. The American Arbitration Association recommends the following procedure for selecting an arbitrator: Each party receives a list of proposed arbitrators and has ten days to eliminate any undesired arbitrators and to rank the remaining ones by preference. The association appoints an arbitrator from those lists that both parties will accept. As an alternative, each party might appoint an arbitrator, who then appoint a third arbitrator.

The formal rules of evidence and procedures for court trials are relaxed in arbitration. Once the arbitrator has made a decision, it is filed with a clerk of court. Arbitration is designed to discourage appeals by requiring the parties to agree to abide by the arbitrator's decision at the outset. However, most states permit appeals if filed within a specified period. If no appeal is filed, the decision is considered equal to a court judgment.

Mediation

Mediation generally involves submitting a disagreement to an impartial third party. A mediator is usually an experienced trial attorney or a retired judge. The mediator's role is to encourage the parties to reach a satisfactory compromise. The mediator has no binding authority but acts as the impetus to the parties to analyze their disagreement, consider possible solutions, and find a compromise. Typically, the mediator meets with each party separately to discuss the disagreement, then brings the parties together, either physically or by phone, to complete the process.

NEGOTIATED SETTLEMENT

In some states, insurers and injured workers can settle workers' compensation claims like any third-party tort claim. States use different terms for these negotiated settlements, including full and final settlement, disputed claim settlement, and compromise and release. Unlike liability claim settlements, the settlement terms must often be approved by the state workers' compensation agency. Workers' compensation commissions or boards usually have the power to reject proposed settlement terms.

In reviewing settlements, commissions evaluate many factors. The settlement amount must appear reasonable given the injury's severity and must appear to be in the worker's best interest. Some adjusters believe that, when a worker is represented by an attorney, the settlement has a better chance of commission approval than a settlement involving an unrepresented worker.

In some cases, an adjuster might want to settle a claim when compensation is questionable rather than expose the employer to a third-party tort action. The law fixes compensation benefits at a set amount, but recovery in tort is theoretically unlimited. Pain and suffering are not compensable in workers' compensation cases but are legitimate general damages in tort claims. The employer might limit its loss exposure by accepting the workers' compensation claim, as in the following two examples:

- A laborer slips and falls on ice when walking into his employer's building. If the employer denies the claim, arguing that the injured worker was outside the scope of employment at the time, it might expose itself to a premises liability claim.

- A hospital worker says he contracted AIDS from his repeated exposure to patients' bodily fluids and substances. The hospital accepts a questionable workers' compensation claim rather than allowing a jury to decide its liability in a tort claim.

Some states have compromise or negotiated settlement statutes that allow employers/insurers to "buy out" the medical benefit loss exposure rather than pay for all future medical costs as they arise. Negotiated settlements offer advantages and disadvantages to the injured worker and to the employer or insurer. Advantages to workers include the ability to do the following:

- Manage medical care without getting adjuster approval
- Use any money saved from the settlement for their own purpose
- Find other employment without having benefits reduced
- Avoid the worry about losing in the adjudication process

The main disadvantage of negotiated settlement for the worker is the possibility of underestimating future needs for medical treatment and of then having to pay medical expenses over the settlement amount out-of-pocket.

The advantages of a negotiated settlement to the employer or insurer are the following:

- It eliminates the uncertainty of litigation.
- It stops the claim administration and legal costs.
- It reduces a company's long-term liability for the claim.
- It can provide significant savings because it avoids the effect of inflation on future payments.

Negotiated settlements are often used when the parties disagree on the right to vocational rehabilitation or when the injured worker appeals a denied claim. Most issues can be resolved if the parties can agree on the monetary value.

Structured Settlements

One variation of negotiated settlement is the structured settlement. While traditional settlements for workers' compensation claims are usually made in a lump sum payment, structured settlements provide payments over time. Structured settlement payments, normally funded by annuities, usually include an initial lump sum payment followed by periodic payments issued over an agreed time at specified intervals. Many insurers have a list of structured settlement vendors they use. The adjuster usually gives the vendor information about the workers' compensation claim, and the vendor develops several proposals with varying payouts. The adjuster presents these proposals to the injured worker during negotiations.

Insurers increasingly choose structured settlements over traditional lump sum settlements because structured settlements present certain advantages for both parties.

One advantage is that a structured settlement combining lump sum payment and continuing periodic payments is one way to keep an injured worker and any dependents financially stable. Many people who receive a large sum of money, whether through a bequest, lottery winnings, or a legal award, tend to spend it in a fairly short time. The money management aspect of a structured settlement can be as important to the injured worker as its estimated economic value.

Another advantage of structured settlements is that they can be designed to fit the specific needs of the injured worker. Payment increases can be targeted to correspond to the worker's changing financial needs, for example, when children enter college or when parents enter long-term care facilities. Regular workers' compensation payments cease immediately on a recipient's death. However, with a structured settlement, an injured worker might be willing to take smaller periodic payments in exchange for a guarantee that dependents will continue to receive payments after the worker dies.

Structured settlements provide guaranteed rates of return, normally higher than banks' interest rates but lower than what might be expected in the stock market. Some injured workers prefer the security of structured settlements' guaranteed rates.

Structured settlements are typically funded by annuities from life insurance companies with AA or better ratings, making them appealing to disabled persons who might not be able to return to work. On the other hand, an injured worker who invests a settlement amount in the stock market expects to earn a higher rate of return than a structured settlement provides. The stock market return, of course, is not guaranteed, and the earnings from the invested lump sum are taxable.

From the insurer's standpoint, structured settlements can bridge the gap between the injured worker's demand and the settlement offer. Sometimes employers/insurers can obtain a discount on a structured settlement annuity if the worker's life expectancy is impaired because of factors such as smoking, hypertension, or diabetes. This discount reduces the settlement's purchase price for the insurer.

Insurers normally make a qualified assignment of the structured settlement, that is, transfer the promise to make the future payments to a third party. The company to which the settlement is assigned assumes the responsibility of issuing the periodic settlement payments. Assignment makes the insurer secondarily liable and adds an additional layer of financial security for both the employer/insurer and the injured worker. The Balanced Budget Act of 1997 included a law (IRC 130) that allows employers or their insurers to use qualified assignments in workers' compensation settlements as well as in physical injury liability claims.

When a claim is settled, either by a court award or by a negotiated settlement, it is often referred to as closed. However, many court awards require medical care and wage loss payments to extend over time. For the adjuster, these claims remain open as long as the benefits are due. To reduce the ongoing administrative costs of maintaining an open claim, many insurers use administrative closures.

Administrative Closures

After a claim has been accepted and a few medical treatments and wage loss benefits have been paid, adjusters sometimes lose contact with the injured worker. The worker might have moved out of the state or have decided that treatment is no longer needed. Most states allow insurers to send a registered letter informing workers that, if they do not contact their adjusters, their claims will be administratively closed. The insurer closes and archives the claim, but must reopen it if the worker returns and proves the need for medical treatment for the workers' compensation accident or illness.

Reopening Claims

Workers might return to work for a time and stop receiving wage loss benefits but might later leave work if their jobs prove to be too rigorous or if they suffer medical setbacks. Such workers might seek to reopen their claims and resume disability benefits. Each state has procedures workers must follow to reopen claims that might include requirements to give formal notice to employers and the compensation commission within a certain period.

Sometimes closed claims are reopened because the worker's condition has worsened. Historically, the term **aggravation** has been used to describe the worsening of a worker's condition, whether because of a second injury or because of normal deterioration. The terminology is evolving to distinguish between these two circumstances by using **recurrence** to mean a worsening because of normal or expected progression of the original injury and aggravation to mean a worsening because of a subsequent injury, even if the prior injury made the worker more susceptible to injury. If the injured worker can document that the condition worsened because of recurrence, then he or she can reopen the original claim and seek workers' compensation benefits from the employer (or insurer) who covered the original injury. An aggravation is considered a separate claim, and the employer of the worker at the time of the aggravation is liable, at least in part, for the increased disability resulting from the aggravation. The following case illustrates a claim involving the progression of an injury that was reopened.

Aggravation
The worsening of an injured worker's condition, whether because of a second injury or because of normal deterioration.

Recurrence
The worsening of an injured worker's condition because of normal or expected progression of the original injury.

Reopening an Old Settlement

In 1974, a worker was injured in an explosion. He suffered a serious brain injury that caused him to have seizures. With medication, the worker could control the seizures, and he returned to work after six months. Five years later, the man contracted bacterial spinal meningitis that doctors associated with his previous brain injury. The man had seizures intermittently until 1981, when they stopped. Doctors were unable to say whether the seizures were related to the 1974 injury. To resolve the issue, the employer entered into an

Continued on next page.

agreement with the worker in 1981 to pay him additional compensation in exchange for a signed agreement to waive his rights to claim a permanent partial disability related to the 1974 injury.

In 1984, the seizures returned. Finally, in 1992 the worker had brain surgery. The doctor who performed the surgery stated that scar tissue related to the 1974 injury had been causing the seizures. Based on this information, the worker requested that his old claim be reopened. The court ruled that the claim could be reopened, despite the settlement, because this was a newly discovered, substantially different condition. The court further ruled that the employer could not rely on the settlement because the worker could not have foreseen the permanent disability when he signed the agreement in 1981. His claim was reopened thirteen years after the settlement.[9]

CLAIM HANDLING ISSUES

Workers' compensation claims are usually more tightly regulated than other types of insurance claims. States often impose licensing requirements and continuing education requirements on workers' compensation adjusters. States might also have more detailed regulations for workers' compensation claim handling.

Adjuster Licensing

Adjusters should be aware of the licensing requirements in the states in which they handle claims. Some states require only workers' compensation adjusters be licensed. Some states require licensing of all adjusters, regardless of the type of claims they handle, and whether they work for an insurer, an independent adjusting firm, or a public adjusting firm. The licensing process can range from completing an application and paying a fee to passing a licensing examination. If a state's insurance regulators discover that an unlicensed adjuster is handling claims, the adjuster's company could be subject to fines and penalties. If an attorney representing an injured worker discovers that an adjuster is unlicensed, the attorney could use that information to attack the adjuster's credibility and claim handling practices.

Penalties for Mishandling Claims

Many states impose penalties for mishandling workers' compensation claims. Some penalties are paid to a workers' compensation fund, but most are paid to the aggrieved party. Some states base penalty assessments on a percentage of the claim payments owed. Other states assess specific dollar amounts, typically ranging from $100 to $500 per day. Penalties can be assessed for various claim errors, such as payment delays, improper denials, or underpayments. These penalties do not necessarily bar the injured worker from seeking damages for bad faith. However, the standard for proving bad faith is usually much higher than the standard for proving that an adjuster mishandled a claim.

Risk Control and Worker Safety

Adjusters can play an important part in risk (or loss) control. Risk control is any action taken to reduce the frequency, severity, or unpredictability of accidental losses. Two forms of risk control that the workers' compensation adjuster can be involved with are:

1. Loss prevention (reducing loss frequency)
2. Loss reduction (reducing loss severity)

Traditionally, **loss prevention** dealt with actions taken *before* the loss occurred to lower the expected frequency of loss from a particular loss exposure, and **loss reduction** dealt with actions taken *after* the loss occurred to lower the expected severity of losses from a particular loss exposure. This distinction is becoming less relevant because the activities of risk control and claims are often intermingled. Rehabilitation of an injured worker could be considered loss reduction because it helps to reduce loss severity. Actions that reduce the amount of medical and wage loss costs through managed care techniques could also be considered loss reduction.

Risk control is related to safety. However, the two terms are not synonymous. Safety is one important aspect of risk control. It emphasizes changing the behavior of workers and their employers to use greater caution in doing their jobs. Risk control is important because insurance does not eliminate loss exposures. If businesses are indifferent toward losses merely because insurance is available, they can soon find insurance too expensive to purchase or too difficult to obtain. Additionally, the level of workplace safety will decrease. Businesses should therefore be encouraged to take whatever means are available to avoid, prevent, or reduce losses.

Adjusters can play an important role in accident prevention through accident investigations and reporting. By interviewing injured workers, their supervisors, and co-workers in the course of an investigation, adjusters often learn the details of how many jobs are performed. This information can be useful to underwriters and loss control specialists, if violations of safety procedures are found. The following case illustrates how an adjuster might interact with a loss control specialist or an underwriter to help prevent accidents.

Loss prevention
A risk control technique that lowers the expected frequency of loss from a potential loss exposure.

Loss reduction
A risk control technique that lowers the expected severity of losses from a particular loss exposure.

Adjuster's Role in Risk Control

At 10:30 PM, a lightbulb over a computerized lathe burned out. Because no maintenance worker was on duty at that time, Bill Jones, the lathe operator for Acme Machinery, was asked by his supervisor to replace the bulb. The bulb was twenty feet in the air and in an awkward location that made it difficult to reach. Bill went to the tool room to get the ladder, but the tool room was locked. Bill found a wooden ladder lying outside the back wall and decided to use it. Bill began to climb the ladder, and when he reached the fifth rung, it splintered and broke. Bill fell backwards and struck his head. The ladder fell

Continued on next page.

against a shelf where completed work pieces were being kept. The ladder knocked over the shelf, causing several completed pieces of work to be damaged.

Following the accident, Bill complained of a headache but decided to continue to work. His supervisor offered to drive him to the hospital if he started feeling ill.

The adjuster came to the accident scene and interviewed the worker and his supervisor. He noted the following:

- Nobody on that shift had been trained to do any maintenance work.
- Nobody on that shift had keys to the tool room.
- During other shifts, as many as five people worked under or next to the unsecured shelving.
- Ladders were not on the safety inspection list.
- The ladder Bill used had been placed there over a month earlier and was intended to be discarded.
- No maintenance schedule existed for replacing lightbulbs.
- No first-aid kit was available, and the supervisor had not been trained in dealing with worker injuries.
- No written policy addressed the medical treatment of injured workers, especially those with head injuries.

These issues developed from the adjuster's investigation and were reported to Acme. Acme contracted with a loss control specialist to review its operations. Based on the adjuster's report and a personal inspection, the loss control specialist made fifty recommendations to Acme on how to improve its risk control. Acme implemented the recommendations and was able to prevent other accidents from occurring.[10]

Workers' compensation adjusters also contribute to the risk control process by reviewing loss runs with the insured. A loss run is a printout of all of the insured's claims showing the current value of the loss (open reserves, wage loss payments, and expense payments) and details about the loss. For a given case, the adjuster might give details about the cause of the accident, the reserve rationale, and the prognosis for the injured worker's return to full duty or transitional duty and might discuss the plan for bringing each claim to a close.

A loss run review can also provide information about the following:

- *Claim frequency.* The number of claims incurred in a given period. Claim frequency should be tracked by area and injury to focus risk control efforts.

- *Average claim size.* Payments and reserves divided by the number of claims handled.

- *Large claims.* This information might include fatalities, claims for more than a specified dollar amount, or specific types of injury such as amputations. These claims are good candidates for detailed examinations of cause to help prevent similar occurrences.

- *Medical only versus wage loss claims.* An increase in the proportion of wage loss claims could indicate a need for a change in procedures or for a better return-to-work program offering modified job duties.

- *Time of day.* This factor is often overlooked, but an investigation might indicate that more claims are occurring on Monday mornings (after weekend recreational activities) or on specific shifts (for example, midnight to 6:00 AM).

SUMMARY

This chapter discussed how an adjuster investigates a workers' compensation claim. The procedure starts with notice of the injury, which can include the following four types:

1. Notice from the worker to employer
2. Notice from the worker to the compensation commission
3. Notice from the employer to the compensation commission
4. Notice from the insured to the insurer

Timely notice of an accident or injury allows the employer/insurer to investigate the claim promptly and to make a compensability determination. Notice to an employer that is not timely is usually insufficient reason to deny a claim unless the delay prejudices the employer's or the insurer's ability to investigate or defend against the claim.

Once notice is received, an adjuster confirms coverage by determining whether the date of loss falls within the coverage policy dates, whether the accident location is a covered location, and whether the injured worker's employment status is covered.

To pay workers' compensation benefits, the adjuster must set the reserve—the amount needed for the payments to be made—for wage loss benefits, medical expenses, and loss adjustment expenses, such as legal fees and the cost to obtain medical records. Reserves can be estimated by one of three methods:

1. *The individual case method.* The adjuster uses his or her expertise to generate the reserve.
2. *The formula method.* A formula based on a ratio between medical cost and wage loss or a compensation rate multiplied by a certain number of weeks is used to generate the reserve.
3. *The round table method.* Several adjusters evaluate the claim, and each suggests a reserve. All of the adjusters discuss the suggestions and reach a consensus on the reserve amount.

Because reserving is more art than science, adjusters must be alert to the pitfalls that can occur in the process. Underreserving, setting reserves that fall short of actual claim costs, is caused by an adjuster's inexperience or inattention or by an unforeseeable claim development. Stair-stepping occurs when an adjuster continually raises the reserve in small increments rather than setting an overall reserve for the claim. Both underreserving and stair-stepping can lead to insurer insolvency. Overreserving, setting reserves higher than necessary in an attempt to avoid underreserving and stair-stepping, can have an adverse effect on the insurer's net income.

To determine coverage and compensability, an adjuster investigates a claim by taking statements from the injured worker, the worker's supervisor, and any witnesses. From the employer, the adjuster seeks information and documents such as the employment application, job description, accident report, and wage information. The adjuster might also obtain medical information about previous injuries. Some investigations require an activity check to determine if the injured worker's activities are consistent with the claimed disability. The adjuster might conduct the activity check or might hire a professional surveillance firm to do so.

The adjuster also investigates a claim's medical aspects, often with the assistance of a nurse or a case manager. The investigation might include reviewing medical records, contacting the worker's current medical providers for a diagnosis and prognosis, and obtaining a history of previous injuries and accidents.

Once a claim is determined to be compensable, benefit payments begin for both wage loss and medical expenses. During the time that benefits are paid, the adjuster is responsible for medical management—ensuring that medical and rehabilitation expenses are appropriate under the circumstances. The goal of medical management is to avoid either undertreating or overtreating the claimant. The adjuster usually works with a nurse or a medical case manager to determine the amount of treatment and rehabilitation the injured worker requires.

Some states have second injury funds to compensate workers with preexisting conditions who suffer subsequent work-related injuries. Second injury funds help to minimize employer reluctance to hire disabled workers by providing a financial safety net for employers.

State laws vary on the procedures and requirements for terminating benefits, but all states define the justifications for termination. To establish a justification, an insurer might use medical opinions or other documentation to show that the worker is no longer disabled.

Most states require the insurer to send written notice of denial of a claim and the reason for it to the injured worker within a specified time. Workers can appeal claim decisions, usually starting with an informal conference or a hearing. Conferences and hearings are usually less formal than civil trials. Evidentiary rules are relaxed. Decisions from hearings can be appealed to the workers compensation commission/board, and, if still in dispute, to the state court. Arbitration and mediation are other ways to resolve claims.

Contested claims can be settled by a court award or by a compromise or negotiated settlement. Such settlements can be for a lump sum or can be structured settlements under which the worker receives a predetermined series of payments over time.

Adjusters handling workers' compensation claims are subject to licensing laws and good-faith claim handling regulations. State laws impose penalties on insurers for mishandling claims by such acts as delaying payment, improperly denying compensation, or underpaying benefits.

Adjusters play an important role in loss prevention and loss reduction by providing information from investigations to underwriters and by reviewing loss runs with the insured.

CHAPTER NOTES

1. National Council on Compensation Insurance, Inc., "Workers Compensation and Employers Liability Insurance Policy," p. 4.

2. *Johnson v. City of Kirksville*, 855 S.W.2d 396 (Missouri 1993).

3. *Oliver v. Stimpson Lumber and Liberty Northwest Insurance Company*, 297 Mont. 336, 993 P.2d 11 (Montana 1999) and *Gileski v. Community Medical Center*, 336 N.J. Super. 646, 765 A.2d 1103 (App. Div. 2001).

4. *Callahan v. Stanley Works and Home Depot, U.S.A.*, 306 N.J. Super. 488, 703 A.2d 1014 (New Jersey 1997).

5. *Oliver v. Stimson Lumber and Liberty Northwest Insurance Company*, 297 Mont. 336, 993 P.2d 11 (Montana 1999).

6. *Survey of Workers' Compensation Laws*, 2003–2004 Edition, Downers Grove, Ill.

7. *Fidelity & Casualty Co. of New York v. State*, 648 So.2d 1054 (Louisiana 1994).

8. *Shassetz v. State ex rel., Wyoming Workers' Safety and Compensation Division*, 920 P.2d 1246.

9. *Sopko v. C&R Transfer Co., Inc.*, South Dakota Supreme Court No. 20012 (1998).

10. This section was adapted from William E. Rogers, *How to Cut Workers Comp Costs: 115 Proven Ways* (Summerhill, Pa.: Country Road Publications), 1991, pp. 8.3–8.6.

Appendix A
Outlines of Statements of Injured Worker, Witnesses, and Employer/Supervisor

Injured Worker Statement Outline

1. What is your full name?
2. What is your social security number?
3. What is your current address and phone number?
4. How long have you lived there?
5. While giving this statement, are you under the influence of any medication or alcohol? If so, what type? For what reason? (Comment: Without this information, the injured worker's attorney might try to explain away inconsistencies in the statement by claiming that the injured worker was not in full possession of his or her faculties because of pain, medication, or other substances.)
6. Are you married? Number and ages of children who are dependent on you. (Comment: Information about dependents is necessary if the claim becomes a fatality.)
7. Where are you currently employed?
8. Is that your only employer? (Comment: Some states may require that, in cases of dual employment, the adjuster use earnings from both jobs when computing the benefit rate for temporary total disability.)
9. How long have you worked for each employer?
10. Before you worked for your current employer, for whom did you work? (Comment: This provides information for subsequent checks on claim and medical history.)
11. What is your work address or location?
12. What is your job title?
13. What are your job duties?
14. What is the name of your supervisor?
15. Are you a union member?

16. Are you a salaried or hourly worker? (Comment: Compare this information with the wage transcript furnished by the employer, the W-2 form, or tax returns.)

17. If hourly, what is your hourly pay rate? How many hours per week do you work on average? Any overtime? How much is the overtime rate? (Comment: Overtime wages might have to be included in the TTD rate.)

18. If salaried, what is your current weekly/monthly/annual salary?

19. Are you paid any noncash wages? If so, describe. (Comment: Some states require that the imputed value of noncash wages, such as housing, company car, or uniforms, be included along with cash wages in computing the TTD rate.)

20. Were you recently injured on the job? (Comment: This sets the stage for the specific claim to be discussed.)

21. What was the date of that accident or injury?

22. What time of day?

23. Where did it happen?

24. When did you start work that day?

25. Did you feel fine, physically, before you started work?

26. How many hours had you been working the day the injury occurred?

27. What were you doing at the time the injury occurred? Is this a regular part of your job? Who told you to do this?

28. Were you working alone or with anyone? What are the names of the people with whom you were working? If you were working alone, what are the names of the people working closest to you? (Comment: This information provides leads for the adjuster's witness investigation.)

29. What happened? Briefly describe the circumstances that led to your injury.

30. Did you feel pain immediately? Where?

31. Did you stop work immediately? If not, why not?

32. Did anyone see you get injured? (Comment: Assists in identifying witnesses.)

33. Did you report the injury immediately to your employer? If not, why not? When did you first report the injury to your employer? What was the name of the first person to whom you reported the injury? (Comment: The greater the delay between the date of the alleged injury and the date reported to the employer, the more the adjuster should investigate the claim's legitimacy.)

34. Did you seek medical care on the day of the injury? If not, why not? What was the first date you sought medical treatment for the injury? (Comment: The longer the gap between the date of injury and the first date of medical treatment, the more tenuous the causal relationship is likely to be between the two.)

35. What are the names and addresses of the medical care providers you first contacted? Did you tell them you were injured on the job? (Comment:

The first part of the query lays the foundation for the adjuster's medical investigation. The second can be surprisingly revealing. Often, workers do not give a description of on-the-job injury to their doctor and then later file a workers' compensation claim.)

36. What did they do for you?

37. Did you see another physician for your injury? What is the physician's name and address? Who referred you to this physician? (Comment: Adjusters might learn that a certain law firm or attorney referred the worker to a particular physician.)

38. When did you start seeing this physician? Are you still under the physician's treatment? What was the date of last appointment? What is the date of next appointment? (Comment: Frequency of treatments can trigger the adjuster's concern about over-billing for unnecessary physical therapy.)

39. Had you ever seen this physician for other accidents or injuries? What other physicians have you seen for this injury? Who referred you to them?

40. Has the physician released you for work? If not, has he or she given you any idea as to when you can return to work? (Comment: The worker's reaction to this question can indicate the worker's motivation to return to work.)

41. Have you worked at all since the injury date? (Comment: If other evidence indicates that the injured worker has been working, the adjuster might be able to use the statement to impeach the worker's credibility.)

42. Were you paid in full for the day on which you were injured? (Comment: In many states, if the injured worker was paid for less than a half day on the date of injury, the employer must pay a full day of TTD.)

43. Have you ever had any problems with this same part of your body before? (Comment: The adjuster should say *problems*, not *accidents*. The worker might have had chronic back pain for many years, but might not consider that an accident. Asking if the worker has had any problems with that same body part prevents hedging. The adjuster can use this information in conducting a subsequent medical investigation and/or in testing worker credibility. If the worker denies prior injuries and further investigation reveals that the worker had some, the adjuster should consider the possibility of fraud and concealment in the current claim.)

44. Have you ever been injured on *any* job before? Give details.

45. Have you ever collected workers' compensation before? Give details. (Comment: If the injured worker denies any prior compensation claims, and prior or subsequent investigation reveals that the worker has made such claims, the adjuster should suspect the possibility of fraud and concealment in the current claim.)

46. Have you ever been injured in an auto accident? Give details.

47. Have you ever filed an insurance claim before? Give details.

48. Have you ever been hospitalized? If so, for what?

49. Any prior surgeries?

50. What part(s) of your body did you injure in this accident? Did you injure any other parts of your body? (Comment: This second question is *very important*. It can limit the claim of some injured workers who might later try to add other aches, pains, and injuries as causally related to the original accident. Although latent injuries do exist, the adjuster can help prevent these "floating disabilities" by having the worker say, "I injured no part of my body in this accident other than my lower back.")

51. Other than workers' compensation, have you filed for benefits from any other source(s) (e.g., health, disability, Social Security, unemployment compensation) as a result of this injury?

52. Is there anything about the accident I haven't asked you that you would like to add?

53. Have the answers you've given been true to the best of your knowledge?

Witnesses Statement Outline

- Name, address, and phone number.
- Social Security number.
- Relationship to injured worker (co-worker, innocent bystander, and so forth).
- If a co-worker, what is your job title and job duties? What were you doing at the time of the event?
- Describe what you saw or experienced regarding the event.
- Did you discuss this event with the injured worker after it happened?
- What did you see after the event happened?
- Do you know the injured worker personally?
- Do you know anything about the injured worker outside of work, such as activities, hobbies, and so on?

Employer/Supervisor Statement Outline

- Name, address, and phone number.
- Social Security number.
- Job title and job duties.
- Relationship to the injured worker.
- Did you witness the event? If so, describe it.
- Was the event reported to you? Who reported the event, when, and how?
- Was the injured worker doing his or her duties at the time of the event?
- What was the injured worker's work attendance record for prior twelve months?
- Are any potential layoffs or reduction-in-force measures being planned that could affect the injured worker?
- Is light duty work available for the injured worker if a physician prescribes it?

Appendix B
Indicators of Workers' Compensation Fraud

Indicators of Workers' Compensation Fraud
Detection – The First Line of Defense

Most claims are legitimate, but some are fraudulent. Therefore, it is appropriate for the adjuster to review all claims for possible fraud. Determining the "fraud probability" of any claim is facilitated when the adjuster is familiar with various fraud indicators.

These indicators should help isolate those claims which merit closer scrutiny. No one indicator by itself is necessarily suspicious. Even the presence of several indicators, while suggestive of possible fraud, does not mean that fraud has been committed. Indicators of possible fraud are "red flags" only, not actual evidence.

Some claims, although suspicious, may have to be paid for lack of conclusive evidence of fraud. However, they should be referred to NICB for further review.

Indicators Related to Claimant, Prior History and Current Work Status

- ☛ Employee is disgruntled, soon-to-retire or facing imminent firing or layoff.
- ☛ Employee is involved in seasonal work that is about to end.
- ☛ Employee took unexplained or excessive time off prior to claimed injury.
- ☛ Employee takes more time off than the claimed injury seems to warrant.
- ☛ Listed number is a mobile/cellular phone.
- ☛ Employee is a drifter and has a history of short-term employment.
- ☛ Employee is new on the job.
- ☛ Employee is experiencing financial difficulties and/or domestic problems prior to submission of claim.
- ☛ Employee recently purchased private disability policies.
- ☛ Employee changes physician when a release for work has been issued.
- ☛ Employee has a history of reporting subjective injuries.
- ☛ Review of a rehab report describes the employee as being muscular, well tanned, with calloused hands and grease under the fingernails.
- ☛ First notification of injury or claim made after employee is terminated or laid off.
- ☛ Disputes the average weekly wage due to additional income, i.e., cash, per diem and/or 1099 income.
- ☛ Has several other family members also receiving workers' compensation benefits or other "social insurance" benefits, i.e., unemployment.
- ☛ Demands quick settlement decisions or commitments.
- ☛ Demands quick payments for medical providers, etc.
- ☛ Is unusually familiar with workers' compensation claim handling procedures and laws.
- ☛ Is consistently uncooperative.
- ☛ Surveillance or "tip" indicates that the totally disabled worker is currently employed elsewhere.
- ☛ Employee has submitted substantial material misrepresentation on the employment application.
- ☛ Employee comes to office for delivery of benefit checks, avoids use of U.S. Mail.
- ☛ Employee refuses to allow visits or rehabilitation at home or specifies plenty of warning time prior to a visit.
- ☛ After injury, employee is never home or spouse/relative answering phone states the employee "just stepped out", or may have to contact him/her by pager.
- ☛ Return calls to residence have strange or unexpected background noises which indicate that it may not be a residence.
- ☛ Employee protests about returning to work and never seems to improve.
- ☛ Employee cancels or fails to keep appointment or refuses a diagnostic procedure to confirm an injury.
- ☛ Employee complains to carrier's CEO or executive management at home office to press for payment.
- ☛ Social Security number provided does not belong to employee.

☞ Applicant refuses or cannot produce solid or correct identification.
☞ Employees' family member(s) knows nothing about the claim.

Circumstances of the Accident

☞ Accident occurs late Friday afternoon or shortly after the employee reports to work on Monday.
☞ Accident is not witnessed or witness to the accident conflicts with the applicant's version.
☞ Employee has leg/arm injuries at odd time, i.e. at lunch hour.
☞ Fellow workers hear a rumor circulating that accident was not legitimate.
☞ Accident occurs in an area where injured employee would not normally be.
☞ Accident is not the type that the employee should be involved in, i.e. an office worker who is lifting heavy objects on a loading dock.
☞ Accident occurs just prior to a strike or near the end of probationary period.
☞ Employer's first report of claim contrasts with description of accident set forth in medical history.
☞ Details of accident are vague or contradictory, have inconsistencies, and are not credible.
☞ Incident is not promptly reported by employee to supervisor.

Medical Treatment

☞ Diagnosis is inconsistent with treatment.
☞ Physician is known for handling suspect claims.
☞ Treatment for extensive injuries is protracted though the accident was minor.
☞ "Boilerplate" medical reports are identical to other reports from same doctor, do not identify by gender or get gender wrong.
☞ Workers' compensation insurer and health carrier are billed simultaneously; payment is accepted from both.
☞ Summary medical bills submitted without dates or descriptions of office visits.
☞ Medical bills submitted are photocopies of originals.
☞ Extensive or unnecessary treatment for minor, subjective injuries.
☞ Treatment directed to a separate facility in which the referring physician has a financial interest (especially if this is not disclosed in advance).
☞ Referral for treatment/testing to facility close to referring facility.
☞ Injuries are all subjective, i.e. pain, headaches, nausea, inability to sleep.
☞ Treatment dates appear on holidays or other days that facilities would not normally be open.
☞ Employee is immediately referred for a wide variety of psychiatric tests, when the original claim involved trauma only. These claims usually present with vague complaints of "stress".
☞ Inappropriate expensive medical equipment prescribed for minor injury.
☞ Alleged injury relates to a pre-existing injury or health problem.

The Claimant's Attorney

☞ Attorney becomes involved early in the claims process.
☞ Attorney lien or representation letter dated the day of the reported incident.
☞ Attorney threatens further legal action unless a quick settlement is made.
☞ Attorneys inquire about a settlement or buy out early in the life of the claim.
☞ Employee initially wants to settle with insurer, but later retains an attorney with increased subjective complaints.
☞ High incidence of applications from a specific firm.
☞ Pattern of occupational type claims for "dying" industries, i.e. lung, asbestos; wholesale claim handling by law firms and multiple class action suits.
☞ Same doctor/lawyer pair previously observed to handle this kind of injury.
☞ Employee receives all mail by and through his/her attorney.

Chapter 7

Direct Your Learning

Workers' Compensation Subrogation

After learning the content of this chapter, you should be able to:

■ Describe the incentives an employer or an insurer has for pursuing workers' compensation subrogation.

■ Given a case, determine if subrogation is economically viable.

In support of this objective, you should be able to:

- Investigate the accident for third-party liability
- Identify potentially liable third parties
- Determine negligence
- Apportion liability
- Determine negligence test and subrogation restrictions
- Determine amount of potential recovery
- Conduct a cost benefit analysis

■ Describe the subrogation process.

■ Describe potential subrogation scenarios for claims involving:

- Vehicles
- Products
- Premises

■ Explain how the insurer can become a party to a claim against a third party.

■ Describe the questions to be answered in determining how to best resolve a lien.

■ Describe the circumstances in which a lien is resolved without stipulation and with stipulation.

Develop Your Perspective

What are the main topics covered in the chapter?

This chapter describes workers' compensation subrogation, including how to identify economically viable subrogation opportunities, how to investigate these opportunities, and how to bring them to a successful conclusion.

Identify the subrogation process at your company.

- Are there workers' compensation subrogation adjusters?
- If not, who looks for subrogation opportunities?

Why is it important to learn about these topics?

Workers' compensation premiums are a major cost to any employer. By pursuing subrogation and making a recovery, the adjuster helps to reduce the employer's cost of claims.

Consider an injury that you might sustain at work.

- Is a third party responsible for your injury?
- If a third party is responsible, is the subrogation opportunity economically viable for your employer/insurer?

How can you use what you will learn?

Examine a workers' compensation subrogation claim.

- Are there any viable defenses to the claim?
- Does the amount of potential recovery outweigh the cost of pursuing subrogation?

Chapter 7
Workers' Compensation Subrogation

In exchange for providing workers' compensation benefits regardless of fault, employers (and their insurers) receive (1) the right to recover benefits paid when the injury is caused by a negligent third party and (2) immunity from suit in most circumstances. The process for recovering the benefits paid from responsible third parties is called **subrogation** and involves substituting one party for another regarding certain rights. This chapter focuses on the subrogation process, which has become increasingly important in the workers' compensation claim business in recent years. Many insurers and claim administrators (called insurers throughout this chapter) have designated subrogation as a specialty apart from adjusting insurance claims. Workers' compensation insurers have also adopted this specialization approach, using specially trained and experienced claim adjusters who work exclusively with subrogation claims. This practice is particularly important in workers' compensation because aggressive and effective subrogation practices can reduce costs, thus lowering workers' compensation premiums, a substantial cost of doing business for insured employers.

Subrogation
The process an insurer uses to recover payment from a negligent third party.

FINANCIAL AND SERVICE INCENTIVES OF WORKERS' COMPENSATION SUBROGATION

Employers expect organizations that administer their workers' compensation claims to take optimum advantage of every subrogation opportunity. If subrogation is successful, the employer's loss experience reflects payments for only those losses that were not recoverable from a third party. Employers can control their workers' compensation costs by taking steps to recover losses whenever possible from third parties. This approach can substantially improve an employer's loss experience and improve an insurer's overall underwriting performance.

IDENTIFYING ECONOMICALLY VIABLE SUBROGATION OPPORTUNITIES: A SEVEN-STEP PROCESS

Even when it can be proven that a third party is responsible for a worker's injury, subrogation might not be viable. Adjusters must evaluate subrogation opportunities to determine if pursuing subrogation is cost-effective. This section sets out a structured framework for determining whether subrogation is economically viable in a given case. Using a structured framework does the following:

- Provides an efficient and effective method to identify which subrogation opportunities are economically viable
- Analyzes those factors (negligence test, subrogation and recovery rights) that affect the subrogation opportunity in a particular state
- Standardizes the methodology, reducing the possibility of a missed subrogation opportunity

Many adjusters use a seven-step process to determine if subrogation is economically viable. The process encourages the adjuster to methodically analyze information that affects the success of a subrogation effort. In each of the first six steps of the process, the adjuster must obtain information that supports a successful subrogation effort in the current step before proceeding to the next step. If the information does not support the insurer's subrogation effort, the effort ends. Even if the first six steps indicate that subrogation is feasible, the adjuster must perform a cost-benefit analysis (Step 7) to determine if, based on the facts, the benefits of a subrogation effort outweigh the costs and the uncertainty about the outcome of the case.

Seven-Step Process to Identify Economically Viable Subrogation Opportunities

Step 1	Investigate the accident for third-party liability
Step 2	Identify potentially liable third parties
Step 3	Determine liability
Step 4	Apportion liability
Step 5	Determine negligence test and subrogation restrictions
Step 6	Determine amount of potential recovery
Step 7	Conduct a cost-benefit analysis

Step 1: Investigate the Accident for Third-Party Liability

In some cases, the adjuster investigating a claim's compensability will simultaneously investigate the possibility of third-party liability. In other cases, a subrogation specialist will conduct the third-party liability investigation, possibly using some of the information from the compensability investigation and supplementing it with further independent investigation.

The third-party investigation should address how, why, when, and where the accident occurred. The *how* and *why* questions help determine the accident's cause. The *how* question focuses on the cause of the injury and the details of what happened. The *why* question addresses fault; who or what acted or failed to act reasonably under the circumstances. The *when* question establishes a time line to determine if a causal connection exists between the fault and the accident's occurrence. The *where* question pinpoints the accident's exact location, a critical fact, particularly for premises claims. For example, for a slip and fall claim, the adjuster should ask, "Who was responsible for maintaining the exact location on the date and time that the injured worker fell?" Identifying the entity that owned and/or controlled the location is not enough. The adjuster must probe further to determine if another entity was responsible for cleaning the area.

After obtaining the accident's details from the injured worker, the employer, and witnesses and securing the evidence, the adjuster decides if the information reveals sufficient subrogation potential to proceed with the next step in the process.

Step 2: Identify Potentially Liable Third Parties

Using the information obtained in the investigation, the adjuster next identifies all third parties involved in the accident. A third party is any person or entity other than the employer or the co-worker. This step comes before determining liability because the adjuster need not conduct a liability analysis if no third party is responsible for the worker's injury.

Step 3: Determine Liability

To determine if the third party identified in Step 2 is liable, the adjuster must review various legal theories, such as negligence and strict liability, that relate to fault.

In establishing a theory of liability, the adjuster uses the reasonable person standard, that is, what a reasonable person would do under circumstances similar to those in the case. In determining foreseeability and preventability, for example, the adjuster asks whether a reasonable person under similar circumstances would have foreseen the accident or would have been able to prevent it.

Step 4: Apportion Liability

Next, the adjuster must apportion the liability among the injured worker, the employer, and the negligent third party(ies) collectively. Although apportioning liability is subjective and is based on the adjuster's experience, it is necessary for two reasons:

1. It will determine if the injured worker can meet the legal test—such as proving the negligence, or lack thereof, of various parties based on the relevant state's law or its case law—to recover damages.
2. It will assist in estimating the amount of recovery possible under the specific statute's definition of negligence.

Factors in apportioning liability are whether the injured worker might have contributed to the injury, whether the third party might be solely liable, or whether the employer might be partially liable. If the injured worker contributed to the injury, then the adjuster should list each separate action of any third party(ies) or of the employer that also contributed to the injury, apportion a percentage of liability to each, add the percentages, and subtract the total from one hundred percent. The result is the amount of liability attributable to the injured worker. In claims that involve multiple defendants, adjusters usually do not apportion liability among defendants; liability examiners, defense attorneys, or plaintiffs' attorneys usually do so.

The adjuster should also determine whether the doctrine of strict liability applies to the case. States vary in how they apply the doctrine. Strict liability imposes one hundred percent liability on a defendant for defects in the manufacture, design, or assembly of a product or in any warnings about a product's hazards. In addition, certain activities, such as blasting, are considered so hazardous by nature that the defendant is strictly liable for resulting damage or injuries, even though the defendant has exercised all necessary precautions to prevent injury.

If a third-party claim meets the statutory requirement for a strict liability action, then the adjuster can skip Step 5 and go to Step 6. Otherwise, the adjuster should complete Step 5 for each third party for which strict liability does not apply.

Step 5: Determine Negligence Test and Subrogation Restrictions

Whether a worker who has contributed to his or her injury can recover damages depends on which of the following four negligence tests apply in the state:

1. *Pure comparative.* The worker and/or the insurer have a right to recover from negligent defendants even if the worker is more at fault than all of the defendants combined. This test presents the most opportunities for subrogation.

2. *Forty-nine percent comparative.* The worker and/or the insurer have a right to recover if the worker's fault is 49 percent or less of the overall fault, that is, less than the fault of all the defendants combined.

3. *Fifty percent comparative.* The worker and/or the insurer have a right to recover if the worker's fault is 50 percent or less of the overall fault, that is, up to equal the fault of all the defendants combined.

4. *Contributory.* The worker and/or the insurer are barred from recovery if the worker contributed at all to the injury. This test presents the least opportunities for subrogation.

Subrogation laws, which vary by state, regulate an insurer's subrogation and recovery rights, including the right to assert a worker's compensation lien.

A lien gives notice to all parties that the insurer has a financial interest in any damages the injured worker collects from a third party. Some state subrogation provisions do the following:

- Prohibit insurers/employers from pursuing an independent action against a third party, that is, an action separate from the injured worker's action against the third party.
- Prohibit insurers/employers from asserting a lien on certain types of workers' compensation settlements.
- Prohibit insurers/employers from asserting a lien against damages awarded in a third-party tort claim or another liability-based claim.
- Permit insurers/employers to assert only part of the lien against damages awarded in a third-party tort claim.
- Permit insurers/employers to assert the full lien, but only against certain types of damages awarded in the third-party claim. For example, states might prohibit insurers from asserting liens against damages paid for loss of consortium or against damages paid for pain and suffering.

Two kinds of laws that either limit or eliminate insurers' liens against damages awarded in third-party claims are employers negligence statutes and statutes that incorporate the "made-whole" doctrine.

Employers negligence statutes apply if an injured worker can prove that the employer contributed to the injury, thereby limiting the liability of other defendants and reducing the amount of damages other defendants would pay in the liability case. In an effort to recover the full amount in damages payable by the third-party defendants, the injured worker tries to reduce or eliminate the employer's lien by the amount the employer was negligent. In some states, if the employer is negligent to any degree, the employer's lien is eliminated. However, in most states with this type of statute, the employer's lien is reduced in proportion to the amount the employer contributed to the worker's injury.

The made-whole doctrine is triggered when injured workers assert that the combined amount of workers' compensation benefits and liability awards will not adequately compensate them (make them whole) for their loss. States do not apply this doctrine uniformly. Because workers' compensation benefits pay lost wages and medical expenses, these cases usually center on damages workers' compensation does not cover.

Adjusters should be aware of any claim that involves a conflict of laws between states. Such a conflict arises when the liability claim is filed in a state other than the benefit state. Usually the liability claim is filed in the **accident state**, the state in which the accident occurred. The accident state usually determines the applicable negligence and strict liability rules. In contrast, the state that governs the workers' compensation claim, also known as the **benefit state**, determines which subrogation law applies.

State subrogation laws pertain to an insurer's right to subrogate and to the amount recoverable. A law might reduce an insurer's recovery amount by

Accident state
In workers' compensation, the state in which the accident occurred.

Benefit state
The state that governs workers' compensation benefit payments and determines the subrogation laws that will apply in a specific case.

requiring it to pay the injured worker's attorney fees and/or legal expenses or the cost of a nurse case manager, for example.

Suppose an insurer asserts a lien against damages awarded for a worker's bodily injury claim against a third party. Also suppose that the insurer has relied (coat-tailed) on the injured worker's attorney to obtain such damages. Most states would require the insurer to pay a share of the injured worker's attorney fee and expenses, calculated as follows:

1. Attorney fee = (Gross recovery − Attorney expenses) × Attorney fee percentage.
2. Insurer's percentage share of attorney fee and expenses = (Attorney expenses + Attorney fee) ÷ Gross recovery.
3. Insurer's recovery amount = Insurer's total lien − (Insurer's total lien × Insurer's percentage share).

The following is an illustration:

Gross recovery:	$100,000
Attorney fee percentage:	33⅓%
Attorney expenses:	$1,500
Insurer's total lien:	$27,000

First, determine the attorney fee, which, for this example, is one-third of the recovery.

$$
\begin{aligned}
\text{Attorney fee} &= (\text{Gross recovery} - \text{Attorney expenses}) \times \text{Attorney fee percentage} \\
&= (\$100{,}000 - \$1{,}500) \times 0.333 \\
&= \$98{,}500 \times 0.333 \\
&= \$32{,}800.50.
\end{aligned}
$$

Second, determine the percentage of the attorney fee and expenses to be deducted from the lien.

$$
\begin{aligned}
\text{Insurer's share of attorney fee and expenses} &= (\text{Attorney expenses} + \text{Attorney fee}) \div \text{Gross recovery} \\
&= (\$1{,}500 + \$32{,}800.50) \div \$100{,}000 \\
&= \$34{,}300.50 \div \$100{,}000 \\
&= 0.343.
\end{aligned}
$$

Third, determine the amount of the recovery to which the insurer is entitled by statute.

$$
\begin{aligned}
\text{Insurer's recovery} &= \text{Insurer's total lien} - (\text{Insurer's total lien} \times \text{Insurer's percentage share}) \\
&= \$27{,}000 - (\$27{,}000 \times 0.343) \\
&= \$27{,}000 - \$9{,}261 \\
&= \$17{,}739.
\end{aligned}
$$

While the total amount of the benefits paid by the insurer is $27,000, the insurer's total recovery allowed by statute is $17,739.

In some cases, rather than recovering money damages, the insurer can recover a credit against future payments of workers' compensation benefits to the worker. The credit allows the insurer either to suspend benefit payments for a time (a dollar-for-dollar credit) or to pay future benefits at a reduced rate figured at the same rate as the insurer's percentage share (pro rata credit). The former acts like a deductible the worker must meet before benefits resume, and the latter acts like a co-payment the worker must make during the credit period.

The amount of the credit is equal to the injured worker's net recovery from the gross recovery. The credit can be calculated as follows:

$$\text{Insurer's credit against future benefits} = \text{Gross recovery} - \left(\text{Attorney Fee} + \text{Attorney expenses}\right) - \text{Insurer's recovery}.$$

Using the figures from the previous example, this credit is calculated as follows:

$$
\begin{aligned}
\text{Insurer's credit against future benefits} &= \$100{,}000 - (\$32{,}800.50 + \$1{,}500) - \$17{,}739 \\
&= \$100{,}000 - \$34{,}300.50 - \$17{,}739 \\
&= \$47{,}960.50.
\end{aligned}
$$

If the credit can be taken dollar-for-dollar, then the insurer is not required to resume benefit payments until the credit is exhausted. If the insurer is required to continue benefit payments but at a reduced rate, future benefits will be prorated, that is, paid at 34.3 percent (insurer's percentage share) until the credit is exhausted. In other words, if the future benefit payments total is $47,928 (from the award to the injured worker), the insurer will make benefit payments of $16,439.30 ($47,928 × 0.343) until the $47,928 credit is exhausted. Thereafter, the insurer will resume full benefit payments if any are still payable. Some states do not allow the insurer to take a credit against future benefits, and others allow a credit only against future wage loss payments.

To help contain medical costs, some insurers employ nurse case managers to monitor files for the relationship between the injury and the treatment, necessity of treatment, and utilization and disability management. These nurses interact with the injured worker, treating physician, and workers' compensation adjuster throughout the benefit period. Some dispute exists about whether the injured worker actually benefits from a nurse case manager's involvement. Most states either prohibit insurers from including nurse case managers' fees in the lien or require the insurer to prove that the injured worker has received some benefit from the nurse's involvement (i.e., that it constitutes treatment).

The results of an employer's or insurer's subrogation efforts are a function of: (1) the subrogation laws in the states in which the employer has operations (although some subrogation claims can occur at incidental locations); (2) the effect of subrogation laws on the employer's operations; and, (3) the quality of the employer's or insurer's subrogation program. All else being equal, an employer with a large machine and equipment loss exposure should have better recovery results if its operations are located in states with a strict liability statute and no employers negligence statute. An employer with a large vehicle loss exposure should have better recovery results if it operates in states with no restrictions on third-party tort claims.

Step 6: Determine Amount of Potential Recovery

Having apportioned the amount of liability among the parties and considered the state laws on negligence and subrogation, the adjuster can estimate the potential amount of recovery from the negligent third party(ies). As part of this step, the adjuster should analyze the likelihood of success at trial and whether the third party(ies) will attempt to negotiate a settlement.

Step 7: Conduct a Cost-Benefit Analysis

The cost-benefit analysis is a function of the following factors: the estimated incurred loss (paid loss plus reserve), the third party's (parties') ability to pay, the costs to be incurred in the recovery action, the strength of the liability case against the third party, and the workers' compensation insurer's subrogation and recovery rights. As long as the insurer's right to assert a lien or recover for the claim is not statutorily restricted, a case with a large estimated incurred loss, high limit(s) of any applicable third-party policies, and a strong theory of liability should yield a favorable recovery. If an insurer is pursuing an independent action, and if the anticipated recovery is greater than the projected cost of pursuing the third party(ies), subrogation is economically viable.

If the adjuster's cost-benefit analysis indicates that the cost to obtain the recovery would exceed the amount of actual recovery, the adjuster will usually not pursue subrogation. However, sometimes, to hold negligent third parties responsible for their actions, an insurer or employer pursues subrogation even though it is not cost-effective. An adjuster should consult with a supervisor before abandoning a potential subrogation opportunity.

Using the seven-step process should not only enhance the efficiency of handling a third-party claim but also improve the effectiveness of the insurer's long-term recovery results by increasing the number of recoveries and the gross dollars recovered. To pursue a recovery, the adjuster must follow another process to initiate and complete subrogation.

SUBROGATION PROCESS

The subrogation process has six elements, as shown in the following box.

> **The Six-Step Subrogation Process**
> 1. Conduct a third-party investigation and a liability analysis
> 2. Notify all stakeholders of lien
> 3. Protect the lien
> 4. Monitor progress
> 5. Negotiate and resolve the lien
> 6. Monitor post-settlement activities

Conduct a Third-Party Investigation and a Liability Analysis

The first element in the subrogation process is the same as the first step in identifying economically viable subrogation. The investigation used to identify a viable subrogation opportunity will have identified any third party(ies) involved in the accident and any possible liability. Third-party liability in workers' compensation subrogation claims typically arises from (1) use of a vehicle, (2) use of a product, or (3) use of a premises. Each type of claim can occur either on or off the employer's premises. The following suggestions for each type of claim investigation provide a basic framework for adjusters to follow.

Subrogation Claims Involving a Vehicle

Most claims that involve the use of vehicles occur off premises, although occasionally, third-party auto claims occur in a parking lot owned or controlled by the employer. A vehicle is considered any mode of transportation registered for use on public roads, primarily trucks and automobiles, and can be owned by either the employer or worker. Policy language determines which vehicle's uninsured motorists (UM) or underinsured motorists (UIM) coverage, if applicable, is triggered. Claims involving vehicles are generally the easiest and least expensive subrogation claims to investigate. If the accident is compensable and a police accident report has been completed, the investigation basically involves securing a copy of the police report from the injured worker, employer, or police precinct. Because versions of the accident can be disputed and other identifying information inaccurate, the adjuster should obtain the following information from the parties involved even if a police accident report was taken:

- Exact location of the accident; if unknown, the name of the closest major street or highway and the city and state.
- Exact date and time of the accident.

- Exact cause of the accident. Information should include the direction of each vehicle; position of each vehicle before, at the time of, and after impact; weather conditions; and traffic controls.
- Name(s) of operator(s) of the other vehicle(s).
- Name(s) of any witnesses.
- Registered owner(s) of each vehicle, if different than the operator(s).
- Name(s) of the insurer(s) of each vehicle.

The adjuster should take statements from the vehicle operators and any witnesses if the facts of the accident are disputed. The adjuster must also conduct a product investigation if the accident investigation reveals any of the following circumstances:

- The accident was caused by mechanical failure of a component part of one of the vehicles.
- The accident was caused by improper repair of one of the vehicles.
- The injuries were more severe because a safety device did not operate properly; for example, an airbag failed to deploy.

All physical evidence must be preserved for inspection by an accident reconstruction expert and a products expert in anticipation of litigation.

Subrogation Claims Involving a Product

Product claims typically involve one of three scenarios.

Scenario 1—Product owned and maintained by the employer

These claims are generally the most complex and the most expensive because of the need for expert inspections and expert testimony. Employers whose operations involve a lot of machinery and equipment generate the largest and most frequent losses. States with strict products-liability statutes provide the best subrogation environment. Strict liability focuses on product assembly, design, and warning defects. Answers to the following questions can help identify a subrogation opportunity for product claims:

- Exactly what was the injured worker doing at the time of the accident, and how did the accident occur?
- Was the injured worker using the product correctly, and had the worker been trained in how to use the product properly?
- Has there been any previous problems with the product? Was the problem documented? If so, when and where did the problem occur, and did it cause any injuries?
- Was the product modified? If so, by whom and when. What type of modifications were made, and why?
- Who installed the product? If the installation required assembly, who performed the assembly?

- In the employer's opinion, what caused the accident? (Only qualified personnel should respond to this question.)

With the answers to these questions, along with product photos, the adjuster should have a fairly good idea about whether a strict liability or negligence claim exists. If so, then the following additional information should be documented for review by a product expert, who might also want to inspect the product.

- Product's brand name, model, and serial number, and the manufacturer's address. The manufacturer and the product should be researched to determine any prior claims against them, and the product should be compared to like products in its class. Web sites advising of product recalls can provide useful information.
- Copies of all purchase documentation (for example, receipts and sales contracts) and product literature (for example, owner's manual, warranties, product labeling, and diagrams).
- Date the product was made and length of time it has been in the employer's possession.
- History of any modifications made to the product and why they were made. The history can be important if the injured worker is alleging that the modification contributed to or caused the injury. Likewise, the adjuster should obtain copies of maintenance records to identify any problems with a particular part and even copies of regular maintenance records.
- Operator's training log. Training logs are important in claims arising from accidents in states with an employers negligence statute. The operator's training and experience are important factors in assessing liability.
- Safety inspection report, if one was completed, from the employer, the Occupational Safety and Health Administration (OSHA), or an outside private inspection firm.

All physical evidence must be preserved and stored. Spoliation of evidence claims are prevalent in product cases if evidence is improperly handled.

Scenario 2—Faulty repair of product owned but not maintained by the employer

These claims arise when the accident is caused by an improper repair or inadequate maintenance work performed by a technician hired by the employer. These claims can require the use of an expert and can involve many of the same issues and documentation as Scenario 1 claims involve and can, therefore, be just as expensive.

However, because the subrogation target is a maintenance and/or repair company, the investigations for these claims focus on the repair technician's actions, and liability is based on negligence. In contrast, strict liability and breach of warranty liability focus on the product itself. In addition to the questions asked in Scenario 1, the adjuster should ask the following questions:

- How often was the product maintained and by whom? Which areas were inspected, when were they last inspected, and what types of adjustments were made, if any?
- Was the product ever repaired? If so, what type of repair was made, and when and why was it made?

In addition to the evidence and information requested in Scenario 1, the following are needed:

- Name, address, and phone number of the firm that performed the product's maintenance and/or repair
- Product's maintenance and repair log, including the type and manufacturer of parts used for repair, type of work performed, and reason for the repair
- Receipts and a copy of the contract for all repair and maintenance work

Employers that have repairs done off premises to a product that has caused an injury should have the repair firm sign an indemnification agreement. This agreement transfers the employer's loss exposure for a possible spoliation of evidence claim if the equipment is lost or stolen while in the custody of the repair firm.

A negligence claim can turn into a strict liability claim. While investigating a faulty repair or maintenance claim, an adjuster might discover that a faulty part caused a malfunction that led to the worker's injury. Faulty parts might relate to a product's design or manufacture and might therefore fall under strict liability rules.

Scenario 3—Product owned and maintained by a third party

This type of claim usually arises when a worker is required to use a product located off the employer's premises. For example, a worker is injured by a construction elevator used to get to the work location. Depending on the cause of loss, the negligent third party could be the elevator's manufacturer or any entities that manufactured any of the elevator's component parts, such as the sensors that regulate the doors' opening and closing. The negligent third party could also be the landlord, the property manager, a general contractor, or an outside firm, depending on who installed and maintained the elevator.

Sometimes the product is located on the employer's premises because the employer has borrowed, leased, or rented it. Regardless of the accident location, the investigations described in Scenarios 1 and 2 must be performed to determine if the worker's injury was caused by the product (because of an assembly, design, or warning defect) or by the product's improper maintenance and repair. If the accident did not occur near the employer's operation, legal action might be required to gain access to the evidence needed to prove liability.

Subrogation Claims Involving a Premises

Scenario 1—Hazard caused by a third party doing work for the employer

These claims arise when the employer hires a third party, such as a cleaning company or a contractor, to do work on its premises. An injury might occur when a worker slips and falls on a substance left on the floor by the cleaning crew or from an obstruction or a hazardous condition left by a contractor. In winter, injuries result from improper plowing, salting, or sanding employers' parking lots. For all premises claims the adjuster should obtain the following information:

- Exact cause of the worker's injury
- Exact time and location of the accident
- Possible contributing factors, such as the speed at which the worker was walking; worker's footwear; slope of surface; size and weight of objects the worker carried; lighting; visibility of the hazard; visibility and location of warning signs; and a general description of the accident location
- Length of time the hazard existed, if known
- Any knowledge the third party had of the hazard
- Whether the third party *should* have known that hazard existed, even if the third party did not have actual notice of the hazard

The adjuster should secure the following documents regarding contractors:

- Certificates of insurance for all general contractors and subcontractors
- Indemnification and hold-harmless agreements between the employer and firm(s) performing the work
- Photos of the accident location and surrounding area from various angles
- Copy of the work plans or diagrams to determine how the work was to be completed
- Log or schedule of which firm worked on a given day, where and what type of work was performed by each firm, and the name of the entity responsible for supervising the work site (for larger jobs or ones with multiple contractors)

When the investigation involves a cleaning firm, a copy of the contract between the firm and the employer is crucial. Contracts with cleaning companies usually provide the time, location, and type of services performed. Contracts for snow removal companies usually specify when and under what circumstances the entity plows and provides other services, such as salting and sanding. Insurance certificates must be secured for both types of companies. The adjuster should also review the contract to determine if it contains a hold-harmless agreement that might relieve a party from responsibility.

Scenario 2—Hazard caused by third party doing work for another third party

These claims usually arise from injuries that occur off the employer's premises, either adjacent, nearby, or far away. Causes of injuries might include substances on or defects in walkways or facilities accessible to workers or obstructions created by third parties, such as construction contractors or cleaning companies. Workers might be injured approaching or leaving their employer's premises or while working or entertaining clients at client locations, restaurants, or sports facilities.

Regardless of the accident location, the investigation is the same. Accidents that occur off the employer's premises are more difficult to investigate because the accident site is outside of the employer's control. Legal action might be necessary to obtain necessary evidence to prove liability. Spoliation of evidence is an issue because the accident location might be altered after the worker's injury to prevent further injury. Early intervention is crucial.

Notify All Stakeholders of a Lien

Lien
A charge or an interest in real or personal property that can be assessed to satisfy a debt.

The second element in the subrogation process is to notify all stakeholders that the insurer is asserting a workers' compensation **lien** on any damages the injured worker collects from a liable third party. A lien is a charge or interest in real or personal property (in this case, damages recovered) to satisfy a debt. The lien notice details the amount of money the insurer has paid in benefits to the injured worker and can also indicate expenses incurred. The parties involved in a workers' compensation subrogation claim are the insurer, the injured worker and attorney, and the defendants (third parties) and their counsel. The lien notification is technically not complete until all parties are aware of the insurer's/employer's right to recovery. See Exhibit 7-1 for a sample Workers' Compensation Notice of Lien letter to the third party. Parties added to the claim later must be given notice of the lien. Once all parties are notified, all necessary statutory measures must be taken to protect the right to that lien.

Protect the Lien

The third element in the subrogation process is protection of the lien. The insurer protects the lien by becoming a party to the action brought by the injured worker against the third party, thus ensuring the insurer's participation in and consent to any settlement of the claim. The requirements to protect (or perfect) a workers' compensation lien vary by state and also by the type of lien. Where the right is statutory, state laws set out the procedure and requirements for protecting a lien. If the right is not statutory, the insurer must file an intervention action to be made a party to the lawsuit. Intervention actions are discussed later in this chapter.

If the insurer is bringing an independent action against the third party rather than joining in the injured worker's action, it files a complaint within the

EXHIBIT 7-1

Notice of Lien to Third-Party Defendant

(benefit state) Workers' Compensation

Notice Of Lien

(third party)

Re: Employer

Claim #

Date of accident

Injured worker

Dear Sir/Madam (or contact person):

(insurance company) is the workers' compensation insurer for *(employer)*. *(injured worker)* is employed by *(employer)* and was injured while working as a result of the negligence of *(third party)*. In compliance with the *(benefit state)* workers' compensation statute, *(insurance company)* is obligated to pay workers' compensation benefits to *(injured worker)* on behalf of *(employer)*.

The *(benefit state)* workers' compensation statute affords workers' compensation insurers the right to pursue at-fault third parties and seek reimbursement for benefits they pay under the Workers Compensation and Employers Liability policy. This letter serves as notice of the workers' compensation lien. Please forward this letter to your liability insurer for its consideration and so that it can communicate with *(insurance company)* directly. If you are self-insured or uninsured, *(insurance company)* will communicate with you or your authorized representative and seek reimbursement directly. As an alternative, if you are insured, you may write the name, address, phone number, and policy number of your liability insurer on the bottom of this letter and mail it to me in the enclosed business reply envelope.

Thank you for your cooperation.

Sincerely,

(name of adjuster)

statutory time frame. For bodily injury claims, a statute of limitations (which limits the number of years after an event that a lawsuit can be filed) applies, and for construction defects claims, a statute of repose (also a law indicating the time period in which a suit can be filed) applies. Some statutes set a time limit, which can be as short as ninety days, for filing a notice of claim (which puts a party on notice that it is going to be sued) and another time limit to file the complaint that initiates the lawsuit.

Many states require an insurer to wait a specified period after the accident date before starting an independent action. This period usually ranges from six months to one year and gives the injured worker time to decide whether to pursue an action. Once this time has elapsed, some states allow the insurer to bring an independent action even if the injured worker has brought one. Other states assign the worker's rights to the insurer if the worker has failed to pursue an action. The assignment means that the worker relinquishes the right to pursue a claim and that the insurer is the only plaintiff in the case. Some assignments are automatic; others require the insurer to notify the worker of its intent to pursue the third-party claims. Usually the worker takes the notification to an attorney who then commences an action for the worker. The insurer can then file an intervention action and/or assert a statutory lien against the third-party claim.

Motion to intervene
A legal mechanism by which a third party, not in the original lawsuit but claiming an interest in the outcome, can be added to the proceedings to protect that party's interest.

An intervention action, or a **motion to intervene**, is a legal mechanism by which a third party, not in the original lawsuit but claiming an interest in the outcome, can be added to the lawsuit to protect the third party's interest. A motion to intervene allows the insurer to become a party to the case and gives it the opportunity to settle independently with the defendant(s). Unlike independent actions, a motion to intervene can be filed after the statute of limitations period, as long as the underlying case has been filed within the statute's time limit.

Protecting the Workers' Compensation Lien

Independent Action States	Intervention States
• Statute gives insurer right to file independent action.	• Statute requires insurer to intervene in injured worker's lawsuit.
• Insurer must file suit within statute of limitations or repose.	• Statute of limitations or repose does not apply to insurer.

Monitor Progress

The fourth element in the subrogation process is to monitor the progress of the subrogation claim. How progress is monitored depends on whether the lien is protected by statute. If so, the adjuster waits for the injured worker to finish medical treatment and for the lien amount to be finalized. By this point, each side will have completed its investigation, and the third party's liability insurer most likely has established its position on liability. The adjuster submits documents substantiating the lien and makes a demand for reimbursement to the liability insurer for the third party.

If the injured worker has already begun a lawsuit against the third party, the adjuster can provide the injured worker's attorney with medical documentation and copies of benefit payments, updating the benefit amounts as needed. Although the worker's attorney is obligated by statute to protect the lien, the attorney's first obligation is to protect the client's interests. The attorney might try to persuade the adjuster to reduce the amount of the insurer's lien, regardless of how large the gross recovery is.

Exhibit 7-2 shows a letter the adjuster can use to monitor a lien in a state that does not require an intervention action.

EXHIBIT 7-2

Letter to Attorney to Monitor Lien

(attorney name)

Re: Employer:

          Policy #:

          Date of loss:

          Plaintiff:

Dear:

Please note that I am handling the subrogation aspect of the workers' compensation claim. I would appreciate your providing me with periodic updates regarding the progress of the third-party liability action. In return, I will periodically update you on the lien figures and assist you in your investigation. Further, I would appreciate your providing me with the following information when it becomes available:

- Name, address, and phone number of the liability insurer(s).
- Stage of the litigation process.
- Amounts of any settlement offers that have been made.
- Next hearing date, if already on the court calendar. If not, when is the anticipated hearing date?
- Copy of the Complaint if a suit has been filed.
- Your theory and apportionment of liability.

The current workers' compensation lien is:

Total medical benefits paid: $

Total wage loss benefits paid: $

Total current lien: $

Please contact me before settling the liability case because the above figures are subject to change. Further, the workers' compensation lien is protected under the *(applicable state)* Workers' Compensation Statute and case law.

Thank you for protecting the workers' compensation lien and kindly respond at your earliest convenience. If you have any questions about this matter, I can be contacted at *(adjusters phone)*.

Sincerely,

(adjuster's name)

If the lien is not protected by statute, monitoring begins when the motion to intervene is filed. To protect the lien, this intervention motion should be filed as soon as the adjuster discovers that a third-party action is pending. Once filed, the motion gives the adjuster more control over the case because the insurer is now a party to the case. An intervention motion has the following advantages for the employer or insurer:

- Settlement proceeds are less likely to be disproportionately allotted to those types of damages that are not subject to the lien.
- At hearings, the insurer's attorney can argue issues of liability not addressed by the injured worker's attorney and can negotiate the lien on the insurer's behalf.
- The insurer's lien is addressed at the hearing and documented in the settlement. If the lien is not asserted, the settlement proceeds would go entirely to the injured worker's attorney who is to satisfy all outstanding liens, a process that might delay dispersing the proceeds to the insured.

Negotiate and Resolve the Lien

The fifth element in the subrogation process is negotiating and resolving the workers' compensation lien. To be effective in negotiating and resolving a lien, the adjuster must be familiar with the facts of both the liability and the workers' compensation cases and the type of lien resolutions available in the state. Exhibit 7-3 is a letter requesting a proposal to resolve a lien from the injured worker's attorney.

Once the adjuster receives a proposal from the worker's attorney to resolve the lien, the adjuster develops a lien negotiation strategy. If the insurer has not hired an attorney to pursue a third-party claim, the adjuster must answer as many as twelve questions *before* attempting to negotiate a lien. In an intervention action, all of these questions must be answered, with the possible exception of the question about the contribution towards the injured worker's attorney fee and expenses because states that require an intervention action usually do not require the insurer to pay for the worker's attorney.

The first five questions pertain specifically to the liability and workers' compensation case under consideration.

1. What is the exact amount of the gross recovery?
2. Is the gross recovery the only source of recovery, or are other actions pending that are subject to the lien?
3. What is the current amount of the lien?
4. What is the total available credit an insurer can take against future benefits to be paid to the injured worker?
5. If there is a credit, what is the projected future lien amount?

The remaining questions are state-specific.

6. Can the lien be attached to the gross recovery at issue?
7. If the lien can be attached to the gross recovery, can it be asserted against the entire award, or are certain types of damages excluded from the lien?
8. Is the injured worker's attorney required to obtain the insurer's consent to settle the third-party claim?

EXHIBIT 7-3

Letter Requesting a Proposal to Resolve a Lien

(attorney's name)

Re:

Employer name:

Injured worker's name:

File number:

Date of accident:

Dear:

Please provide me with the following information, so I can properly evaluate your proposal to resolve the lien.

- Amount of the proposed liability settlement
- Your fee percentage and amount of expenses
- Your theory and apportionment of liability
- Amount of reimbursement and credit to be taken against future benefits, if applicable
- Amount of the cash waiver and/or cash payment, if applicable

Please note that the current lien is:

Total medical benefits paid: $

Total wage loss benefits paid: $

Total current lien: $

Without all of the above information, I will be unable to evaluate your proposal and discuss resolution of the lien.

Thank you for your cooperation.

Sincerely,

(adjuster's name)

9. In lieu of taking a credit, does the insurer have the option of resolving both the lien and all or part of the workers' compensation claim by stipulation? Essentially, by stipulating, the insurer waives or compromises all or part of its lien (reimbursement and credit) in exchange for eliminating all or part of its future exposures (uncertainty).

10. What is the priority of distribution of the third-party settlement proceeds after the injured worker's attorney fee and expenses are paid?

11. What is the insurer's contribution toward the injured worker's attorney fees and expenses?

12. Are there any special considerations?

Answering the first set of questions begins after the injured worker has a tentative settlement with the defendant(s) and the insurer has received a proposal to resolve the lien.

Questions Specific to the Liability and Workers' Compensation Case

Question 1: What is the exact amount of the gross recovery?

The gross recovery, the amount of the settlement without deduction of the attorney's fee, is one of the most important figures in preparing a case for negotiation and for completing the recovery analysis. This figure determines the negotiation strategy, the recovery composition (i.e., the blend of cash and credit), and whether stipulation is appropriate (see Question 9). The amount of the gross recovery is of primary concern to insurers that have paid benefits in a state that requires the injured worker's attorney to obtain the insurer's consent before settling the liability case (see Question 8). Because settlement negotiations might continue and the gross recovery might increase after the adjuster resolves the insurer's lien, the adjuster should obtain a copy of the hearing's closing statement. This statement itemizes the terms of the third-party liability settlement, such as the gross recovery amount and disbursements and would let the adjuster know if more of the lien should be paid.

Question 2: Is the gross recovery under consideration the only source of recovery, or are other actions pending that are subject to the lien?

Most of the defendants in a suit settle with the injured worker at the same time, and the individual settlement drafts are disbursed from an attorney's escrow account at the same time. However, if the claim involves a third-party auto, one or two additional sources of recovery might exist: the injured worker's underinsured motorists (UIM) coverage and the employer's fleet policy. The adjuster should inquire about the possibility of these additional sources of recovery because the worker's attorney is not required to inform the adjuster of their existence. This step is particularly important if the initial gross recovery was not enough to satisfy the current lien and/or future exposure.

Question 3: What is the current amount of the lien?

The current lien represents the amount of benefits an insurer has paid at the time the liability claim settles. All wage loss payments and medical treatment benefits are considered part of the current lien and are reimbursable to the insurer. However, the workers' compensation statute might require the insurer to reduce its current lien under certain circumstances. For example, in medical malpractice cases, many states that allow subrogation give the insurer the right to assert a lien only on workers' compensation benefit payments that were made as a result of the physician's negligence. The adjuster and the injured worker's attorney must estimate and agree on what the lien would have been without malpractice and subtract this figure from the total benefits paid.

Question 4: What is the total available credit an insurer can take against future benefits?

As mentioned, the total credit available equals the injured worker's net recovery from the liability case. Most states allow an insurer to take a credit against future benefits if the workers' compensation case and lien are not resolved by a stipulation. State law determines how the credit can be applied and to what type of benefits. The credit period starts after the settlement draft is issued by the third party's insurer(s).

Question 5: If there is a credit, what is the projected future lien amount?

The projected future lien amount equals the insurer's future exposure up to the amount of the total available credit. If the workers' compensation case is still open or is administratively closed but, in the adjuster's judgment, is likely to be reopened, care should be taken in estimating the future exposure and how the credit is included in the negotiation of the lien.

Often, too much attention is paid to the reimbursement portion of the recovery and too little, if any, is paid to projecting the future lien. A possible reason for this is that many insurers enter only the cash portion of the recovery into their recovery results. Nevertheless, even though most statutes are clear on the right to take credit, attorneys usually either try to persuade the adjuster to waive the credit or do not address the issue during the negotiation process. Because the insurer's silence can be construed as a waiver, the adjuster should discuss the credit amount and confirm both the reimbursement and credit portions of the recovery in writing. Doing so prevents disputes and unnecessary litigation.

Questions That Are State-Specific

Questions 6 through 12 are specific to the state and should be considered in every subrogation claim.

Question 6: Can the lien be attached to the gross recovery at issue?

An insurer can assert a lien against the damages awarded in most types of liability claims. If the injured worker's attorney is disputing the insurer's right to assert a lien, the adjuster should ask for the supporting statute or case law citation. The adjuster should also do research and/or request assistance from defense counsel to verify what the attorney's position is based on. New cases might favor the adjuster's position; the worker's attorney's interpretation of the law might be incorrect; or the attorney's argument might not be supported by the case(s) provided.

Question 7: If the lien can be attached to the gross recovery, can it be asserted against the entire recovery, or are certain types of damages excluded from the lien?

While an insurer might have a right to assert a lien against the damages awarded in the injured worker's liability claim, certain types of damages cannot be subject to the lien. For example, if a liability claim is made by both the worker and the worker's spouse, the portion of the damages awarded to the spouse for pain and suffering and loss of consortium is usually not subject to an insurer's lien. Courts reason that because the spouse did not receive benefits from the workers' compensation claim, damages apportioned to the spouse's liability claim should not be attached to the insurer's lien. Another example is damages awarded to dependents in a wrongful death or survival claim. An insurer is entitled to reimbursement for benefits paid before the worker's death (medical and wage loss) and after death (burial and funeral costs and dependency benefits for wage loss). However, some states do not allow damages awarded to the dependents for pain and suffering or loss of consortium that results from the loss of companionship to be attached to a lien.

As with Question 6, if the injured worker's attorney disputes the insurer's right to assert a lien against the entire recovery, the adjuster should consult with the insurer's defense counsel and should also request a copy of the settlement order apportioning damages. An insurer can take legal action against a worker's attorney who allocates settlement funds to avoid satisfying the insurer's lien, directing the funds instead to the damage claims that the lien does not cover. To prevent such disproportionate allocation, particularly in large, complex cases, the adjuster can direct the insurer's legal counsel to intervene.

Question 8: Is the injured worker's attorney required to obtain the insurer's consent to settle the third-party claim?

Some states require the worker's attorney to obtain the insurer's consent to settle the third-party claim for two reasons. First, it forces the attorney to notify the insurer that the third-party claim is about to be settled or near resolution. Second, it gives the insurer an opportunity to ensure that the third-party claim is being resolved for an appropriate sum, because the amount of the settlement affects the insurer's recovery. It prevents an attorney from trying to settle the third-party claim prematurely and/or for an undervalued figure when the current lien is large and/or when future exposure is significant.

Question 9: In lieu of taking a credit, does the insurer have the option of resolving both the lien and all or part of the workers' compensation claim by stipulation?

Many states allow the insurer to use its lien rights to resolve all or part of the workers' compensation claim by stipulation, that is, to agree to relinquish its right to reimbursement for past payments in exchange for release from any further benefit obligations to the injured worker. Liens resolved by a stipulation are subject to the approval of the Workers' Compensation Commission or Board. Because a stipulation closes all or part of the workers' compensation claim, no future benefits against which to take a credit would be available. However, an adjuster must still calculate the amount of the credit as if the workers' compensation claim remained open to determine if a stipulation is a favorable option. Before deciding to stipulate, the adjuster should carefully estimate the insurer's future exposure to make sure the reimbursement relinquished does not exceed the future exposure.

Question 10: What is the priority of distribution of the third-party settlement proceeds after the injured worker's attorney fee and expenses are paid?

The worker's attorney fee and expenses are always compensated in full before any distribution is made to the worker and the insurer. Obviously, the party who has priority of distribution is in a superior negotiating position before trial. If the case is tried, the jury might be given instructions about how to apportion the settlement. In a made-whole state, the jury decides whether the insurer is entitled to anything (see Question 12). If the jury is not required to make any decision about the lien and the law clearly specifies that the insurer has priority, a small settlement could mean that the worker is left with nothing.

Question 11: What is the insurer's contribution towards the injured worker's attorney fee and expenses?

Typically, the insurer pays a pro rata share of the worker's attorney fee and expenses, as discussed previously. Some states impose maximums on the fees and expenses that can be assessed on the insurer. The adjuster should be aware if any maximums apply to a given case.

Question 12: Are there any special considerations?

As previously mentioned, some states have either a made-whole doctrine or an employers negligence statute. Because these laws are generally misunderstood and are not uniformly applied, they can put an insurer in an inferior negotiating position. Under the made-whole doctrine, an insurer's lien can be either eliminated or reduced to "make whole" an injured party, that is, to adequately compensate the worker for all losses. Employers negligence statutes prohibit any insurer recovery if the employer's negligence has contributed to the worker's injury.

The rationale for an employers negligence statute is twofold. First, it gives the employer incentive to provide a safe work environment by inhibiting the employer's subrogation and recovery rights if it has contributed to the worker's injury. Second, it prevents the worker from being penalized for the employer's negligence regardless of the worker's negligence.

An adjuster who fails to answer all of the preceding questions and analyze the responses could risk the insurer's recovery, despite a comprehensive third-party investigation and a strong liability case.

Once the adjuster has successfully negotiated the lien, the lien resolution must be recorded. Lien resolutions fall into two categories: those without stipulation and those with stipulation. Three possibilities exist for both lien resolutions without stipulation and those with stipulation, but not all states allow both stipulation and nonstipulation lien resolutions, and, as previously mentioned, some states do not allow stipulation to apply to both medical and wage loss benefits. The difference between the two categories is that lien resolutions with stipulation resolve the lien and permanently close out all or part of the workers' compensation claim. In nonstipulation lien resolutions, both the medical and wage loss portions of the workers' compensation claim are left open or can be reopened. The adjuster should consider negotiating a credit against future benefits as part of a nonstipulated lien resolution.

Lien Resolutions Without Stipulation

The first type of lien resolution without stipulation, the cash-only lien resolution, applies when the total lien (current and future) is greater than, or at best, approximately equal to the gross recovery.

Many cash-only recoveries are equal three-way splits of the gross recovery (i.e., one third each to the attorney, the injured worker, and the insurer). This result occurs when, after the worker's attorney fee and expenses are paid, insufficient money is left to pay the insurer's full statutory *current* lien and to adequately compensate the worker for the types of damages not paid under the workers' compensation claim, such as pain and suffering. The insurer compromises its current lien (receives less cash) and does not take a credit (waives its future lien) against future benefits even though the worker has received a complete settlement from the third-party case.

Sometimes waiving the credit is the only way to resolve the lien so that all parties can avoid the possibility of losing the case at trial. Accepting a cash-only recovery is appropriate for the insurer if one of the following conditions exist: the future exposure to the insurer is small, or the workers' compensation claim is closed and no future benefits are expected.

The second type of resolution without stipulation, the cash and credit lien resolution, can apply when the worker has a positive net recovery from the third-party case. However, the size of the gross recovery relative to the current lien determines the composition of the insurer's recovery (i.e., the amount of cash and credit) and the adjuster's lien negotiation strategy.

If the gross recovery is not significantly larger than the current lien, that is, no more than one-third greater, and if the third-party case is not strong (but probably stronger than for the cash-only recovery), the adjuster might be satisfied with a cash-only recovery. Neither the insurer nor the worker's attorney is likely to want to pursue a larger recovery at trial. Both parties risk ending up with little or no recovery. However, the larger the future exposure, the more the adjuster should consider retaining its credit, especially for cases requiring lifetime medical and/or wage loss benefits.

If the gross recovery is more than one-third larger than the current lien, the adjuster might want to negotiate a recovery that includes cash and credit. However, when the gross recovery is some multiple of the current lien—that is, the liability on the third party case is strong—the insurer should demand full statutory reimbursement of its current lien and assert its full credit against future benefits (its future lien). Under these circumstances, there is sufficient money to reimburse the insurer for its current lien, compensate the claimant for other damages, and cover the attorney fee and expenses. Further, if the insurer's future exposure is less than the total available credit, it should not enter into a stipulation-type lien resolution to close the entire workers' compensation claim; the insurer's total available credit will absolve the insurer from its obligation to make future payments. If, for whatever reason, a compromise is made on the cash portion of the recovery, the total available credit would increase dollar for dollar by the amount the cash is reduced.

The third type of lien resolution without stipulation is the credit-only lien resolution, which is appropriate regardless of the size of the gross recovery as long as all of the available credit will be used. In other words, the insurer's future exposure should be greater than or equal to the total available credit. Like waiving credit in a cash-only resolution, an insurer must realistically quantify its future exposure before considering this type of resolution. Conservative estimates of future exposure are more likely to be accepted by workers' compensation courts. The adjuster should also calculate the credit in present value terms. Cash has more value than credit because current dollars purchase more than the same amount of future dollars, assuming continuing inflation.

During the credit period, the burden of paying either all or part of the future benefits shifts to the injured worker; the insurer pays little or no benefits during this time. Therefore, in serious and complex cases, fewer disputes are likely between the insurer and injured worker about the nature and frequency of future medical treatment or disability management.

When injured workers are paying their own expenses they often spend less, thus using the insurer's credit at a slower rate or never exhausting it. The insurer might be able to lower its reserves or close the claim. Therefore, a credit-only lien resolution, if properly used, is just as valuable to the insurer as either a cash or a cash and credit lien resolution.

Lien Resolutions With Stipulation

Insurers use lien resolution with stipulation to facilitate resolutions, but they should also consider settlements that do not use stipulations. Sometimes the prospect of closing a difficult, complex claim can be viewed so favorably that resolution of the lien without a stipulation is not seriously considered. For example, an adjuster might compromise or waive the cash portion of the recovery in exchange for a stipulation when the total available credit would be large enough to absorb the future exposure without the stipulation.

Just as for lien resolution without stipulations, the adjuster resolving a lien with stipulations must ensure that the insurer is receiving at least as much (and, ideally, more) than it is giving. To properly evaluate whether a stipulation is favorable, the adjuster analyzes what the outcome would be without a stipulation. The following formula can be used to determine if a stipulation would be favorable and when the credit, with a nonstipulation lien resolution, would be taken dollar for dollar:

$$\text{Future exposure being stipulated} - \text{Total credit assuming no stipulation} > \text{Cash recovery waived} + \text{Cash paid}.$$

The formula shows that the savings on future benefits from the stipulation should be greater than or equal the current cost of the stipulation. The left side of the formula, the benefit to the insurer of a stipulation, quantifies the future benefits subject to the stipulation (medical and/or wage loss benefits) that would have to be paid after the credit is exhausted if there were no stipulation. That is, without a stipulation, the insurer would be relying on its credit to extinguish part or all of its future benefit obligation (i.e., perform the same function as stipulation).

The right side of the formula, the cost of the stipulation, quantifies the concessions demanded by the injured worker's attorney. An insurer might be asked to either reduce its cash recovery or waive it completely. If the cash recovery is waived, the insurer must decide whether it is appropriate to make a lump sum payment in addition to forgoing the lien (cash recovery). A concession(s) is, by definition, always part of a stipulation. The worker's attorney would never agree to reimburse an insurer its full statutory lien, allow the insurer to take full credit against future benefits, and waive the client's right to future benefits.

The formula is useful in those states that allow an insurer to take a dollar-for-dollar credit against future benefits. The formula can be modified slightly to accommodate situations in which the insurer is required to pay future benefits at the pro rata rate during the credit period. The following is the pro rata payment version of the formula:

$$\left(\text{Future exposure being stipulated} - \text{Total credit assuming no stipulation}\right) \times (1 - \text{Pro rata rate}) > \text{Cash recovery waived} + \text{Cash paid}.$$

The formula includes a multiplier, one minus the pro rata rate, which determines the percentage the insurer saves on each payment during the credit period. Savings from the stipulation are actually higher under the co-payment formula because the insurer is saving the co-payment as well as the future exposure after the credit is exhausted.

When using these formulas, the adjuster should be aware of the following rules:

- *Future exposure ≥ 0*: The future exposure is a nonnegative number, which is the insurer's estimated future exposure on the workers' compensation claim. The future exposure is positive if the insurer currently owes or believes it will owe future benefits. It can be zero if the insurer believes no future exposure exists.

- *Total credit* ≥ 0: The total available credit is a nonnegative number. It is positive if the third-party case results in a gross recovery. It can be zero if the third party wins the case or the claim is abandoned. Total credit is a function of the size of the gross recovery and the insurer's recovery. The higher the gross recovery and the lower the insurer's recovery from the third-party case (i.e., the more cash it forgoes), the larger the total available credit (i.e., injured worker's net recovery).

- *Cash recovery waived* ≥ 0: The cash recovery waived is a nonnegative number. It is positive when the insurer has paid benefits before resolution of the third-party case. It is zero if no benefits have been paid. In the latter situation, if benefits are expected to be paid, the amount appears on the left side of the equation in the future exposure estimate. Lastly, this figure represents what the insurer would have collected from the third-party case and can range from zero to the insurer's statutory recovery. It is a function of both the gross recovery's size and the current lien's size. The larger the gross recovery and current lien, the larger the insurer's statutory recovery. A small gross recovery and large lien means the insurer nets less from the third-party case and has less cash to waive if it compromises or waives its lien (i.e., cash recovery).

- *Cash payment* > 0: The insurer's cash payment is greater than zero. It can be paid in addition to a complete lien waiver or paid by itself, if the lien is zero. For example, the insurer might stipulate to waive the lien in exchange for making no future benefit payments. The waiver, however, might not be sufficient to resolve the lien, that is, the amount the injured worker has netted from the third-party settlement does not cover what the worker will have to pay to replace the future benefits that have been waived. In this case, the insurer might agree to a lump sum payment in addition to the lien waiver.

The amount of the lump sum cash payment is a function of the formula's other elements. It is related to the difference between the future exposure and total available credit. As mentioned, the amount of the total available credit is related to the amount of the insurer's recovery, which is determined by the amount of cash the insurer forgoes.

An insurer's maximum benefit from a stipulation is to reduce or eliminate its future exposure. An obvious example is when the total available credit is zero, a result that occurs when the gross recovery is zero. The insurer's benefit of a stipulation ranges from zero to elimination of the future exposure. Even if the left side of the formula is positive, the stipulation does not benefit the insurer if the cost of the stipulation, or the right side of the formula, is greater than the left.

Estimating the future exposure is not an exact science and is more difficult in complex cases. For example, wage loss benefits are always easier to estimate than medical benefits because permanency and lifetime tables help quantify wage loss benefits. The adjuster might want to add an error factor for future uncertainty to the left side of the formula before making a final determination about whether to accept or reject the stipulation's terms. The size of the error factor might be influenced by the size of the workers' compensation claim and the third-party case.

The future exposure should include not only benefits expected to be paid, but also administrative costs to monitor or defend the case, such as independent medical exams and defense costs.

The three types of lien resolutions with stipulation are the following:

1. Compromised lien with stipulation
2. Waiver of lien with stipulation
3. Waiver of lien with cash payment and stipulation

In a compromised lien with stipulation, the insurer reduces the cash portion of its recovery in exchange for closing all or a portion of its workers' compensation claim. The net result should be that the future saving (the left side of the formula) is at least as large as the amount of cash forgone.

In a waiver of lien with stipulation, the insurer completely forgoes the cash portion of its recovery in exchange for closing all or a portion of its workers' compensation claim. The net result should be that the future saving should be at least as large as the cash recovery forgone.

In a waiver of lien with cash payment and stipulation, the insurer pays a lump sum in exchange for closing all or a portion of its workers' compensation claim. This resolution is appropriate if the future exposure is substantially larger than the total credit, and the insurer is determined to close as much of the claim as possible. In other words, the injured worker's attorney believes that waiving the lien is insufficient. The adjuster might consider a lump sum cash payment to bridge at least part of the difference between the future exposure and the total credit. The cash payment lowers the benefit (raising the cost) from the stipulation; however, the settlement is more equitable for the injured worker, who is concerned about being adequately compensated for injuries. The net result should be that the insurer's future saving is at least as large as the cash recovery waived and the lump sum cash payment.

The type of resolution that ultimately satisfies the lien is the amount of the gross recovery and the result of the interplay between the injured worker's attorney's lien proposal and insurer's estimation of its future exposure. The insurer should wait for the worker's attorney's lien proposal, evaluate it, review the third-party case and workers' compensation claim, and then decide what type of lien resolution is most advantageous and equitable. The worker and his or her attorney are negotiating with better information because they know more about the intentions of the worker that affect the insurer's *actual* future exposure. The attorney's demand will reveal valuable information about the insurer's *actual* future exposure, which can be very different from the insurer's *estimated* future exposure, and which, if kept current, is reflected in its reserve.

The adjuster should keep the following four points in mind when negotiating a lien:

1. Regarding nonstipulation lien resolutions, if the cash portion of the recovery is compromised, the adjuster should ensure that the future exposure is large enough so that the insurer receives the benefit from the increase of the credit portion of the recovery.

2. The adjuster should never enter into a stipulation if the third-party case has not resolved. Predicting the outcome of the third-party case is difficult.

3. The adjuster should ensure that the insured's benefit from the stipulation is greater than the cost.

4. If the total available credit is greater than or equal to the future exposure, a nonstipulation lien resolution is preferable because it can conclude the claim in the same manner as a stipulation without the concessions.

The claim file should carefully document the amount of the credit and how it will be applied against future benefits, whether dollar for dollar or pro rata. Documenting the terms of lien resolution in as much detail as possible prevents future file handling difficulties, such as overlooking the credit and paying benefits that should not be paid. Money saved on future benefits as a result of a credit is just as important as money received for reimbursement of the current lien.

Monitor Post-Settlement Activities

The sixth element in the subrogation process is to monitor the post-settlement activities. Many adjusters overlook this final step because they are under the impression that once the settlement draft is received, their subrogation duties are complete. However, monitoring must continue if the settlement includes a credit to be applied against future benefits currently owed or future benefits to be paid if the workers' compensation claim is reopened.

SUMMARY

Because workers' compensation premiums are a substantial cost of doing business, employers look to their insurers to optimize subrogation opportunities, thereby reducing their loss experience.

This chapter discussed the analysis an adjuster must perform to determine if subrogation is economically viable. This analysis uses a seven-step process.

The seven steps are:

1. Investigate the accident for third-party liability
2. Identify potentially liable third parties
3. Determine negligence
4. Apportion liability

5. Determine state negligence test and subrogation restrictions
6. Determine amount of potential recovery
7. Conduct a cost-benefit analysis

Each of the first six steps provides information that the adjuster uses in the final step—conduct a cost benefit analysis. For many insurers, the amount of the recovery must exceed the cost to pursue subrogation.

Having determined that an economically viable subrogation opportunity exists, the adjuster begins the subrogation process. The first element in the subrogation process is to investigate the accident for third-party liability. The most common types of third-party liability arise from claims involving vehicles, products, and premises. Each type of claim has investigation unique to it.

The second element in the subrogation process is to notify all stakeholders of a lien. A workers' compensation lien notice is sent to potentially liable third parties detailing the workers' compensation benefits paid and, sometimes, additional expenses incurred.

The third element in the subrogation process is protecting the lien. The lien might be protected by statue, in which case the lien notice is sufficient to protect the lien. If no statutory protection applies to the lien, the adjuster might choose to file an independent legal action (not connected to any legal action that the injured worker has filed against the third party) or to instruct the insurer's attorney to intervene in the injured worker's lawsuit against the third parties.

The fourth element in the subrogation process is monitoring the progress of the suit and updating the lien information as necessary. At the appropriate time, the adjuster will participate in the fifth element, negotiating and resolving the lien. As part of this process, the adjuster must consider various factors, some state-specific and some specific to liability issues and workers' compensation. The adjuster must also decide whether to resolve the lien with or without stipulations. Formulas are available to help the adjuster perform a cost-benefit analysis to determine whether to use stipulations. The adjuster must properly document the terms of the lien resolution, particularly if they involve credit, to avoid overpayments to the injured worker.

The sixth element of the subrogation process is to monitor post-settlement activities. This is particularly important if a credit is to be applied to future benefit payments.

TEXTBOOK SUMMARY

This textbook examines the principles of workers' compensation and how to adjust workers' compensation claims by discussing:

- The common-law duties of employers to their workers and defenses available to employers
- The common features of state workers' compensation statutes
- Federal workers' compensation statutes
- Employments and injuries covered by workers' compensation statutes
- Compensability requirements of (1) arising out of and (2) in the course of employment
- Statutory benefits
- The coverage provided by the Workers Compensation and Employers Liability Insurance Policy
- Loss investigation and claim practices
- Workers' compensation subrogation

The text focuses on the statutorily required benefits and how the WC&EL policy provides coverage for them. It examines how to investigate a workers' compensation claim, make a compensability determination, calculate benefits, and pursue subrogation.

The framework for investigating workers' compensation claims presented in this text can be applied to most workers' compensation claims. Because each loss presents its own unique set of facts and issues, the workers' compensation adjuster applies his or her expertise and knowledge to bring each claim to a timely, fair, and equitable conclusion.

Index